MEDIA AND CRIME

MEDIA AND CRIME

Vivek Sehgal

CYBER TECH PUBLICATIONS
4264/3, Ansari Road, Daryaganj, New Delhi-110002 (India)
Ph.: 011-23244078, 011-43559448 Fax: 011-23280028
E-Mail: cyberpublicationsdelhi@yahoo.com
Website: www.cybertechpublications.com

MEDIA AND CRIME

Vivek Sehgal

First Edition 2010

Published by :

G.S. Rawat for **Cyber Tech Publications**
4264/3, Ansari Road, Daryaganj, New Delhi-110002 (India)
Ph.: 011-23244078, 011-43559448 Fax: 011-23280028
E-Mail: cyberpublicationsdelhi@yahoo.com
Website: www.cybertechpublications.com

Printed at: Asian Offset Printers, Delhi-53

Preface

This book explores the situating of law and crime within the vast range and scope of contemporary media forms. It begins from the premise that the whole of society, including crime and criminal justice, is embraced by media culture. 'The media' are viewed not as a set of institutions, but as a myriad of communicative forms or expressive techniques ranging from soaps to cyberworlds. The author shows how crime and the law, or our understanding of them, are produced, reproduced, disturbed, and challenged in and through media culture.

A lively and engaging text, this book contains a wide range of topical examples and provides a theoretically coherent examination of the field, providing an accessible critique of cultural theory along the way. It opens up the boundaries between the more traditional aspects of law and criminology, and the broader concerns of sociology and cultural studies. The result will be essential reading for students and a key reference for researchers as well as those with a wider interest in crime and the media.

— *Author*

CONTENTS

Preface

1. Introduction 1
2. Off Balance: Youth, Race and Crime in the News 20
3. Youth, Race and Crime in the News 38
4. Crime in the News 56
5. Media in India 86
6. Violence in the Media and it's Effects on Society 102
7. A Psychological Assessment of Crime Profiling 113
8. Causes of Crime 122
9. Crime Scene Investigation 126
10. Introduction to Crime Scene Reconstruction 161
11. Evidence Dynamics: Locard's Exchange Principle and Crime Reconstruction 191
12. The Importance of Careful Interpretation of Shell Casing Ejection Patterns 209
13. Sex and Crime in the Media 237

Bibliography 253

Index 255

1

Introduction

It is quite vicious how each time the media reports a sensational crime. First, it berates the police for not solving the crime immediately and then follows it up by ridiculing the probe. The media satisfies itself by launching its own investigations, which are generally at variance with the police findings. It does not seem to matter if eventually the conclusions of the media sleuths turn out to be way off the mark.

There is no question that the murder of Aarushi Talwar, 14-year-old daughter of a Noida-based dentist couple, Dr Rajesh and Nupur Talwar, is a horrendous crime. Since her parents happen to belong to the upper strata of the society the incident required wide coverage in accordance with the media obsession with the lives of the haves. A similar case of murder in a slum family would be forgotten the same day.

After the news of the tragic death of Aarushi Talwar broke, the visual media focused all its attention on the crime at the cost of all other events of the day. It continued the next day with the emphasis shifting on details furnished by the police as also neighbors, and friends, all of which built up a story that sounded like a script for a Bollywood film. The police had carried out nothing more than a cursory investigation of the crime scene. That was an angle that certainly required to be played up to show how callous and irresponsible can the police be in carrying out investigations.

The sleazy coating of the murder story may be good for ratings but is that really germane to the main story-the murder of a teen-age girl? By emphasizing certain aspects of the private lives of the victim and her family the police with the aid of media hype were actually murdering the lives of many living ones. The entire media latched on to those details as if the teenager was inviting trouble by disapproving the alleged extra-marital affair of her father and the conduct of her own relations with a domestic help.

By the time the media took note of the subsequent denials of the doctor's amorous pursuits the damage had been done to the reputation of three living persons-the dentist couple and their female colleague-not to mention the poor slain girl. If the police had not been in such a haste to name Dr Rajesh Talwar as the alleged murderer of his daughter and spice it all up with some details about his personal life the extent of damage would have been perhaps limited.

Media has the responsibility of informing the public about the development's going around. Whatever is the turn of events in the nation, it has to be reported by the media. Media also spreads awareness about the existing facts which influence the society. Precisely, media is an integral part of the society, which functions nonstop for its betterment. It keeps people in touch with the events happening around. It also voices people's grievances against the system. Wherever the executive or the legislation falters, it's the media who takes up the issue as in a democracy it's the people who have the power in their hands. But sometimes, this power of being able to reach to the masses and the ability to shape the public opinion is not aptly handled by the media.

MASS MEDIA AND CRIME - JOURNALISM

The relationship between the criminal justice system and the media system has been the subject of research, speculation, and commentary throughout the twentieth century. This relationship may be understood in terms of dependency relations operative between these massive systems (Ball-Rokeach and De Fleur). Put most simply, neither the media nor the criminal justice system could operate effectively without the other. The criminal justice system is a resource for the media system in that it affords one of the common sources of news and entertainment stories. The classical surrogate scout role of the media, whereby they monitor the environment for actual and potential threats to individual and collective welfare, affords a powerful way for the media to attract their audiences. People must constantly update their understanding and ability to orient themselves to the environments in which they act.

Media crime stories, whether the news or entertainment genre, instruct and update these understandings. Commercial media organizations translate this relationship with their audience into the profit that flows from advertisers. The media system's capacities to reach vast audiences of citizens and policymakers also positions it as an essential resource for the criminal justice system and all of its attendant judicial and law enforcement organizations.

For the criminal justice system to operate effectively, it must have the authority that derives from people's willingness to grant it legitimacy, and media storytelling can profoundly affect this process. Allocation of scarce resources to the criminal justice system also depends upon success in the struggle to get "its" story positively framed and widely disseminated to media audiences. These macro dependency relations serve as context for examinations of specific aspects of media, criminal justice, public, and decision-maker relations.

Research attention has been given to the dependency relations between journalists and the police, courts, and jails. The impact of journalism on public perceptions of the criminal justice system, and on public attitudes toward specific cases—including the attitudes of potential and actual jurors—has been another frequent focus. The right of journalists to protect sources by not disclosing their names has also come under scrutiny from time to time.

While journalism may be the media profession with the most legitimate claim to exercise influence over the criminal justice system, it is by no means the only way the media exercise such influence. Entertainment media have also been studied and criticized for their influence over public perceptions of the people and institutions that comprise the criminal justice system. A striking amount of television programming has in one way or another (e.g., through comedy, mystery, drama, biography, docudrama, and soap opera) been centered on police, lawyers, judges, criminals, and victims of crime. The effects on public attitudes and behavior that these portrayals may have brought about have received considerable research attention. Media portrayals of violence, largely in television but also in movies and—increasingly in the 1990s—recorded music, have been studied in part for their potential to inspire real-life criminal behavior. Exposure to violent media content has been argued in criminal defenses as a mitigating factor in the guilt of defendants.

Since the early 1980s a television genre has emerged that is part journalism (in that it purports to deal with reality and with important subjects) and in no small part entertainment (in that it is dramatic, enhanced with music and special effects, and often includes actors playing various roles). Shows such as *Cops, America's Most Wanted,* and *Unsolved Mysteries* combine footage of actual arrests, interviews with people involved in crimes, and other documentary information with an assortment of dramatic elements to create a new sort of quasi-journalism scorned by professional journalists but very popular. While not yet the focus of much research attention, the emergence of such shows is occasionally credited for a perceived decline in the quality of broadcast journalism, which may have an indirect effect on the justice system.

The possibility that exposure to mass media entertainment—from comic books to the Internet—can inspire criminal behavior was the subject of research, speculation, and debate throughout the twentieth century. Some content is considered more suspect than others, particularly depictions of violence. Since 1950, violent television fare has been the subject of a great deal of research, and meta-analyses of this body of research tend to conclude that there is a consistent, moderate causal relationship between exposure to televised violence and aggressive behavior in the real world (Hearold; Paik and Comstock; Hogben). Various theoretical explanations for the link have been offered, notably including social learning (Bandura), excitation transfer (Zillmann, Hoyt, and Day), and disinhibition, or desensitization (Berkowitz and Rawlings; Thomas, Horton, Lippincott, and Drabman).

Not all aggressive behavior is criminal, of course. The laboratory studies that lead to the conclusion that exposure to televised violence causes more aggressive behavior in real life are frequently criticized for not being sufficiently realistic to be generalized to the potential for truly dangerous, criminal behavior outside the laboratory. This criticism is deflected somewhat by research using other methods, including large sample surveys, quasi-experiments (using a more realistic setting with naive subjects unaware that they are under observation) and "found experiments" (in which public records are searched for evidence of pre- and post-exposure effects) (Phillips), all of which tend to support the conclusion that a persistent but moderate effect on aggressive behavior can be traced to exposure to violent media.

Three particular subjects receive the bulk of research attention where entertainment-related effects are concerned: (1) the effects of any violent media on children; (2) the "cultivation" of beliefs about crime and the criminal justice system that results from viewing television; and (3) the effects of pornography on adults. It is frequently noted that by the time an American child reaches adolescence he or she is likely to have seen thousands of murders depicted on television (e.g., Huston et al's, calculation that by the time a child leaves elementary school he or she will have seen eight thousand murders) (cited in Bogart, p. 351). In the 1990s the increasing popularity of computer games that simulate wholesale slaughter of human beings (e.g., *Doom* and *Quake*) has led to speculation that the wave of school shootings of the late 1990s has roots in part in the skills (such as arming, evaluating killed or wounded status, and strategizing) cultivated by playing such games and in the indifference toward suffering that leads to success in the games (Grossman).

Cultivation theory hypothesizes that television's depiction of the world leads heavy viewers of television to believe that the real world resembles the television world in key respects, including the likelihood of crime and the proportion of people involved in the criminal justice system (Gerbner, Gross, Morgan, and Signorielli). Carlson (1985) studied the content of crime shows in the late 1970s and the attitudes toward the criminal justice system held by viewers of these shows. He found that the crime shows on television in the late 1970s presented a very unrealistic view of the criminal justice system, specifically including the effectiveness of police, the rights of suspects and defendants, and the general level of criminal activity in the world.

People who watch these shows report more support for authorities such as police, less support for civil liberties, and more political cynicism. Carlson notes that the consistent messages of crime shows may result in "an increase in demand for police protection" (p. 195) since police are portrayed as extraordinarily effective and crime as rampant. It should be noted, however, that the sort of crime shows Carlson examined were qualitatively different from the shows that emerged in the 1980s, beginning with *Hill Street Blues*. These later shows, many produced by Stephen Bochco, have featured flawed police who often fail to catch their suspects, and open criminals as recurring characters who appear immune to capture. The effects of such programs would, by Carlson's logic, result in mistrust of police and perhaps even more generalized cynicism.

Shrum and Mares each have attempted to explain the psychological processes by which cultivation occurs. Shrum points to the accessibility of heuristics, whereby it is easier for heavy viewers of television to rely on the impression TV makes on them when they answer questions about the real world than it would be for heavy viewers to search their minds and make a more elaborate—

and perhaps accurate—calculation. Mares argues that respondents are not always aware of where their information comes from, and thus "source confusion" accounts for people's tendency to describe the real world in television terms. Potter, Warren, and others point out that even if viewers limit their exposure to non-fiction programs, such as news and news magazines (e.g., *20/20*), they are likely to end up with distorted impressions of the real world.

The authors compare nonfiction TV depictions of antisocial behavior to real-world statistics. "If we rely on non-fiction programming to tell us about the parameters and nature of our society, that programming is constructing narratives that are not particularly useful for that purpose. Nonfictional television presents a very high rate of antisocial activity, and the most serious forms of that activity (physical violence and crime) are presented at rates far above the rates in the real world" (p. 86).

While fears regarding children's exposure to violent media are mostly centered on the likelihood that children will imitate or learn the criminal behavior they see, concerns about adults' exposure to pornography also include the impact of such exposure on such decisions as jury verdicts in rape trials (Linz, Donnerstein, and Penrod) and acceptance of "rape myths," for example, that women only pretend to resist rape (Allen, Emmers, Gebhardt, and Giery). Adults play many roles in the criminal justice system that make their attitudes toward crime important. If, as Linz and others demonstrate, exposure to pornography can affect jurors' decisions, voir dire in rape cases might benefit from questions about such exposure (if potential jurors could be counted on to respond to voir dire inquiries on this subject truthfully).

It is not always easy to define the ideal relationship between the media system and the criminal justice system. The goals and resources of the media do not mesh perfectly with those of prosecutors, defendants, judges, and police. The goals and resources that people possess as audiences and readers are different from the goals and resources those same people possess in other roles they play, as citizens, jurors, suspects, and consumers. The ongoing negotiation between the media, the justice system, and people in their various relevant roles produces the media effects observed in the research fields reviewed here (Ball-Rokeach). Many of these effects may be unintended or undesirable, but mitigating such effects as prejudicial pretrial publicity is often not possible without threatening goals that others consider paramount, such as press freedom or the desire of a prosecutor to try a case locally (i.e., avoiding a change of venue).

When goals are in conflict, and resources are scarce or fought over, the relative power of the parties to the conflict becomes the central issue. There is doubt that the ability of the media to influence the course of criminal justice is entirely legitimate or desirable, especially when that influence stems from the increasing dominance of the media's entertainment over its journalistic function. But the media are powerful enough to resist intrusive public policy and defend their resources (such as access to sources, control over their broadcast schedules, and use of information-gathering tactics such as hidden cameras). The justice system has powerful resources of its own to use to pursue its goals when they conflict with the media's. It is the public, particularly when the public is atomized, whose goals are least likely to receive support and benefit from rich resources when they are threatened by the goals of the media or the justice system. As Potter and Warren point out in their discussion of policies regarding the regulation of sex and violence on television, the political influence of the broadcasting industry allows the media to tie up regulators over definitional issues (What is sex? What is violence?), rendering public policy to limit such content ineffective.

We began and ended the twentieth century with a nervous tension of conflict and cooperation between the media and criminal justice systems. In nontotalitarian societies this tension is unavoidable as the goals and interests of these systems differ. A question for the twenty-first century is whether the delicate balance of power between these players will give way. A major concern is the trendline of increasing distrust of major social institutions, especially when combined with an apparent decline in the strength of commitment to civic society (Putnam, 1995). In other words, the relationship between the media and criminal justice systems is a dynamic one that reflects changes in the larger social and political environment where conceptions of justice and community are formed. For the criminal justice system to have legitimacy for its just administration of the criminal law and for the media system to have legitimacy for its contributions to civil society, each must be regarded as playing vital roles in furtherance of a democratic order that commands the allegiance of its citizens. In short, justice must remain part of the crime story, whether told by the criminal justice system or by the media.

PANICS AND MEDIA CRIME

Definitions

A moral panic 'is an overreaction of the mass media, police and local community leaders to delinquent offences which are in fact relatively trivial, both in terms of the nature of the offence and the number of people involved' B Turner et al, Dictionary of Sociology, Penguin.

Examples of trivial offences that are escalated: Vandalism; Mods and Rockers; nuisance neighbours; welfare scroungers; lager louts; fighting dogs; savaging toddlers; glue sniffing; joy riding; mugging; bag snatching; mobile phone snatching in streets; millennium bugs; disorderly plane passengers; fly posting; violent strikers; football hooligans; anarcho travellers; gypsies; 'Peeping Toms'.; 'Tides of Porn'.

A more general concept for the process in which the media produce overreactions with all sorts of crimes, from the trivial to the major.

Examples of serious offences that are amplified and escalated: Pedophilia priests; car highjacking; pot smoking; crack cocaine; heroin;

HIV; computer virus's; Serial Sniper; International Terrorism; illegal immigration; Credit card fraud; 'chocolate drop girls' - girls in prostitution; rent boys; Gang warfare; Intentional infectors of HIV;

History of the Debate and its Theoretical Base

1950's Inclusion and Exclusion - Cohen, Lemert and Becker begin to study the process by which the powerful manage to define some groups as outsiders; delinquents; deviants; as abnormal; as dangerous. This mirrored studies of how powerful groups were able to reproduce their own status as insiders, the establishment; as normal; and as the guardians of law and order e.g. C W Mills 1951 White Collar; 1956 the Power Elite. E Lemert introduced the power that lies with those who can 'define the situation' and the way the labeled react by adopting the stereotypes (secondary deviance). Deviance is not natural but constructed by the powerful in the search for social control. Arthur Miller's play on The Crucible (1953) explained how a moral panic in a small town of Salem led to the trial and execution of witches in an allegory of the McCarthy anti communist trials in the 1950's. Later used by Christopher Hill to account for Witch Trials in C17th Britain. (West Side Storey)

1960's Symbolic Interactionism and Labelling – Howard Becker in the Outsiders (1963) Boys in White (1961) and Making the Grade (1968) identifies the key dynamic in the process as 'labeling' groups so as to justify controlling and excluding them. Deviance and exclusion is not structural (Marxism) but due to the way groups interact and who wins the battle to define themselves as legitimate and normal. Mods and Rockers loose; boisterous medical students win. Ernest Goffman introduced the idea of 'stigma' as part of the process of gaining power over others and their behaviour by stigmatization, imposing your critical labels (1964). Meanwhile the work of George Mead was resurrected to explain how this happened. We all have an ego or 'I' plus a self that accommodates itself to role and society– the 'me'. During interactions between self and others the self has to negotiate between 'I' and 'me' at the same time. We develop gestures, body language and vocabulary that symbolize the way we are accommodating with others. So once defined by others as a 'mod' or 'rocker' you either retreat into normality or role-play the character.

1970's Deviancy and Amplification – originally coined in 1964 by L T Wilkins this concept is made famous by Stuart Hall and the Birmingham Centre for CCS. They redirect focus from the police and powerful to the media, and introduce the idea of media 'amplification', or the spiraling of panics, stories, and exaggerations that only subsides when the CJS react with authoritarian measures e.g. Jason Ditton.

The stimulus is the identification of the deviant act by the police, a politician or the media. They amplify, and generate more panic. The labeled then choose to respond conversationally and symbolically to the depiction e.g. Mods and Rockers storm Hastings after Brighton, then other seaside towns. The interactions then spiral upwards as stakeholders try to gain the power by defining reality.

Case Studies of Moral Panics

Jock Young, Folk Devils and Moral Panics, 1980, Blackwell

Picks up on the demonisation of youth groups i.e. Teddy Boys; Mods, Rockers, Hells Angels; Hippies 1964-5

They are identified as a 'threat' to society – so 'the rule makers create the rule breakers', Howard Becker. 'Warnings' of disaster are made

They are stereotyped in a simplistic and negative manner and 'unruly' acts identified.

The 'moral guardians' of society are mobilized and man the barricades and demand tough action. Experts and professionals then define, diagnose and prescribe responses i.e. leaders of professional bodies who try to fit into their agendas.

The groups then react, interact, escalate, respond in cycles of amplification Brighton, Clacton, Margate.

Some shocking event is then used to precipitate a massive response i.e. a fight or riot.

The authorities devise a response, implement (stop scooters outside the towns; heavy policing; provoke an incident; arrest ring leaders; run groups out of town; film it all and use it to justify illegal actions by the police).

See film 'Quadrophenia', The Who with Sting.

Mugging as moral panic 1972-4.

Stuart Hall (1978) Policing the Crisis; Mugging, the State and Law and Order; critiqued by Peter Waddington ch 12 in Caffrey and Muncie reader pp 235-247.

See especially D Kidd- Hewitt and R Osborne, Crime and the Media: A Postmodern Spectacle, ch's 1-6.

Britain in decline – so someone has to get the blame i.e. trade unions; welfare scroungers, thieves and petty criminals. Images of black riots in US cities, violent anti-Vietnam demonstrations created a narrative to replicate.

The Conservative part with the a right wing media decide to *manufacture a public image of chaos and danger that requires authoritarian responses.*

Examples are found. The film Clockwork Orange is used to illustrate the threat.

The media highlight a series of street robberies in London and apply an American term 'mugging'. This catches on and is amplified.

Psychologists blame lax parenting in the 1960's, drugs, sexual liberation, left wing ideology and welfare nannying, end of National Service.

Quickly the provocateurs are identified as 'young black men'. Message - The white poor can handle economic crisis – but not black youth. Blame blacks for the crisis –'false enemy'). Solution – stop and search; SUS policy; drugs raids; harassment (Leads to the Brixton Riots and Winston Silcote prosecution)

Observations

The media act as agents and conductors of moral indignation– they create media 'fantasies' or a criminal 'hyper-reality' of produced and consumed images (Baudrillard). They create 'social censure'. They investigate, muck rake then point the finger via gross cases that challenge the publics tolerance - scapegoating. The effect is to create disquiet, worry, fear and anxiety – then a desire for security, for order to be returned. This is their constructed reality. So is the corollary of a mythical law abiding and orderly past – to return to and envy.

Amplification raises the tension demanding release by authoritarian measures, law and order, swift justice and harsh punishment. A public end up calling for their own repression, they desire and demand 'get tough' action created by panics. The media can quickly move on to other vulnerable targets

Criticisms

- Until Hall, structural inequalities (race, colour, sex, class) are down played and psychological factors overplayed
- Outsiders and law breakers are made into victims; and actual victims are ignored or marginalized
- Places agency with interactions not individuals; ignores moral choices
- Underestimates the power of excluded groups to re-label and reconstruct themselves e.g. gay men
- Perhaps overstates the power of the media and its conspiratorial liaison with right wing politicians
- Historically inaccurate, ignores official statistics - Waddington

CRIME AND THE MEDIA (NOTES FROM SIMON WINLOW)

The 'Moral Panic' Argument: Media, Social Imagery and Deviancy Amplification.

This perspective has achieved a very high profile in criminology for over 30 years, and, although looking rather intellectually tired and worn, continues to inform much practice in the criminal justice system. It can be categorised as part of the 'effects perspective' in media studies and concentrates on how fictional and non-fictional media representations feedback on to the perceptions and behaviours of individuals. The basic critical claims of this perspective is that media imagery creates apparent increases in the amount of deviance, thereby creating moral panics which justify authoritarian law and order policies which are really the product of the 'respectable fears' of middle classes. This process also has the effect of reinforcing deviant identity, and, like a self-fulfilling prophecy, creating more crime.

There is a large literature based on this perspective. Palmer (1973) examined the role of fiction, particularly how specific portrayals of villains justify the 'dirty tricks' of the police. Because the villains are so downright nasty and evil, according to Palmer, the police have such a tough job that bureaucratic legal niceties, such as regulation, procedure and accountability are projected as a hindrance to the real job of protecting the public (Dirty Harry, Regan and Carter etc.). Thus legal safeguards and civil liberties are secondary and the police should be granted more powers.

Cohen & Young (1981) see moral panic and deviancy amplification as part of a 'one-way' communication process of media. Disproportionate access is given to the self-appointed 'moral guardians' of society, and deviants' own accounts are rarely heard, therefore they are explained by the discourses of more powerful groups, e.g. magistrates, police chiefs, judges, MPs etc. who claim a mandate as the moral guardians of society. Becker calls this a 'hierarchy of access' to the media.

The perspective relies on the claim that the media is the principal, dominant mode of communication and generation of meaning in a modern society. It is extremely difficult for the general public to check out media representations and compare them with direct experience of deviancy. Most of us have very little or none at all; even those who work directly with offenders, like police or probation officers, have no experience of the historical background and cultural meaning systems of the deviant. Wilkins, in Cohen & Young, cites the example of the pre-industrial village community, where knowledge of problems was direct, where, for instance, young and old were in direct contact with each other. Now, because of the development of a commercial mass media under the control of a dominant elite our knowledge is the one-dimensional product of a one-way meaning system.

So how does deviancy amplification work?

- Societal reaction; media images cause a reaction in the public.
- Labelling; images and social typing strengthens deviant identities.
- Deviancy amplification; feeds back into support for criminal justice policies of criminalisation, heavy handed policing, sentencing, punishment etc. that actually cause more crime and delinquency.

Hall et al note the disproportionate media attention given to 'black muggers' which resulted in correspondingly more attention given to black youth by the criminal justice system. The concepts of 'blackness' and 'youth' began to be used as a symbolic shorthand for troublemaker (remember indexical relationships, naturalisation, myth etc.). Other symbols were haircuts, leather jackets, boots, etc. This resulted in the creation of outsiders, a process whereby black youths, already marginalised, became more so. Other 'labelled' groups suffered the same fate:

Halloran et al (1968) - anti-war demonstrators as subversives.

Golding & Middleton (1982) - welfare claimants as scroungers.

Young (1971) - drug takers as heroin addicts or criminal dealers.

Cohen (1972) - Mods and Rockers as inherently violent gangs (fear of the mob).

Marsh, Rosser and Harre (1978) - football hooligans as above.

Folk devils - Ideological climate - news sense - political agenda setting.

A word of caution; what we are talking about here goes beyond the psychological concept of the stereotype (prejudice, attitude, personal belief, a simple inaccurate and negative image, locked within the individual, e.g. Adorno's 'authoritarian personality'). Rather, it is not merely an idea in the individual's head to which they habitually refer, but a shorthand way of referring to social relationships, and these are socially produced and often contain a large element of reality - e.g. women do find themselves in subordinate positions, it is not just a false idea in people's heads. Realities like the subordination of women are naturalised by the media and attributed specific underlying causes by buying into those myths which provide them. The same thing happens with crime and the criminal. One of the problems with this is that labelling theory would claim that these 'realities' are produced by symbolic interaction in the first place. In order to throw light on this sort of problem, we need to know something about the theoretical background

THEORETICAL BACKGROUND

The moral panic argument has its roots in the theory of symbolic interactionism. This, in turn, is based on Mead's formulation of the dualistic subject - the 'I' and the 'Me' - which defines itself and constructs it's own identity in a sort of internal conversation with itself. What intrudes in this conversation is the 'significant other', whose response to the 'I' can influence the process of symbolic interchange. This provides the initial link with the outside world, and the process therefore becomes social. Significant others can be parents, members of peer groups, public of, cials, and, of course, those characters who inhabit the media world with whom the 'I' identifies.

This theory was transposed into criminology via the work of people like Lemert, Becker and Cohen in the deviancy studies of the '50s and '60s. Primary deviance, which, it is claimed, is largely petty, sporadic and committed by young males, is picked up by a mass media in the control of the value system of the dominant white, male, middle class whose attitudes to a certain social 'type' of working class people, since the beginnings of the urbanisation and industrialisation processes, have been traditionally based on fear, loathing and hostility - Pearson's 'respectable fears'. Thus the media tends to exaggerate these primary acts; this has two principal effects:

(1) It provides an exaggerated and reactionary image of deviance with which young people can identify, intruding into the process of identity construction and reinforcing the image. This makes it more likely that the deviant, especially the young deviant, will construct this identity in a more durable and resistant form and tend to commit more crime - secondary deviance.

(2) This reactionary and exaggerated image constitutes the public's view of the deviant, socially constructing (or cultivating already existing reactionary conceptions) the myth of the 'folk-devil', social typing or 'labelling' rule-breakers as threatening and dangerous. Thus all of their actions come to be interpreted according to the status produced by the label, and they receive discriminatory and unwarranted attention from the criminal justice system - singled out, observed, hassled, wrongfully arrested and heavily sentenced. Young people who began by committing minor acts of deviance become often unnecessarily implicated in the criminal justice system - remand, secure care, probation, prison etc., - and this becomes the new terrain for identity formation, again tending to produce secondary deviance if the lifestyle is embraced and adopted. A deviant career can be the outcome.

Problems

As we have seen, sociological attention is drawn to the criminalisation process as an essentially symbolic activity carried out by the agencies of a repressive State in reaction to any activity that it construed as potentially subversive (Pearson,1983,1985). In these formulations the causes of youth crime lie in the intrusion of the dominant group's idea of criminality into the subordinate group's conversation with itself, and the subsequent adoption of an imposed identity - the much-vaunted 'label'. Thus the young criminal was the product of someone else's idea, a temporary symbolic entity that could be allowed to define itself as something else and assert it's inalienable human rights if the tap of negative symbols could only be turned off. This formulation is problematic:

(1) Voluntarism on the part of the middle class. Do the middle class control the media to such an extent and are they malevolent enough to deliberately cause the working class grief? Or are they themselves implicated in a prevailing social structure which determines the social imagery of both classes?

(2) Romanticising deviants, ignoring victims. This perspective, from the beginning, has displayed a tendency to concentrate on 'exotica' and ignore serious, persistent criminal activity and also ignore the 'lived reality' of those victims who suffer from it and don't rely entirely on the media for their interpretations. There may be a rational, experiential basis for fear.

(3) Ignores the possibility of moral choice. Despite the label, do not people possess the morally informed power to choose their actions? Is it invariably true that young people always allow labels to stick?

(4) Over-reliance on the power and oppressive/repressive nature of social control agencies, particularly the media. Why is it that certain young people readily embrace the negative and repressive images of the media and other agencies such as education and criminal justice, yet resolutely resist anything positive they try to project? Does this not indicate a pre-existing disposition to take on board a deviant identity?

(5) Relies on the pre-existing, independent rational individual - the Rousseauian notion of the human being who is naturally good if left to construct a truly benign, humanistic identity outside of the corrupting and repressive influence of society. Stop the labelling, and the good person will emerge, as an act of nature, in front of our eyes.

(6) Can be seen as either voluntaristic (the 'I' as an independent entity) or deterministic (the 'Me' as a determined entity).

(7) Ahistorical and acultural in that it ignores the development of deep traditions and ways of life that develop in more direct, practical response to material conditions and pass their meaning system down over generations (cultural transmission), thus maintaining and reproducing themselves. In this formulation, they don't need to be labelled and are highly unlikely to accept the imposition of any meaning apart from their own.

2

Off Balance: Youth, Race and Crime in the News

This is the fourth in an ongoing series of analyses published by Building Blocks for Youth, a multiorganizational initiative whose goal is to promote a fair and effective juvenile justice system. In January, 2000, Building Blocks issued its first report, "The Color of Justice" which found that youth of color in California were more than eight times as likely to be incarcerated by adult courts as White youth, for equally serious crimes. Building Blocks' comprehensive national study, "And Justice for Some", reported that youth of color are treated more severely than White youth at each stage of the justice system, even when charged with the same offenses. In October, 2000 Building Blocks' third report, "Youth Crime, Adult Time" an in-depth study of youth prosecuted as adults in 18 of the largest jurisdictions in the country, found racial disparities similar to the earlier reports, and raised serious concerns about the fairness and appropriateness of the process. The initiative has five major components:

- Research on the disparate impact of the justice system on minority youth, on the effects of new adult-court transfer legislation in the states, and on the privatization of juvenile justice facilities by for-profit corporations;
- Analyses of decisionmaking at critical points in the justice system, including arrest, detention, adjudication, and disposition;

- Direct advocacy on behalf of youth in the justice system, particularly on issues that disproportionately affect youth of color such as conditions of confinement in jails, prisons, and juvenile facilities; access to counsel and adequacy of representation in juvenile court; and "zero tolerance" and other issues relating to school suspensions and expulsions;
- Constituency-building among African-American, Latino, and Native-American and other minority organizations, as well as organizations in the medical, mental health, legal, law enforcement, child welfare, civil rights, human rights, religious, victim's rights, and domestic violence areas, at the national, state, and local levels;
- Development of communications strategies to provide timely, accurate, and relevant information to these constituencies, public officials, policymakers, the media, and the public.

The partners in the initiative are the Youth Law Center, American Bar Association Juvenile Justice Center, Center on Juvenile and Criminal Justice, Juvenile Law Center, Minorities in Law Enforcement, National Council on Crime and Delinquency and Pretrial Services Resource Center. The initiative is supported by the federal Office of Juvenile Justice and Delinquency Prevention and the Bureau of Justice Assistance, the Annie E. Casey, Ford, Mott, MacArthur, Rockefeller and William T. Grant foundations, and the Center on Crime, Communities & Culture of the Open Society Institute. This project was supported by award No. 98-JN-FX-K003 awarded by the Office of Juvenile Justice and Delinquency Prevention, Office of Justice Programs, U.S. Department of Justice. Points of view or opinions in this document are those of the authors and do not necessarily represent the official position or policies of the U.S. Department of Justice or the supporting foundations.

INTRODUCTION

Despite sharp declines in youth crime, the public expresses great fear of its young people. Although violent crime by youth in

1998 was at its lowest point in the 25-year history of the National Crime Victimization Survey, 62% of poll respondents felt that juvenile crime was on the increase. In the 1998/99 school year, there was less than a one in two million chance of being killed in a school in America, yet 71% of respondents to an NBC/Wall Street Journal poll felt that a school shooting was likely in their community. Despite a 40% decline in school associated violent deaths between 1998 and 1999 and declines in other areas of youth violence, respondents to a USA Today poll were 49% more likely to express fear of their schools in 1999 than in 1998.

In an environment in which fear of youth crime and actual youth crime are so out of sync, policies affecting young people are bound to be impacted. Since 1992, 47 states have made their juvenile justice systems more punitive by eroding confidentiality protections or making it easier to try juveniles as adults. In one estimate, more than 200,000 youths were prosecuted in adult court in America in 1998. Americans are also more likely to exaggerate the threat of victimization by minorities. Twice as many White Americans believe they are more likely to be victimized by a minority than a White, despite the fact that Whites are three times more likely to be victimized by Whites than by minorities.

What is the News Media's Role?

More than 70 years ago, in his classic work, Public Opinion, Walter Lippmann wrote that it was impossible to know through direct experience everything that it was necessary to know to function as a citizen in our modern democracy. Instead, Lippmann explained, we depend on "pictures in our heads," many of them delivered by the news media, to tell us about the world.

Our decisions about how to behave and how to construct our society have to be based on those pictures, Lippmann believed, because the world was too vast to experience personally. The public depends on the media for its pictures of crime. Three quarters (76%) of the public say they form their opinions about crime from what they see or read in the news, more than three times the number who state that they get their primary information on crime from personal experience (22%).

In a Los Angeles Times poll, 80% of respondents stated that the media's coverage of violent crime had in-creased their personal fear of being a victim. These survey results are consistent with communications research that confirms that the news media largely determine what issues we collectively think about, how we think about them and what kinds of policy alternatives are considered viable. News portrayals of juvenile justice issues are significant for how they influence policymakers and the public regarding what should be done to ensure public safety. The public and policy makers do not consider issues unless they are visible, and they are not visible unless the news brings them to light.

Most people have little or no personal experience with juvenile crime since adults commit most of the crime in the nation: adults commit about 89% of all crimes cleared by arrest. The public depends on the media even more for its pictures of crime done by or to minority youth, since most of the public doesn't have personal experience with it. Eighty-six percent of White homicide victims are killed by other Whites and, overall, Whites are three times as likely to be victimized by other Whites as by minorities. There is a very small likelihood that a White adult will have the unfortunate opportunity to form an opinion about Black youth violence based on personal experience. Consequently, America's dominant voting and opinion setting block — its White adult population — simply must rely on the news to explain minority youth crime to them.

The news media should help as many citizens as possible make sense of the world around them. But does the current approach to covering youth and crime maximize public understanding of reality? What information on youth and crime does the American public get from the news? In view of the powerful impact news coverage of crime has on public opinion and the dependence of most Americans on the media for depictions of crime, there are several important questions we have about the accuracy of the picture Americans are receiving from the news media:

- Does news coverage reflect actual crime trends?
- How does news coverage depict minorities and crime?
- Does news coverage disproportionately depict youth of color as perpetrators of crime?

METHODS

Our objective was to compile and examine the best social science that has analyzed the content of crime news to answer the questions above, particularly analyses that included examinations of race and youth. Toward that end, we conducted a comprehensive, computerized search of criminal justice and communications data bases on content analyses of crime news, which we augmented with additional studies gleaned from references in the computer-generated articles. Altogether, the search yielded 146 articles that we reviewed, abstracted, and categorized. We eliminated any articles that were about single events (e.g. O.J. Simpson), "reality" shows, or non-US news. We also eliminated articles that did not offer primary data analyses and books that were not peer-reviewed.

Ultimately we focused on the 77 studies that directly assessed the content of crime, race and/or youth in the news. Once we had summarized and condensed the findings about news content, we compared those findings to crime trends reported by law enforcement agencies.

For example, if studies of the news showed an ever-larger proportion of the "news hole" (the amount of newspaper or television time devoted to news) occupied by violent crime, was that simply a reflection of actual increases in violent crime during the same time period? According to the best scientific analyses of media content, is the news providing an accurate reflection of crime trends? We ascertained whether the studies themselves made the relevant comparisons to crime trends, and, if they did not, we collected the appropriate crime data to compare to the content of the news.

The studies we surveyed covered a range of media — local and network television, newspapers, and broadcast and print news magazines — from 1910 through 2001. Most studies analyzed newspapers (N=55), followed by local television (N=25). Nineteen studies analyzed network television news. Only three studies analyzed print news magazines and two analyzed the content of TV news magazine programs. (The numbers add to more than 77 because several studies analyzed more than one medium). Studies that examine race and crime find that the proportion of crime committed by people of color (usually African Americans) is over-reported and that Black victims are under-represented. Other studies find that crimes committed by people of color are covered in proportion with arrest rates, but that crimes committed by Whites are under-covered.

Finding #1: The news media report crime, especially violent crime, out of proportion to its actual occurrence.

Studies of newspapers and television identified three clear patterns. First, and most consistent over time, is that newspapers and television emphasize violent crime. Second, the more unusual the crime, the greater the chance it will be covered. Third, the rate of crime coverage increased while real crime rates dropped. While all media emphasize violence in their news, newspapers do it to a lesser degree than network television, which does it less than local TV news. There are fewer studies of Spanish language newspapers and television news broadcast in the US, but those that exist also demonstrate an emphasis on crime consistent with studies of Englishlanguage US news.

Violent crime dominates crime coverage. Crime is often the dominant topic on local television news, network news, and TV news magazines. In general, TV crime reporting is the inverse of crime frequency. That is, murder is reported most often on the news though it happens the least. Several analyses of the evening news found that, although homicides made up from one to two-tenths of one percent of all arrests, homicides made up more than a quarter (27% - 29%) of the

FINDINGS

Overall, the studies taken together indicate that depictions of crime in the news are not reflective of the rate of crime generally, the proportion of crime which is violent, the proportion of crime committed by people of color, or the proportion of crime committed by youth. The problem is not the inaccuracy of individual stories, but that the cumulative choices of what is included in the news — or not included —presents the public with a false picture of higher frequency and severity of crime than is actually the case. Furthermore, the studies show that crime is depicted as a series of distinct events unrelated to any broader context. Most crimes reported on the evening news. While it is to be expected that a homicide will receive more media attention than a petty theft, overcoverage of violent crime can give viewers the sense that the world is a more dangerous place than it actually is.

The more unusual the crime or violence, the more likely it is to be covered. Factors that increase the likelihood of a homicide being reported in the news are multiple victims, multiple offenders, an unusual method, a White victim, a child, elderly, or female victim, or occurrence in an affluent neighborhood. One study found that the least frequent murders—homicides between strangers and interracial homicides—received more coverage when, in reality, most people were murdered by someone they knew and someone of the same race. Crime coverage has increased while real crime rates have fallen. Overall the rate of crime coverage in the news did not reflect crime trends. Nationally, crime dropped by 20% from 1990 to 1998 while network TV showed an 83% increase in crime news. While homicide coverage was increasing on network news — a 473% jump from 1990 to 1998 — homicides were down 32.9% during the same time period.

Finding #2: The news media report crime as a series of individual events without adequate attention to its overall context.

Presumably, if the emphasis on crime is satisfying viewers' desire to know about it, print and broadcast journalists should also be explaining it. Yet most crime news is episodic, describing crime events as if they are isolated from larger social, historical or environmental contexts.

Studies spanning almost 100 years—1910 to 2000—were consistent in their findings that news reports describe what happened with little reporting about why the crime and violence happened or what could be done about it. In one example, researchers found that the nation's dominant news magazines portrayed the race riots of the late 1960's as "random, unpredictable and most of all, unjustified" events outside a larger social context, despite Kerner Commission findings that there were many identifiable— and justifiable— reasons for the riots. The lack of explanations for crime and violence complicates the problem of exaggerated frequency in news stories by leaving the impression that the violence is inevitable.

Finding #3: The news media, particularly television news, unduly connect race and crime, especially violent crime.

A disproportionate number of perpetrators on the news are people of color, especially African Americans, and the strongest evidence shows that people of color, again primarily African Americans, are underrepresented as victims in crime news. African American perpetrators are depicted as dangerous and indistinguishable as a group, and they appear more frequently in crime news stories than Whites. Interracial crime is also covered disproportionately. Invisible Black victims. Six out of seven studies that clearly identify the race of victims found more attention was paid to White victims than to Black victims. Homicides of White victims not only resulted in more articles, but also longer articles than homicides of Black victims. This prompted one researcher to coin the term "worthy victims" to describe the greater coverage received by White crime victims compared to people of color. Visible Black suspects.

Overall, while the coverage of perpetrators of color is out of balance with actual crime trends, it is less so than the coverage of minority victims. In nine of twelve (75%) studies, minorities were overrepresented as perpetrators of crime. Some studies found distinct disparities, while others found perpetrators of color represented in numbers that matched their local arrest rates, but found Whites underrepresented. For example, a study of murder coverage in Indianapolis newspapers found that the percentage of articles about Black suspects reflected the percentage of Blacks arrested for murder (60% and 61%, respectively), but if the suspect was Black, the average article length was longer than for a White suspect. Close looks at local TV news in a large urban center found disparities as well. Blacks were 22% more likely to be shown on local TV news in Los Angeles committing violent crime than nonviolent crime, while according to police statistics, Blacks were equally likely to be arrested for violent crime and nonviolent crime. Likewise, Hispanics were 14% more likely to be depicted as committing violent crime than a nonviolent crime, whereas Hispanics were 7% more likely to be arrested for a violent crime than a nonviolent crime.

Some might argue that this is simply because violent crime is more newsworthy than non-violent crime. But Whites were 31% more likely to be depicted committing a nonviolent crime than a violent crime, whereas Whites were only 7% more likely to be arrested for a nonviolent crime than a violent crime. While Blacks and Hispanics were overrepresented as violent offenders, Whites were underrepresented as violent offenders on the same evening news. In addition, researchers found that when stories featured a Black perpetrator, reporters included sources hostile to the perpetrator half the time, whereas with White perpetrators, reporters included hostile sources 25 percent of the time. How are African Americans depicted in crime stories? In his extensive work on portrayals of African Americans on local television news, Robert Entman documents that Blacks are most likely to be seen in television news stories in the role of criminal, victim, or demanding politician.

Black suspects were less likely to be identified by name than White suspects; were not as well dressed as White suspects; and were more likely to be shown physically restrained than Whites. In sum, Entman concluded that Black suspects were routinely depicted as being poor, dangerous, and indistinct from other non-criminal Blacks. Interracial crime. Our nation has an ugly history of treatment of interracial crime, dating from slavery through the "Jim Crow" era to the well-documented fact that today Blacks have a higher risk of receiving the death penalty for killing Whites than any other victim-offender racial mix. That history is reflected in public opinion polling on race and crime that shows that Whites overestimate their likelihood of being victimized by minorities by three to one. Studies of TV news coverage of crime in Philadelphia, Los Angeles and Chicago found that interracial crime was substantially more likely to be reported than its actual percentage of crime statistics would predict.

These findings are disturbing since people of all races are far more likely to be killed by someone of the same race. Summary. While every content analysis of media coverage of crime by and against people of color does not show disparate coverage, a clear majority of the research reveals a disturbing pattern of disproportionate coverage. Consequently, it is likely that most Americans form an erroneous picture of which groups are violent and who suffers most often from crime and violence. In particular, the absence of Black victims, coupled with the repeated presence of Black suspects across different sources of news, reinforces stereotypes about African Ameri-cans as a group audiences should fear.

Finding #4: Few studies examine portrayals of youth on the news. Those that do find that youth rarely appear in the news and when they do, it is connected to violence.

There is substantially less research that focuses on portrayals of youth in the news. Though the findings are consistent, there are fewer of them. Of the 146 articles we originally identified, only 16 examined whether and how youth were portrayed on television news or in newspapers. The findings on the coverage of youth crime are consistent with overall crime coverage – when youth appear in the news, it is in connection with violence. A few of the studies also uphold the findings on race and the news. Young people of color seem to fare as poorly as their elders on the news — perhaps worse. Finally, some studies find that violence perpetrated by adults upon youth is underreported. News involving youth is violent. Stories about youth in newspapers and on television news are scarce. When they do appear in the news, youth usually are in stories about education or violence. Relatively few youth are arrested each year for violent crimes, yet the message from the news is that this is a common occurrence. One study of newspaper coverage of youth in Minnesota concluded that youth "are presented as inevitably bad, and, if left untreated, they will inevitably go wrong."

An analysis of Hawaii's major dailies over 10 years showed a 30-fold increase in coverage of youth crime, despite declining rates of youth crime. An analysis examining 840 newspaper stories and 109 network news segments in 1993 showed one out of every 50 (2%) young people in that 40% of all newspaper stories on California were either victims or children were about violence, as were 48% perpetrators of violence in 1993. Nearly of network television news, whereas seven in 10 news stories (68%) on violence nominal attention was given to topics of in California involved youth, whereas family, health, or economic concerns. youth made up 14.1% of violence arrests There was more overall coverage of crime in California that year.

By and violence than of all other policy issues contrast, young people had to perform combined. In a later study that examined extraordinary feats to appear on local 3,172 randomly selected stories on youth television news in non-violence-related in one year of the Los Angeles Times, circumstances. When youth crime receives Sacramento Bee, and San Francisco a far larger share of all crime coverage Chronicle, the newspapers focused largely than youths actually commit, and when on two topics: education and violence. No youth crime coverage dramatically other topic rated even a third as much increases while actual youth crime is attention. Education stories comprised decreasing, the public that relies on media 26% of all stories involving youth.

The coverage as its primary source of authors concluded that this is appropriate information about youth crime is since the vast majority of youth between misinformed. the ages of 5 and 17 attend school and about half continue after high school. But violence Seven out of 10 local TV news stories made up 25% of all stories on violence in California involved youth coverage, when only youth, but young people only made up 14.1% of violent arrests three young ,people in 100 perpetrated or became victims of violence.

Young people made up the circumstances in which youth are seen on television news are similar. A study of youth on local television news in 1993 examined 214 hours of local television news broadcast over 11 days on 26 stations through-out California. More than two-thirds of violence stories involved youth while more than half of all stories that included youth involved violence. One out of every two (53%) TV news stories concerning children or youth involved violence, while California crime data show that.

Youth of color fare worse than their white counterparts. The one study that examined youth portrayals in magazines had the most to say about race. A qualitative analysis of all cover stories in Time and Newsweek between 1946-1995 determined that the term "young Black males" became synonymous with the word "criminal" during the late 1960's when Blacks were struggling for equality. A March 1965 Newsweek article was the first to connect crime with Black crime. In later stories in the 1970's, both Time and Newsweek portrayed crime as "largely perpetrated by 'young Black males'".

Later, Hispanic males were added to the picture. A study of youth crime portrayals in the New York Times found that Black or Latino youth were never quoted directly, while White youth were quoted in all five stories in which they appeared. Furthermore, defense attorneys for White youth were quoted 13 times, but attorneys for youth of color only twice. Crime news is where all youth are most likely to be seen on TV news, but youth of color appear in crime news more often than White youth—52% and 35%, respectively. White youth were present more often in health or education stories (13%) than were youth of color (2%). Youth victims & perpetrators. Only a few studies distinguished between youth victims and perpetrators. One found that homicide victims under age 15 received more coverage in the Los Angeles Times than would be expected based on the frequency of homicides in that group. Researchers examining the San Francisco Chronicle found more depictions of youth perpetrators than youth victims, despite crime data that show three crimes committed by adults against teens for every violent offense committed by youth under 18. In another examination of the Los Angeles Times in 1997, researchers found that nearly one in four murder suspects (23.9%) whose ages were identified in the Times were youth, while only one in six homicide arrestees (15.8%) in Los Angeles were youth that year.

Violence against youth is underreported. Two studies assessed whether crimes against young people were being covered; both studies found that crimes perpetrated by adults against youth are underreported. Several other studies that examined depictions of youth in the news generally did not detect substantial coverage of youth as victims of violence.

The relative lack of reporting on violence against youth can be juxtaposed with the overreporting of homicide by youth as compared to adults. In a comparison of youth portrayals in 327 stories from the 1997 Los Angeles Times (Orange County edition) to crime reports from the Los Angeles Police Department, researchers found youth homicides were nearly three times more likely to be reported in the Los Angeles Times, despite the fact that adults commit and are victims of far more murders.

The authors conclude that the Times' coverage scapegoats youth, since they commit far fewer crimes than adults. Journalists ponder why. There are reasons the coverage looks as it does. One is that crime news is easy — everyone knows what it looks like, how to gather it, and how to report it. Some journalists argue that audiences want news about violence, though most polls dispute that argument.

Another reason is that news is a business, and reporters, producers, and editors have learned to choose the news they believe will draw the most attractive audience for advertisers. The study of Denver's "Summer of Violence" offers some insight into newsroom decision-making about which homicides warrant coverage. After interviewing editors, producers, and reporters, the researcher concludes that, in covering Denver's "Summer of Violence" in 1993, journalists viewed these mostly White, middle class victims killed by minority youth through a predominantly White middle class lens. Denver Post reporter Steven Lipscher said, for example: Take a look at our editors over there.

Take a look at the news editors at the TV stations. Most of them are White middle class. Most of them are men but that doesn't make a whole lot of difference here. They live in these nice middle class neighborhoods and when those neighborhoods start having random crime…and it gets close to the suburbs or even in the suburbs where these news editors live, you know that deeply troubles them. When the crime was centered solely on the inner city if we had minority editors, people who lived in the inner city, we might have covered it. But we didn't and we still don't. Inner city crime is not nearly as shocking as suburban crime and the only reason why is look at who is writing the stories and look at who is assigning the stories. The White, middle class lens means that some murders are more important than others, as explained by this Rocky Mountain News reporter:

There are homicides and then there are homicides on the police beat. There are homicides I can work hard on and only get this much into the paper. And then there are the kind that all you have to do is mention to the editor, "Gotta former district attorney who just killed his wife," and we're all over it…And as a colleague of mine once said, he had this theory that there were misdemeanor murders. That's not a theory I subscribe to, but he had a point. Obviously, there are some murders that don't count as much as others. A misdemeanor homicide according to Tony was typically a drug dealer

[who] wipes out another drug dealer in an alley somewhere over a business deal gone bad. That is considered a low interest homicide (Emphasis in original). Ultimately, individual news workers make decisions about what to include in the news of the day based on whether they personally care about the story. Reporters, editors, and producers have finely honed internalized mechanisms that are triggered by their personal values and emotional responses, tempered by news judgement, experience, and expectations of audience response. Standard selection criteria for news stories — controversy, conflict, novelty, proximity, significance, timeliness, visual appeal, practicality — are processed through the personal filters of journalists.

Discussion – Creation of a "Misinformation Synergy"

The public relies on news for its knowledge of crime. We suggest that a "misinformation synergy" occurs in crime news that profoundly misinforms the public. The synergy results from the simultaneous and consistent presentation of three significant distortions in print and broadcast news. It is not just that African Americans are overrepresented as criminals and underrepresented as victims, or that young people are overrepresented as criminals, or that violent crime itself is given undue coverage. It is that all three occur together, combining forces to produce a terribly unfair and inaccurate overall image of crime in America. Add to that a majority of readers and viewers who rarely have any personal experience with crime by Black youth, and a White adult population who must rely on the media to tell them about minority youth crime, and the result is a perfect recipe for a misinformed public and misguided power structure.

Each study's findings, taken alone, may not be cause for alarm. After all, crime is a serious problem that demands news attention and political action. But if news audiences are taking the crime coverage at face value, they are accepting a serious distortion. They are likely to believe that most crime is extremely violent and that perpetrators are Black and victims, White. If news audiences have little contact with young people, they are likely to believe that youth are dangerous threats, in part because there are so few other representations of youth in the news to the contrary. Since every news outlet can't cover every crime, the question then becomes, how should editors, producers, and reporters choose which crimes to cover? How can the picture be made more accurate? How can print and broadcast journalists make choices that minimize the distortions documented by researchers since 1910? How can their cumulative choices better reflect the crime and violence they cover? When they make those choices, how can the media add more context to crime coverage so as to improve the viewers' understanding of the causes and solutions to violent crime? And what, if anything, can the public do to get more accurate information in the news?

RECOMMENDATIONS FOR THE NEWS MEDIA

The overwhelming evidence is that in the aggregate, crime coverage is not reflecting an accurate picture of who the victims and perpetrators are. The most consistent finding across media and across time is the gross distortion of the types of crime reported in the news. Rather than informing citizens about their world, the news is reinforcing stereotypes that inhibit society's ability to respond to the problem of crime, including juvenile crime. This is an admittedly difficult problem to fix, given the many constraints of daily journalism. Nonetheless, it is way past time to try to create a more accurate overall picture of crime, who suffers from it, and what can be done to prevent it. To begin to address this dilemma, we suggest that reporters, editors, and producers expand their sources; provide context for crime news; increase enterprise and investigative journalism; balance stories about crime and youth with stories about youth generally; conduct and discuss content audits of their own news; and examine the story selection process, adjusting if necessary.

1. Expand sources beyond police and courts. Health departments and coroner's offices are good sources of homicide data. Hospital admission data, though not always available for a breaking story, can help reporters put crime and its consequences in perspective. Other social agency

employees and community residents have information about neighborhood life pertinent to crime stories. Reporters need to cultivate these sources the same way they cultivate the local beat cops.

2. Provide context for crime in regular reporting. In almost every area of news — sports, business, politics, entertainment— general information is integrated with spot reports and the news makes sense of events for audiences by placing them in a larger context, if not in the same article, then with additional graphics or sidebars or standing reports. Stories on crime and youth could be treated with equal depth and breadth.
3. Bolster enterprise and increase investigative journalism. This recommendation requires adequate investment in the practice of journalism. Reporters need the time and resources to cultivate sources, investigate leads, and identify the connections between seemingly isolated events. They need support for understanding the patterns in a community so that they recognize when an event is important and interesting, not just interesting.
4. Balance stories about crime and youth with stories about youth in general. News organizations must pull back their lens to get a broader picture of what else young people are doing. When it comes to youth, violence is as prominent in the news as education. This exaggerates the rate of violence, particularly since 52 million young people go to school but only 125,000 are arrested for violent crimes each year. What issues affect them? What other newsworthy activities are they engaged in?
5. Conduct periodic audits of news content and share the results with readers and viewers. Newspapers and television newsrooms should periodically pause to examine their content. An audit would look beyond the evening ratings and sales numbers to ask the question: If the only information

our readers and viewers got was from our news, what would they know about youth and violence? What wouldn't they know? Assess whether the news gives readers and viewers enough information to deliberate their community's problems.

6. Examine the story selection process, and use restraint when necessary. Who qualifies as newsworthy in the newsroom? Who doesn't? Of course, news outlets cannot stop telling unusual stories, but they need not tell every one, thereby overwhelming readers and viewers with a cumulative misrepresentation, especially when it means there is not room for less sensational but more important news. Is perceived victim "worthiness" the unspoken criteria for whether a murder is selected for the news? Reporters should ask themselves: Who qualifies as a worthy victim in my newsroom? Who doesn't? If reporters limit themselves to reporting what just happened without considering how that crime fits into larger patterns, the news is doomed to be distorted.

3

Youth, Race and Crime in the News

RECOMMENDATIONS FOR CHILD ADVOCATES, YOUTH GROUPS AND CIVIL RIGHTS ORGANIZATIONS

While most of this report and these recommendations have focused on what the news media can and should do to improve crime coverage, there is much that the community can do to help generate a fairer depiction of youth crime.

1. Work with the media to give a more accurate picture of youth crime. Because of the juvenile justice system's historic confidentiality protections, many child advocates refuse to talk to reporters about the context of individual cases. This places a serious and sometimes insurmountable burden on reporters when they try to tell a more complete story. It can also result in depictions of youths as monolithic criminals whose delinquency is presented without important contributing antecedents. Child advocates and lawyers must develop creative ways to tell a more contextual story about youth crime without jeopardizing their clients' confidentiality. Advocacy groups can conduct their own audits of crime coverage, as some youth groups have done, and directly engage media outlets in dialogue about youth crime coverage. Civil rights groups which have successfully demanded diversification in entertainment media should now turn their attention and creativity to the disparate coverage of youth crime.

2. Engage the media in a dialogue about their coverage. Further, child advocates, youth groups and civil rights groups need to begin to engage news outlets as consumers to educate the media about their needs and to jointly seek solutions to the complex issues raised in this and other reports about coverage of youth crime. We Interrupt This Message, an advocacy group that conducted two of the studies discussed in this report, took its findings on disproportionate youth crime portrayals directly to the San Francisco Chronicle and the New York Times. In 2000, Suffolk University's law school held a forum which brought together reporters from the Boston Globe, the Boston Herald, and several electronic media with lawyers and community groups that work with young people for a productive exchange of ideas about coverage of youth crime. In recent years, civil rights groups like the NAACP and the National Council of La Raza have highlighted the scarcity of minority representation on network programming. Although these efforts concerned entertainment media, there is no reason to believe that similar efforts to educate news media about depictions of minority offenders and victims would fall on deaf ears.
3. Make data available. Journalists need local data to make national problems relevant for their audiences. Share information with the media so journalists can learn about local patterns, incorporate that information into daily stories, and give citizens the information they need to make better decisions about violence prevention policy.
4. Prepare young people to speak for themselves, then give them the opportunity to do so. Youth are becoming involved in advocacy efforts about juvenile justice and violence prevention from coast to coast. Give young people the training and support they need to speak confidently about the work they are doing to improve their communities for themselves and others. Increasing the visibility of young people in the news will help balance the current picture.

Create situations where you can introduce young people to journalists so they can begin establishing themselves as sources on their own.

5. Make yourself available to the media. Youth advocates and researchers cannot have an impact on the coverage of youth crime if journalists don't know they exist, if they cannot find spokespeople when they need them, or if advocates do not respond to their requests for information in a timely manner. Sometimes, this will be difficult, because breaking stories about youth crime do not always arise at convenient times. But advocates' availability as experts or alternative voices prior to deadline can help shape coverage and put youth violence into its proper context.

Topic Seven: Marxist Theories of Crime/conflict Theories of Crime

Section 1. Introduction to Marxist theory as a 19th century positivist theory Marxist sociologists, like consensus sociologists, see crime as related to a basic structural feature. But they have a different metatheory of society – the conflict view – which considers all historical and existing societies to have inequality of power, leading to conflict or potential conflict as a basic structural feature.

Referring back to earlier topics, social scientists in the 19th century were presuming that social change was leading in the direction of progress, towards "better" societies. It was presumed, also, that social scientists could objectively study societies. From this objective study they could determine how societies are basically structured and organized, and what was the process of change that was occurring. If such process of change was occurring rather slowly, or was going slightly off track, sociologists could help in bringing desirable progress sooner.

Marx and Marxist sociologists shared this general idea (which has nowadays been termed the "modernist" project). However, Marx considered that progress was not a smooth unrolling of one type of society into another, of more and more progress (of more and more "modern-ness), with just the occasional problem aspects to be got rid of, like crime. Rather Marx considered that (1) every historical society, except the very earliest egalitarian societies, was based on a strong internal conflict, which was not truly recognized as such due to the prevailing ideas and values, and that (2) to move from one societal stage to the next, and to eventually reach the "best" society, a series of actual physical manifestations of this conflict would have to occur.

Section 2 : Marx's theory.

Sub-structure and super-structure : The basic conflict that existed in every society was between those who owned and/or controlled the basic necessities of life, (called means of production) like land, labour and tools, and those who did not own them.

Marx considered that the sphere of activities that was involved in production of necessities (and often luxuries), what we would mostly term the economic sphere, was the basis of social life, and can be termed the sub-structure. (see diagram). The people and their relationships in the economic sphere, the owners and non-owners, formed two separate classes, somewhat complementary to each other and yet essentially in conflict.

In each society the patterning of legal, political, social, family and religious relations (called the superstructure) supported the owners of means of production with ideas that were relatively compatible with the distribution of the means of production. These prevailing systems, ways of life and ideas, if accepted by those in the lower class, would mean that they accepted their position and did not see their situation as "inferior" and/or "unjust". They saw it as reasonable or natural.

Stages of societies (social formations) According to Marx, history has involved change from one type of society (social formation), with one type of means of production, into another society, stage by stage.

Each change into the next type of society was not smooth. It involved a physical resolution of the essential conflict or conflicts between those who owned different types of necessities of life, and/ or those who did not, and it involved a change from one set of legal and religious ideas and systems to another.

Marx did not see his contemporary 19th century capitalist society as the last stage of history, but as the penultimate stage, with an egalitarian society living at a high standard of living created by machine production as the final stage. It would need a drastic change, a revolution to bring it about.

Marx's stages of social change were broadly:

1. Primitive communism - where everyone owned their own labour and made their own tools, and no-one owned the land or what the land provided.
2. Ancient society - based on agriculture worked by more-or-less slave labour, where a few owned the land and the tools and the life-long labour (and total life) of others. A small, urban, literate population benefited to enjoy a high standard of living, literacy and leisure (what would be termed "civilization"). An example would be the Roman Empire, where first urban Romans dominated rural dwellers, and later as it turned into an Empire, slaves were acquired from conquered territories.
3. Feudal society (medieval European society) – where peasants "held" (had perpetual tenancy of) their pieces of land "in perpetuity" (for ever) but had to give some of its produce to their landlord and also some of their time each year to work on the landlord's own land. They also had rights to graze their animals on common land, or to hunt in common forests, etc. They were not allowed, however, to leave the land – they were "tied" to it. But reciprocally, landlords were tied to the land, could not sell it, could not get more land unless it was granted by the King, could not get their peasant tenants off the land.

4. Capitalist society where land was private property of an owner, and could be bought and sold, where tools were also private property, and where labour of an individual belonged to himself or herself and could be sold. "Energy" could now be produced by machines, and "tools" were now mechanized, involving large-scale investment by their owners. Because the basis "tools" were mechanized and cost a lot of money (investment), the difference in ownership of this means of production, and non-ownership of it, involved a wide gap between two classes of people.
5. Advanced communism – where the high standard of living and leisure time enabled by mechanized production was enjoyed by all, due to communal ownership of the land, machinery, etc., and where all were also equally involved in decision-making, development of the arts and so on.

Overall, the process of history is one of greater and greater productivity, allowing for higher and higher standards of living and of literacy, the arts and leisure, but up to and including capitalism this higher standard of total living is not achieved by everyone. The final stage of history, to which all the other stages have been "logically" moving, is advanced communism – a stage of egalitarianism such as occurred at the beginning of history, but now experienced at a much higher standard of living, with the "heavy" work all done by machines.

Ideas, Values and Laws in each Stage of History

In each of the four historical stages of society already experienced, the relationships and ideas of society that are called the superstructure had to be compatible with those that are called the sub-structure. For instance, you could not have a religion in which gods negotiated and discussed with people, and allowed people to have views of their own, if in the economic system one set of people owned and totally determined the lives of others (slavery). Nor was it likely that male slave owners would exist in a system where women dominated men at home, and daughters chose their own husbands. The political ways of doing things would have to be relatively compatible with the pattern of relationships in the economic sphere, and the laws would have to allow and support the forms of "ownership" or "distribution" of the means of production. Generally prevailing ideas in all aspects of the superstructure would "back up", give legitimacy to, the pattern of relationships in the economic sub-structure. Ideas that justify a situation of power holding are usually termed "ideology".

This means that in each of the stages of history that Marx outlines - ancient society, feudalism and capitalist society - the ideas and laws have been different – the ideas about religion, families, laws, political power and so on. Thus the laws we have now are not "eternal" laws, they used to be different.

Marxists thus share with interactionists the idea that laws are socially constructed. However, additionally Marxists see them as arising from the overall social structure, basically representing the interests of various economic and political power holders in an unequal society, rather than of just moral crusaders.

Conflict involved in social change from stage to stage A further corollary of the differences of ideas and laws, as well as the patterning of the economic sub-structure, in each stage of history, is that to move from one stage to another involves new ideas and economic interests developing and challenging the previous system. You cannot have a smooth transition from one stage to the next stage. Those people and groups with vested interests in the older stage will want to maintain it, and will use economic power, political power, and control over law, ideas, religion and values to try to maintain it. Those people and groups within a stage who develop new forms of economic activity, and who want to challenge the earlier form, or who develop new ideas, will have to move through a stage of real physical conflict.

Such developments, conflicts and resolutions of conflict might not occur quickly, but might themselves take time and involve a number of mini-stages – e.g. in Europe, especially in England, the gradual rise in power of merchants in the cities, who bought and sold houses and trading goods, and who gradually challenged the power of the aristocratic feudal landlords and the king, took many hundreds of years, the loss and restoration and reloss of the powers (and sometimes the heads) of the monarchy, and of the Catholic Church, and later the Anglo-Catholic Church.

So far we have just looked at Marxist theory as an analysis of history and a prediction of the future. The theory, however, did in some cases lead to political activity – the idea was that you could hurry up the change into the final stage through revolutionary political action.

The connection of Marxist analysis with political revolutionary activity is now outmoded, since we are aware that creating an egalitarian society from "the top down" is both difficult (if not impossible) in economic terms, and also tends towards totalitarian rule. However, analysis of historical and contemporary societies with the conceptual tools provided by Marx, and their refinements and developments, allows us to make useful contributions to social science.

Furthermore, it has been argued that the responses to Marxist analysis, in terms of the development of democratic processes that would give some power to the non-owners of capitalist production, occurred precisely because the existing analysis was accurate. In other words, precisely because Marx was so correct about the extent of the conflict in capitalist societies, the existing power-holders had to act to prevent revolution, by allowing universal suffrage and gradual welfare benefits.

Section 3 – the conflict theory (Marxian) analysis of laws and crimes

Introduction, and basic explanation of crime: Marx, himself, did not say a great deal actually about crime, or why people committed it. But obviously if the laws were merely supporting the existing distribution of property, then non-property owners might not feel very committed to them. In fact, overall from those sociologists who focus on conflict theory, there is a general expression that committing crime is perfectly rational in response to the nature of the societies that people live in.

Marxian criminologists have worked on a number of issues in relation to crime and law.

Law

As stated above, Law as an expression of the interests of the owners of the means of production, and of the state which represents those interests.

Historical examples: see Haralambos reading:

Chambliss' analysis of colonial tax laws in East Africa.

Vagrancy laws of feudal England, from 1349

Carrier's case of 1473.

The Carrier's Case - 1473

A Carrier, hired as a bailee (carrying goods on trust), broke open the bales of cloth he was carrying and took the goods.

According to the law at that time, he had not broken any law, since entrusting goods to someone gave them the right to dispose of them. (Normally one entrusted to a known person, family member, etc.) But definitely he had personally betrayed the trust of the person who had (stupidly) consigned the carrying of the goods to him. However, he was convicted of larceny (theft) in a criminal court – in fact in the top criminal court, the Star Chamber – on the basis that he had committed trespass on the bales when he opened them.

There was a law against trespass.

This created a precedent for future similar convictions.

Importance:

1. decision made by top criminal court, meant that monarchy **was pressuring** judges to make the decision. But **why?**

2. trade in wool and cotton was developing at this time. Monarchy and others wanted to be involved in this long distance trade, and needed to be able to control 'unknown' carriers.

Discussion of laws that protect consumers - Kolko, Graham studies. Do the laws we have now in capitalist societies which appear to protect ordinary consumers indicate that the Marxist analysis is wrong? Or do they actually benefit the capitalist owners as much as the ordinary workers as consumers?

Kolko – laws about meat packing, around 1900 in USA. Sanitation laws to protect consumer.

The large business corporations favoured them because it put the smaller ones out of business, and also ensured the European market.

Railroad industry – asked for laws fixing standard prices to guarantee profits to industry. Officially justified so that it would prevent monopolies which could put prices up for the consumer, it actually prevented prices going down, and also created a monopoly.

Graham, 1970, controls on manufacture of amphetamines, in order to prevent them reaching illegal users, were not as strict as they might have been because of the drug company.

Discussion of laws that protect workers. Are these laws against the capitalists and for the workers, or are they as much in the interests of capitalists?

e.g. allowing trades unions; safety laws, minimum wage laws.

Well, somewhat in the interests of workers, but they are also in the interests of capitalists because they keep the workers happy, and also show the workers and wider society in general how responsible the capitalists are. So they serve an ideological function.

There is some, a small but necessarily real, commonality of interest – because in a class system each needs the other. To some extent (or perhaps to a very great extent) the small but real commonality of interest can explain how a situation full of conflicts survives.

Moreover, like laws that protect consumers, they are widely violated. Sutherland has documented that – but more recently, if you look at your Giddens readings, so has a study by Slapper and Tombs of corporate crime (1999) that it is pervasive and widespread

Separation of government bureaucracies and interest groups. Is there a true separation of government and the working of its agencies from capitalists, such that they work for all citizens, or do they essentially represent the interests of the capitalists?

The answer is probably "somewhat for everybody, but more so for capitalists". The point is that even if the government and the bureaucracies are completely separate, since capitalists are ultimately the basis of the economic system, laws will on balance be in their favour.

The actions taken by interest groups of a "moral" type or a "class" or "ethnic" type will only be successful if they are also in the interests of the main corporate owners. E.g. Civil Rights laws passed at the time of Martin Luther King occurred at the time when mechanization and chemical weed killers used in the cotton fields of the south meant that low-wage, passive labour was no longer needed.

But also were a response to a deep Black movement building up in the South as well as in the urban Northern black ghettos.

Concessions - democracy and the welfare state as a concession, such that there is slow change, at least in the Western societies, with capitalists earning less of their profits at home. One of the analyses of colonialism.

Crime

Crime as unequally punished – only the poor get punished, because the law is essentially operated by those who share the viewpoint of the capitalists and genuinely cannot "see" others as criminals. As with Sutherland's analysis, Pearce in Haralambos – Violations are widespread, prosecutions few – by why have any? Because they serve the ideological function of showing that the law does get the rich too (sometimes)

Another reason for some punishment is that fact that nowadays,individuals are owners of means of production, through share-holding for pension funds, for personal savings, etc. As such, ordinary people have an interest in certain aspects of the activity of corporations and corporate decision-makers, and are able to enforce rules. Also the state cannot provide pensions to the level of people's desires – they want private investment to occur.

Necessity of the poor/underclass as a reserve army of labour. In order for the capitalist system to continue to exist, there must be a reserve of labour available. These people obviously have little or no income at times when they are not needed, and so inevitably some will turn to crime.

Crime and punishment as a source of employment for policemen, prison officers, social workers and so on.

Crime and punishment as a form of ideological consensus building, or legitimation of the prevailing order. It is useful to be able to focus on a small group of wrong-doers, or their actions, which are considered to be harming society, so as to be able to draw the majority of people around the leadership. You need a group of "outsiders".

Section 4:Issues in relation to conflict theorists.

Issues: Marxist theory uses a range of data in its analyses – some quantitative, measureable data and some qualitative data. In particular it analyses "objective interests". But like all social science it also puts an interpretation on the data, which may or may not be accepted by others.

However, for Marxists and other conflict theorists, even if the analysis was correct, how can the situation be changed? What policies would be drawn from the analysis?

Because the analysis is based on issues of power, there would have to be real changes of power for policy to follow. Some people would say that in fact such changes of power have occurred in the twentieth century, especially after the Second World War. They would say that in fact the development of democracy has meant that political parties that are left of center have been in power some of the time and have enacted laws in favour of ordinary people, as citizens and consumers. Because of the control and influence of such parties, there are now in existence penal policies that include rehabilitation programmes, probation programmes and so on, as well as policies that aimed to raise the general standards of education, health and living. They would argue that there is an ongoing trend in this direction. Marxists or strong conflict theorists would argue that these are only "modifications" within a capitalist framework to ensure a loyal and motivated workforce.

Concluding Points

Topic 8 on media and Topic 9 will look at the use of conflict theory (as well as interactionist theory) in studying media and women's crimes or victimization. In Topic 10 the developments called "Realism", especially "Left Realism" will show how some Marxists have recently developed their thinking.

CONFLICT AND CONSENSUS THEORY

In Summary: The difference between consensus theorists and conflict theorists in relation to crime can be stated in terms of the relative emphasis put on such universally agreed goals as "equality", "justice" and "order" ("law and order"). Consensus theorists will usually put greater stress on "order", conflict theorists would put greater stress on "equality" and "justice". In terms of the political terms "left" and "right", which are not used in Singapore and therefore are not very familiar to Singaporean students: conflict theorists are to the "left" and consensus theorists, depending on their precise theories are around the "center" or a little towards the "right". The extreme right has no time for sociology at all.

Section 5 – the example of casinos in Singapore – moral values and economic interests

As we know, the debate is now more or less finished. The decision was in favour of casinos, because we need the tourists to come here. The casinos will be part of integrated resorts, so the investment will not be just in casinos but in a wider range of tourism facilities, but it is acknowledged that the resort-builders would not invest in the resorts without casinos. Meanwhile the government will attempt to answer the moral issues, by limited access of Singaporeans, and providing all sorts of counseling centers, etc. to help gamblers get over their addiction. Here is an example from the early part of the debate: Article from: Straits Times, September 25th, 2004.

THE CASINO TOSS-UP

RETIRED teacher Soh Chiew Peng hates the idea of a casino here even as she recognises that people already gamble here, like at the 4-D and Toto outlets scattered all over the island.

'I'm dead set against them too, but when they introduced those things, they didn't ask us what we thought.'

Mrs Soh, 54, says she knows from personal experience how gambling addictions can tear families apart.A relative of hers and one former classmate went to jail after they turned to crime to support their gambling habits. 'If the Government wants to boost the economy, there are other ways,' she says.

Mrs Soh has the backing of 47 per cent of the population, according to a recent Straits Times survey.Their reasons for opposing a casino? The belief that it will cause gambling addiction, family problems and crime to escalate.

But the other half of the population - 53 per cent - see it differently. They believe Singapore should have its own casino as this will help boost tourism, generate revenue and create jobs.

In this group is Mr Tan Eng Hong, 47, an advertising professional.He says: 'Casinos are no longer sleazy, shady gambling dens of vice, but glitzy and impressive mega tourist attractions.'Just look at countries like Australia, says the father of two. It has casinos in many cities and they have not degenerated into crime-ridden hot spots. Mr Tan is sure a casino's economic benefits will outweigh the social costs but there's little data to back his view, or Mrs Soh's opposing one for that matter.

While the Ministry of Trade and Industry (MTI) has been studying the casino proposal for some months, it has yet to release figures on potential benefits and costs.What it would say is that no decision has been made yet on whether or not to proceed. It reiterated that it is considering proposals to build an integrated resort with a casino component and not a standalone casino.Similar developments overseas have resulted in large investments, significant increases in visitor numbers and the creation of jobs, the ministry tells Insight.It says that it is also mindful of the potential social impact of the casino component and 'will put in place appropriate social safeguards if we decide to proceed'.

National University of Singapore economist Choy Keen Meng says what makes the casino decision different from other public policy issues is the difficulty in carrying out a cost-benefit analysis. 'No one denies the social consequences of a casino but how do you measure them? How do you quantify the cost of a ruined family, for example?'This problem could explain why the Government has for so long resisted calls from the business community to allow a casino here, he says.

A MINUS?

THE lack of conclusive evidence on how casinos affect communities is not for want of trying. Researchers in countries like the United States, Australia and New Zealand have in recent years attempted to measure casinos' social and economic impact.These studies show that casinos affect different communities differently and commonly-held assumptions about how casinos are supposed to help or hurt societies often do not hold water.

Take for example the view that casinos will cause crime to escalate. A 1998 study commissioned by the New Zealand Casino Control Authority, on the impact of newly-opened casinos in Christchurch and Auckland, found this was not the case.In Christchurch, for example, rates of certain types of crimes, such as liquor offences, burglary and fraud, fell after the casino's opening, although it remains unclear what prompted the better behaviour.

Yet another study, this one funded by America's National Institute of Justice, covered seven cities or counties in the US where casinos had opened recently. It too found few consistent trends in crime. In three of the areas studied, more types of crimes increased than decreased. In another three, more types of crimes went down rather than up. In the last city, there was little change for most crimes. The results were also mixed when the researchers compared suicide and divorce rates in these communities against rates in similar communities without casinos. However, personal bankruptcies went up significantly in five of the seven casino communities when compared to the control groups.

Another big worry among critics of casinos is that they will cause more people to become addicted to gambling. This was indeed the top concern among the 47 per cent who said 'no' to a casino in the recent Straits Times survey.The New Zealand study found that the number of people seeking help for gambling addiction did in fact increase after the two casinos opened. But part of this jump could have been due to increased publicity on problem gambling and the support services available, researchers said.

A similar upsurge in the number of gamblers seeking help can be expected if a casino opens here, says Dr Munidasa Winslow, who heads the Institute of Mental Health's Community Addictions Management Programme.That has been the trend whenever a new form of gambling is legalised, he says, and, for that matter, whenever local newspapers run stories on problem gambling.Whether a casino will significantly increase the number of gambling addicts is in his view difficult to tell.

It will depend on whether the casino enlarges the total pool of gamblers or draws largely on the existing pool of regular gamblers, he says. 'Studies show that when people take part in potentially addictive activities like drinking or gambling, the percentage of those who develop problems is always about the same. 'So the higher the total number of gamblers, the more addicts there will be.'

That is why Dr Winslow thinks there is a basis for restricting casino access to minimise impulse gambling, which is what can cause the pool of gamblers to swell.

OR A PLUS?

HE economic benefits of casinos may be easier to quantify but the interpretation of the results can spark a debate that is as open-ended as the one over social costs.Of those polled in the Straits Times survey, 53 per cent said 'yes' to a casino here because they expect it to boost tourism, revenue and job creation. Gaming industry players certainly agree with this reading.Those in Singapore recently, for a conference on gaming, projected that by 2010, Asians will spend US$23 billion (S$39 billion) a year to gamble in the region and beyond.

So is it a matter of build it and they will come? Dr David Marshall of the Australian National University's Centre for Gambling Research doubts so.Singapore will face tough competition from established casinos in Macau and Australia and new casinos being planned in countries in the region, such as Thailand and the Philippines, he points out.'So the question is why would tourists who want to gamble choose to go to Singapore instead of somewhere else? 'Furthermore, in terms of encouraging non-gambling tourists to gamble, well, maybe that could occur but generally, it is agreed that casinos do not necessarily produce extra spending but simply displace spending from other sectors,' he tells Insight via e-mail.

And while tourism is often used to justify the building of a casino, Dr Marshall says that from what he knows, the bulk of casino earnings in Australia comes from locals. In South Korea too, where the revenue from the one casino that admits locals exceeds the total revenue of the 13 foreigner-only casinos.

MTI is distancing itself from the experiences of such standalone casinos by emphasising that its proposal is for an integrated resort that will also feature world-class entertainment shows, theme attractions, convention facilities, luxury retail outlets and fine dining.It is these other amenities that are likely to draw larger numbers of international visitors to Singapore, it says, especially now that casinos are being legalised in so many parts of the world.'For many world-class resorts, it is the non-gaming amenities that attract large numbers of visitors,' it says.The gaming and non-gaming facilities complement each other, it adds, and become viable because of the number of visitors drawn to the wide range of entertainment options.

Examples of such integrated resorts include Atlantis on Paradise Island in the Bahamas, a tropical resort with a marina, giant water park and spa; and the luxurious Bellagio complex in Las Vegas, with its opulent lobby and fountains, world-famous restaurants and shows by Cirque du Soleil. About 7.2 million people visit Bellagio every year while Atlantis draws one million visitors annually.The revenue for Bellagio is close to US$1 billion a year, and it is just over US$500 million a year for Atlantis. The resorts employ 8,000 people each.MTI says major international investors have expressed keen interest in developing a similar resort here. It plans to invite proposals from them within the next few months.

In line with Prime Minister Lee Hsien Loong's promise that the Government will consider all views before deciding, the Feedback Unit has been conducting dialogue sessions with various parties, including religious groups, grassroots leaders and the business community.Given the strong arguments on both sides, and the fact that the population is split almost right down the middle, this is one issue that will surely test the Government's powers of persuasion. Its challenge is to forge a final compromise that is acceptable to most, if not all, Singaporeans.

4

Crime in the News

This study examines the representation of crime stories in the news. Using 71 matched pairs, we examine the constructed elements in the reporting of crime stories between newspapers and local television to document similarities and differences across the mediums. Although considerable work has been devoted to discerning differences in reporting across types of media, little research has investigated how the same crime story "gets told" in one medium compared to another.

With matched-pairs of stories, we are able to do this. In this study, we also use content analysis to examine a subset of cases that focus on juveniles to ascertain how atypical victims and offenders are portrayed in the media. Although youth are much less likely to commit crime and to be victimized compared to adults, their stories are disproportionately "the stuff of news." Collectively, the findings indicate that news reporting follows the law of opposites—the characteristics of crime, criminals, and victims represented in the media are in most respects the polar opposite of the pattern suggested by official crime statistics. This was especially the case in news reports involving juvenile victims and offenders. Keywords: media, victims' studies.

INTRODUCTION

Everyday people consume the news from a variety of sources including television, radio, newspaper, and the Internet but few are aware of potential biases in the construction and reporting of news stories. All news, no matter the source, has a constructed newsworthy quality. There are important reasons why one story is selected for coverage when another is not. "Events that appear to disrupt expectations [or are] deviant occurrences are the stuff of news" (Reiner, Livingstone and Allen 2003:13).

These "disrupted expectations" and "deviant occurrences" are particularly characteristic of crime news stories. Critical attention to how crime is reported in the news is necessary given the way in which the media represent these events heavily influences our understanding of crime in society. "Media images help shape our view of the world and our deepest values; what we consider good or bad, positive or negative, moral or evil" (Kellner 1995:24). The extent of influence depends, to some degree, on characteristics of the different types of mediums (Weitzer and Kubrin 2004). Jeffres (1986) defines a medium as "any device that carries messages between people...but what makes a medium a mass medium is its ability to carry messages not just from one person to another but from one person to thousands or millions of others" (pg. 1). This study examines the representation of crime stories in the mass media, in newspapers and television in particular, to reveal how crime is characterized in the news.

Using 71 matched pairs, we examine the constructed elements in the reporting of crime stories between newspapers and local television to document similarities and differences across mediums. Although considerable work has been devoted to discerning differences in reporting across types of media (Barak 1994; Burton 2005; Doyle 2003; Ericson, Baranek and Chan 1991; Jensen 1997; Schlesinger and Tumber 1994), little research has investigated how the same crime story "gets told" in one medium compared to another. With matched-pairs of stories, we are able to do this. In this study we also use content analysis to examine, in detail, a subset of cases that focus on juveniles to ascertain how atypical offenders and victims are portrayed in the media. Although youth are much less likely to commit crimes and to be victimized compared to adults, their stories are disproportionately "the stuff of news."

The Social Construction of Crime in the Media Reality is socially constructed, in large part, through the media, which provide a way for dominant values in society to be articulated to the public. In particular, the news media constitutes an arena for the powerful institutions of society to disseminate information to a large audience. Gramsci (1971) argues that 'media hegemony' refers to the dominance of a certain way of life and how it is diffused through the public (see also Barak 1994:238-243).

In other words, "media systems tend to privilege the ideological perspective of the powerful—in particular those of the holders of state power, exponents of establishment politics, and representatives of major capitalist economic interests" (Schlesinger and Tumber 1994:7). The news, therefore, favors some groups over others (e.g., affluent whites vs. poor inner-city blacks) so media bias is not random (Barak 1994:4; Jensen 1997:27). Lipschultz and Hilt (2002) suggest there are two levels to the social construction of reality with regards to news media. At the first level, producers construct reality through the bureaucratic decisions they make about which events to report and how they will report them (Chermak 1997:711).

In this process, biases are inevitable. "The process of gathering information and deciding what's news are the primary concerns of critics, who argue that there is no way news can be 'value-free' because a series of value judgments have been imposed on the event along the way" (Jeffres 1986:110). The second level suggests that viewers construct their own reality based on how they understand and interpret the news.

Not everyone receives and processes news in the same way; audience characteristics and experiences can be influential. As Weitzer and Kubrin (2004:499) claim, "The field of communication studies has increasingly regarded the reception of media messages as a dynamic process in which viewers actively interpret and perhaps reconstruct those messages in light of their personal backgrounds and experiences." The social construction of reality thus begins when the producer decides what story to cover and continues all the way to the consumer's living room, where social reality is (re)constructed.

If the media construct a general sense of reality, they also construct a reality of crime. In fact, the media are "among the most important agents in the diffusion of criminal conceptions. Crime coverage in the newspapers [and] television affects a person's estimate of the frequency of crime as well as the interpretations that he attaches to crime" (Quinney 1970:281; see also Miller Potter 2005).

In fact, over 75 percent of the public claim they form their opinions about crime from what they see or read in the news, which is more than three times the number who say they get their primary information on crime from personal experience (22 percent) (ABC News 1996). The language used in a news report is critical in constructing the consumer's reality and perception of crime. Relating the framing of language to the social construction of reality, Loge (2005) uses the metaphor of a camera stating that "the same photograph of the same scene looks different depending on the filter used on the camera.

And, of course, just as the camera lens and filter include information, they also exclude information; one cannot see what is outside the camera frame or see the photograph in a different light. Language, therefore, is both a reflection and a deflection of reality" (pg. 695). The language used in a newscast or in the newspaper, the information that is included and the facts that are omitted, greatly influence how the public perceives crime. Jewkes (2004:40) describes how crime stories become newsworthy by focusing on several news values specific to crime including the level of predictability of the crime (or how common or uncommon the crime is), risk (or the sense that consumers may be at risk of similar victimization), whether the crime has a sexual aspect to it, whether the offender or victim is a celebrity or high-status person, whether the crime occurred locally, the level of violence, the presence of spectacle or graphic imagery, and whether youth are involved, among others. The extent to which a story contains these elements influences the likelihood that it will be reported.

Of course "a story does not have to conform to all the criteria in order to make the news – although events that score highly on the newsworthiness scale (that is, conform to several of the news values) are more likely to be reported" (Jewkes 2004:40). Crime news values can change over time. Ultimately, the discussion of news values for both general and crime news focuses on the idea that dominant values are placed on the audience and that these ideals inform the selection and construction of specific stories into news (Burton 2005).

This study is not concerned with where these values stem from, but rather how they shape the stories produced by the media. Crime Reporting in the Media No matter the country, the day, or the time, "crime is an important news topic" (Chermak 1994:95). According to one content analysis of six print and three broadcast media organizations, "print media present nine crime stories a day, on average, and electronic media four crime stories per day" (Chermak 1997:711). Despite potential differences across mediums, there are general ways the media portray crime. Ultimately, decisions the media make typically create a distorted view of reality held by the public, one that differs in many ways from reality (Sacco 1995:143). According to Reiner, Livingston and Allen (2003), the portrayal of crime in the media compared to official crime statistics is referred to as the "law of opposites," meaning that "the characteristics of crime, criminals, and victims represented in the media are in most respects the polar opposite of the pattern suggested by official crime statistics or by crime and victim surveys" (pg. 15).

There are several dimensions of crime stories to which the law of opposites applies. Prevalence and Content of Crime Stories Since the Second World War, an increasing proportion of news stories have focused on crime. And the last two decades, in particular, have witnessed a redefinition of what is considered an appropriate subject for crime news reporting. "Changes in mores relating to public discussion of sex and violence have allowed respectable media outlets to report crimes that would have previously been seen as taboo and to do so at a level of detail that would once have been considered lurid" (Sacco 1995:145). Nowhere is the law of opposites more applicable than with respect to the types of crimes reported in the media. Official crime statistics indicate that most crime is nonviolent yet the news media suggests just the opposite (Chermak 1997:696; Garofalo 1981; Schlesinger, Tumber and Murdock 1991), often creating the perception of an "epidemic of random violence" (Sacco 1995:142).

"About two-thirds of crime news stories are primarily about violent or sex offenses, but these account for less than ten percent of crimes recorded by the police" (Reiner, Livingstone and Allen 2003:18-9). A study by Sheley and Ashkins (1981) found that a St. Louis newspaper gave "crimes against the person" thirty five times more attention than property crimes, and murder ninety times more coverage than other major offenses. At the same time, attention to property crimes in the news has declined "unless they involve celebrities or some highly quirky features" (Reiner, Livingstone and Allen 2003:19), yet property offenses constitute over 90 percent of crimes recorded by the police. Offenders and Victims Many news sources give little information about criminal offenders but when they do, they are typically older than in actual crime reports (Lotz 1991; Reiner, Livingstone and Allen 2003; Sacco 1995). In the media, the majority of reported offenders are between the ages of 20 and 40, yet according to official statistics "more than 40 percent of convicted or cautioned offenders are under 21" (Reiner, Livingstone and Allen 2003:20).

An increasing trend, however, has been the reporting of crimes, particularly violent crimes, by juveniles (Dorfman et al. 1997; Perrone and Chesney-Lind 1997). A meta-analysis of 77 studies that examined crime news reports found that when youth appear in the news, it is often connected to violence. "Relatively few youth are arrested each year for violent crimes, yet the message from the news is that this is a common occurrence" (Dorfman and Schiraldi 2001:17). One analysis examining 840 newspaper reports and 109 news segments documented that 40 percent of all newspaper articles on children were about violence, as were 48 percent of television news stories (Kunkel 1994). On the other hand, evidence indicates that youth victims receive much less attention than youth offenders (Dorfman and Schiraldi 2001:22).

As might be expected, the media depict a large proportion of offenders as racial and ethnic minorities, even though a much smaller percentage are involved in the criminal justice system (Reiner, Livingstone, and Allen 2003). Minorities, therefore, are overrepresented as offenders in the news (Barlow 1998; Gilliam and Iyengar 2000). Research by Entman (1990, 1992, 1994) finds that in television news stories, black (compared to white) suspects are less likely to be identified by name, are not as well dressed, and are more likely to be shown physically restrained. Yet while blacks are overrepresented as offenders, they are typically underrepresented as victims in the news (Weiss and Chermak 1998; Pritchard and Hughes 1997).

One study found that newsworthiness increases when the victim of a crime is white and another found that homicides with white victims resulted in more and longer articles than homicides with black victims. The media and official statistics are in agreement on one aspect of criminal offenders: they are more often males (Reiner, Livingstone and Allen 2003; Sacco 1995:143). Regardless of race, a general problem with the portrayal of victims in crime news stories has to do with what Sacco (1995:149) refers to as "the random character of victimization," or the media's tendency to imply that anyone at anytime may fall victim to crime. He notes, "While the best social science literature indicates that the risks of crime…are not equally shared, media images often convey a different message" (pg. 149). The random character of victimization is underscored to increase the dramatic value of a story.

As the preceding discussion indicates, the news media does not reflect actual crime statistics on several dimensions. The previously mentioned meta-analysis concluded, "Overall, the studies taken together indicate that depictions of crime in the news are not reflective of either the rate of crime generally, the proportion of crime which is violent, the proportion of crime committed by people of color, or the proportion of crime committed by youth" (Dorfman and Schiraldi 2001:7). While much of this discussion applies to the reporting of crime in all types of media, it is also the case that mediums differ in various ways regarding the construction of crime news. Comparing newspapers and local television news, we highlight these differences below and argue that such differences have potential implications for the construction of the social reality of crime. Crime Reporting Differences in Newspaper and Television The news media allow for private events, or individual crimes, to become public concerns.

"The news media, in particular, provide an important forum in which private troubles are selectively gathered up, invested with broader meaning, and made available for public consumption" (Sacco 1995:142). This study determines whether these "private turned public" events are in fact represented differently depending on the medium in which they are reported. There are numerous reasons to believe that differences in representation exist depending on whether the crime story is written-up in a newspaper or broadcast on local television news. Doyle (2003) describes television as a "shared arena." Unlike newspapers, television allows for a wider and more diverse audience. Since it requires a less specialized skill from viewers in decoding and understanding, the audience has a more passive role when it comes to television news; viewers sit and watch, without a choice as to what is covered, taking in information they are given as truth (Doyle 2003:14-15).

As for newspapers, readers make more choices regarding which stories they will focus on, thereby playing a more active role in their news consumption. Newspapers are completely visual. Headlines and pictures attract the reader and both are designed to catch the eye. Television, on the other hand, is based on sound as well as sight, thus appealing to numerous senses (Jeffres 1986:5). The notion of graphic imagery, a crime news value previously mentioned, is of higher importance for television news. While newspapers can include black and white pictures, a streaming color video from the news station adds more sensation to one's consumption. In particular, "seeing something on television may have a much stronger emotive impact than…reading about it in the newspaper" (Weitzer and Kubrin 2004:501). With regards to emotion, newspapers focus on ideas whereas television emphasizes "feeling, appearance, mood…there is a retreat from distant analysis and a dive into emotional and sensory involvement" (Doyle 2003:15).

Television takes already formed cultural stereotypes and uses them to its advantage, tapping into human emotions. For example, the belief that juvenile offenders are becoming increasingly violent is often used. Because of this stereotype, a story that involves a youth offender will receive greater attention in the news. Another major difference between newspapers and television is that newspapers use space to get their message across whereas television uses time. Television values timeliness more than newspapers because of the short amount of time available for a given program or news segment. In essence, "broadcasters emphasize events that occur within a given day and highly value those occurring within the most recent few hours while daily newspaper journalists deal with material that appears as 'yesterday's news'" (Jeffres 1986:109). In addition to these differences, newspapers and television are distinct in terms of the organization and production of content.

There are differences between the mediums "where most of the 'media work' is accomplished" (Jeffres 1986:86). Actual news makes up a large percentage of the content in newspapers whereas for a television station, news constitutes only a small portion of the coverage. Moreover, pressure for ratings and internal competition is much greater for television than newspapers (Weitzer and Kubrin

2004). Internal competition reflects the reality that there are several local television stations compared to typically one major newspaper in a city. Thus, a heavy reliance on ratings and competition among local news channels can "lead to a greater stress on marketable, shocking news in television" (Weitzer and Kubrin 2004:501). In sum, television and newspapers are not identical media sources, in large part because they have different "structuring agents" (Ericson, Baranek, and Chan 1991), or ways in which information is presented. Before news even becomes available for public consumption, the mediums start on different playing fields.

All in all, newspapers have a relatively limited arena or readership, have space as their "structuring agent," produce only news, do not rely heavily on technology for production, and have a distance barrier to overcome. On the other hand, television has a much larger and more diverse audience, produces more than just news broadcasts, relies heavily on technology for production, uses time as its "structuring agent," and has the feel of being much closer to the audience. We argue that these differences are likely to influence the content and nature of crime news reporting, resulting in the finding that the same crime story will be presented somewhat differently in newspapers and television. The Current Study The current study focuses on the representation of crime stories in newspapers and television to compare similarities and differences in the reporting of events across mediums. In this study we also examine a subset of cases that focus specifically on juveniles to ascertain how atypical offenders and victims are represented in the news. In our analysis, we adopt the framework advanced by Singletary and Lipsky (1977) that focuses on the nature of errors present in a news story.

Singletary and Lipsky (1977) classify reporting errors as "objective" or "subjective," where objective reflects the factual characteristics of a story and subjective reflects the interpretive aspects of the report. Here we use a modified version of this framework that accounts for the inclusion and/or omission of objective versus subjective story characteristics or facts. Specifically, objective facts are the indisputable facts of the crime, some of which are essential for understanding what happened and some of which are not essential but tend to be reported to provide greater detail about the course of events. Subjective facts, on the other hand, include the unnecessary aspects of the story that more often than not add a layer of bias. Further discussion of objective and subjective facts is provided in the methods section.

Using this framework, we address three research questions: First, what type of information about crime is provided to consumers in both newspapers and television? Are objective or subjective facts most common? And to what extent do crime news stories reflect the "law of opposites," where the focus of attention is on uncharacteristic crimes/offenders/victims? Second, do differences in reporting exist across newspapers and television? Given differences between these mediums, will newspapers and television report in different frequencies objective and subjective facts for the same given story? And third, how do portrayals of juvenile offenders and victims—unusual candidates for news stories according to official statistics—vary in newspaper and television news? Are differences in reporting and the types of "facts" presented diminished in such cases? Methods From October 19th through December 2nd 2005 we collected crime stories from the Washington Post and the 11o'clock local television news on the Washington, D.C. ABC affiliate.

We define a crime story as "a program segment which features one or more acts of breaking the law as central to the narrative" (Grabe 1999:38). Each day during this period we read the Post and clipped crime stories from the first section (coverage of national, international, and a small number of local stories) and Metro section (complete coverage of the local news). At 11:00 pm each night, we recorded the local television news. The following day, all crime reports were transcribed. In order to be in the sample, a crime story had to be included in both mediums. If the television news covered a murder in Northeast D.C. but it was not covered in the Washington Post either the next or the following day, then the story was not included in the sample. Over the study period, we collected and coded 71 crime stories resulting in our sample of matched pairs. In this study, a "matched pair" consists of two news reports of the same crime, one from television and the other from the newspaper.

With matched pairs, we are able to determine whether, and to what extent, crime stories are reported differently across mediums. It is important to note that the unit of analysis for this study is the report of a crime story, not the crime itself. In other words, our sample consists of 71 matched crime reports, some of which include reports of the same crime over a period of time. In this sense, some crime stories are presented multiple times in both mediums given repeated reports on these events. We selected the Washington Post because it is the most highly circulated newspaper in the D.C. metropolitan area. The local ABC station was randomly chosen between ABC, NBC, CBS, and FOX stations. The 11 o'clock news was coded because there is little, if any, coverage of traffic, which constitutes a large portion of the morning and evening news.

Without traffic included, there was the likelihood that more crime stories could be reported. Also, by 11:00 pm most crimes for the day have occurred and could be reported on. All television recordings were transcribed word for word to determine the precise word count. After crime reports from both mediums were matched and the television news was transcribed, we read the stories line by line and, using SPSS, coded them "on what was portrayed, reported, suggested or implied in the context" (Grabe 1999:38). We coded a variety of variables: Date case reported, List of crimes that occurred (e.g. murder, sexual assault, robbery), Most serious crime type (1 = violent, 2 = property, 3 = drug, 4 = other), multiple crimes (0 = no, 1 = yes, 99 = missing), multiple offenders (0 = no, 1 = yes, 99 = missing), multiple victims (0 = no, 1 = yes, 99 = missing), Is crime story part of a string of crimes (0 = no, 1 = yes, 99 = missing), Did the crime occur in DC (0 = no, 1 = yes, 99 = missing), DC quadrant of crime (1 = NW, 2 = NE, 3 = SW, 4 = SE, 5 = Did not occur in DC, 99 = missing),

State crime occurred in (0 = Washington DC, 1 = Virginia, 2 = Maryland, 3 = Florida, 4 = California, 5 = Washington State, 6 = Massachusetts, 7 = Tennessee, 8 = Pennsylvania, 99 = missing), aggravating circumstances (0 = no, 1 = yes, 99 = missing), List of aggravating circumstances (e.g., police involved shooting, offender is female, victim is a child), Number of offenders, Number of victims, Race of offender reported (1 = White, 2 = Black, 3 = Hispanic, 4 = Asian, 5 = Other, 6 = No Race Reported, 99 = missing), Race of offender implied (1 = White, 2 = Black, 3 = Hispanic, 4 = Asian, 5 = Other, 6 = No Race Implied, 99 = missing), Age of offender, Sex of offender (0 = male, 1 = female, 99 = missing), Race of victim reported (same coding as offender), Race of victim implied (same coding as offender), Age of victim, Sex of victim (same coding as offender), Victim/offender relationship (1 = Family Intimate, 2 = Family Nonintimate, 3 = Friend/Acquaintance Intimate, 4 = Friend/Acquaintance Nonintimate, 5 = Strangers, 99 = missing), Word count, Was the story a lead story (0 = no, 1 = yes).

These variables were coded twice for each crime story—once for the television report and once for the newspaper report. For all race variables, no race reported or implied means that the offender or victim was mentioned in the article, yet no race was explicitly mentioned (reported) or shown through pictures (implied). A variable coded as "missing" indicates that the article made no mention of that factor. For example, if the police had no suspects, therefore having no offender to assign characteristics to, then the reported race, implied race, sex, and victim/offender relationship, among other factors, all would be reported as "missing."

As noted above, in line with Singletary and Lipsky (1977), this study adopts the terms "objective" and "subjective" with slightly modified definitions. Again, an objective fact is an indisputable and unbiased aspect of a news story. Some objective facts are essential for understanding the story while others are not equally essential. In the latter case, without these facts the audience can still comprehend what happened however they provide another layer of coverage, supplementing the essential facts. Regardless, the media cannot skew this information, unlike with subjective facts; the offender can either be male or female, there can only be one time the crime occurred, and the victim can only be one age. Most important, however, is that objective facts minimize personal bias or judgment in the report. For example, reporting the offender's race, which provides additional meaning to the story in a manner similar to the reporting of offender age or sex, is often an unnecessary element of the story that mostly serves to reinforce existing stereotypes of race and crime.

Thus, offender race is considered subjective rather than objective. The variables that fit under the objective heading are: most serious crime type, state crime occurred in, time crime occurred, sex of offender, sex of victim, age of offender and age of victim. Subjective facts refer to aspects of a news report that are unnecessary for a complete understanding of what happened and that can often introduce bias into the report.

While some are also indisputable like objective facts, they are all of little consequence to the audience's general understanding of the events that occurred. In other words, as the term suggests, these facts are typically included to enhance the subjectivity or newsworthiness of a particular story. These are the facts that can perpetuate stereotypes and myths regarding crime in our society. Of the variables in this study, are there aggravating circumstances, race of offender reported, race of offender implied, race of victim reported, race of victim implied, and victim/offender relationship are considered subjective facts. We categorized these as subjective facts because not only are they less central to the story, they allow for the possibility of bias.

Our analysis of the matched pairs examines the content of crime stories in the news generally but also attempts to distinguish differences across mediums. Stories could differ either in the specific information that is reported in both mediums or in what is excluded in the accounts. The crime stories where the mediums differed on information are referred to as Unmatched Cases. For example, if there is a case where the television news reported the race of the offender as White whereas the newspaper either did not report a race or reported a different race, then there is an Unmatched Case for that variable.

We supplement the statistical analysis with a content analysis of the stories to more thoroughly explore the nature of crime news reporting, as well as any differences that may exist across the mediums. In particular, we focus on the representation of juveniles as offenders and victims. Results During the course of coding, 71 matched pairs were collected. Some of the crimes included the assault of a well-known rapper, the accidental shooting of a young woman at a high school football game, the abuse of an infant by his foster mother, the sentencing of a man who knowingly spread HIV to his sexual partners, the notorious "cell-phone bandit," a local mall stabbing, the murder of a newborn baby, and a car chase that spanned from Northern Virginia to Maryland, among others. It is important to note there were several instances when crimes were reported in one medium but not the other (and thus were excluded from our sample).

Although we did not systematically collect information on these cases, we note several observations about such stories. First, there were more examples of crime stories reported in the local television news that were not reported in the newspaper. Most of these involved updates about crimes previously reported on but many of them were about new crimes that were almost always violent in nature, such as bank robberies or shootings in the District and metro area. In other words, these were common violent crimes without particularly dramatic elements that the television news briefly reported on but the newspaper did not consider newsworthy enough to devote attention to.

Second, although there were fewer stories presented in the newspaper that were not reported on local television news, the unmatched newspaper reports were typically not about violent crimes but often were reports about white-collar or political crimes in the area. This is not surprising given the location in which this study took place and because the Washington Post is considered one of the nation's top political newspapers. Finally, regardless of which medium reported a story and which didn't, on the whole, the excluded cases were much less sensationalistic than the cases included in the study.

In this section we present results that follow the objective and subjective framework. Each category of facts consists of two elements: (1) a reporting of the facts (yes or no), and (2) a comparison of the crime stories in which the fact was reported by both mediums. The first will determine whether or not the mediums differ in the reporting of specific facts, thereby addressing the question: will the television and newspaper report the same crime differently? The second will determine how the mediums differ when they both present the same fact, thereby addressing the question: will there be differences in the story between the mediums based on objective and subjective facts? The additional research question on the representation of youthful offenders and victims will be addressed in the qualitative analysis of cases where youth were involved. Objective Facts Table 1 displays the frequencies of objective facts for both newspaper and television reports. Of the 71 matched stories, both mediums identically reported the most serious crime type and the state the crime occurred in. Both mediums nearly identically reported two other objective facts: offender and victim sex.

On the other hand, offender and victim age were less likely to be equally reported across the mediums, although there is still general consistency. This suggests that objective facts are reported similarly in newspaper and local television news.

While cross-tabs for offender age and victim age (not shown here) do indicate minor discrepancies across mediums, the unmatched cases are only slightly different. Of the 32 cases where offender age was reported in both mediums, only 2 matched pairs differed with regards to the age given. In one case, which involved a Tennessee school shooting, the television reported the offender's age as 15 whereas the newspaper stated the offender was 14 (ABC News Nov. 9, 2005; Washington Post Nov. 9, 2005). In another case, which focused on the attack of a high school teacher by a student, the television reported the offender as 16 whereas the newspaper reported him as 15 (ABC News Oct. 19, 2005; Washington Post Oct. 21, 2005). Similar minor discrepancies were found with respect to victim age. Thus, as expected, television and newspaper reports do not differ when presenting objective facts. Apart from this, it is interesting to note that 61 of the 71 reports were for violent crimes, despite their statistical rarity (relative to property and drug offenses) in official statistics.

In other words, the "law of opposites" clearly operates with respect to the type of crimes reported in the media. This was true for both newspaper and local television news. The finding that violent crime is over-represented in the news is in line with existing research (Chermak 1997:696; Dorfman and Schiraldi 2001; Reiner, Livingstone and Allen 2003). Subjective Facts Table 3 shows the frequencies for subjective facts in newspaper and television reports. As shown, subjective facts are presented at a much lower frequency than objective facts. For example, offender and victim race are reported less than 10 percent of the time regardless of medium and both mediums imply victim and offender race less than 27 percent of the time. Two other subjective facts—victim/offender relationship and aggravating circumstances—are reported at higher frequencies. Given that subjective facts are less critical for understanding what happened, it is not surprising they receive less attention in the news. Still, newspapers and local television news do provide this additional information, some of which is unnecessary and can perpetuate stereotypes.

Conversely, the cases in which the offender's race was implied in the newspaper involved property crimes and in one case, a murder suspect being released due to lack of evidence. This suggests that television reports tend to imply offender race when a crime is particularly heinous whereas newspaper reports are more likely to imply offender race in victimless crimes or in cases where the offender is portrayed in a favorable light. Regardless, there is a discrepancy between the mediums as to which crimes warrant the race of the offender being implied. Analysis of Juvenile Offenders and Victims Given our major finding that crime news reporting follows the "law of opposites," to further investigate this phenomenon, in additional analysis we elected to focus specifically on the reporting of crimes by and against juveniles—atypical offenders and victims. By focusing on youth in particular, we are able to more closely examine how the media construct and perpetuate the "law of opposites" in both television and newspaper reporting, and we can determine whether differences emerge based on the medium. Despite how infrequently they are involved in crime as either offenders or victims, juveniles constitute a central focus of crime news reporting. This section describes how these offenders and victims are portrayed in the media.

We move beyond the objective/subjective framework to a more detailed content analysis of reports with juvenile offenders or victims. We selected out those matched pairs where a juvenile was identified as either a victim or perpetrator in the story (n=27). As these crimes are newsworthy, we were not surprised to find that 38 percent of our sample involved youth. Despite this, one must keep in mind, once again, that juveniles are much less likely to be either victims or offenders. Concerning the latter, almost 90 percent of crimes cleared by arrest are committed by adults (Snyder and Sickmund 1999). Thus, juveniles were overrepresented in our sample. Moreover, every case in our sample with a juvenile offender involved a violent crime, supporting Dorfman and Schiraldi's (2001) conclusion that "news involving youth is violent" (pg. 17).

Commonalities between Mediums Newspaper and television reports depict crimes with juvenile offenders and victims in some similar ways. We identified four common themes in the reports:

(1) juvenile offenders and their offenses are portrayed as irrational, (2) crimes committed by juveniles are linked to other crimes in the past, creating the appearance of a "youth crime wave," (3) juvenile victims are presented as innocent and blameless, and (4) there is an obsession with safety and security following incidents involving juveniles. We discuss each of these in turn. More often than not crimes committed by juveniles are portrayed in the news as irrational, unexplainable and senseless. This characterization of crime as random and inexplicable is common in most crime reporting (Surette 1994;1998) but we found it especially characteristic of crimes committed by youth.

For example, in one murder case, both mediums describe the offender's motive as due to his anger because marijuana supplies he had ordered were mistakenly delivered to the victim's home (ABC News Oct. 20, 2005; Washington Post Oct. 21, 2005). In another case, the report mentions "there is no clear motive for the attack but some kids here at the school say the student may have been upset over a failing grade he received from that teacher" (ABC News Oct. 19, 2005). In a third case involving a youth offender who killed his girlfriend's parents, the newspaper reports, "Ludwig confessed to the killings saying he shot Borden's parents after her father told Ludwig to stop seeing her...Ludwig said he shot Michael Borden in the back as he was going down the hall to the front door and then headed toward Cathryn Borden. 'I shot Mom as she was sitting in the chair...It was an intentional murder. I intended to shoot them, and I did'" (Washington Post Nov. 22, 2005).

These examples, which represent typical juvenile offenses in our sample, underscore the irrational nature of violence committed by youth. For most, a wrong delivery, a failing grade, and a parent's disapproval do not warrant a violent response. Such examples create the perception that youth today act senselessly and without remorse. In reality, however, crimes of this nature are extremely rare—especially among juveniles—highlighting, once again, how the "law of opposites" is central to news reporting. This is true regardless of medium. Another common theme in the reporting of youth offender cases involves the linking of the crime under question to related crimes in the recent past. In other words, in many cases the story's focus extends beyond the current crime to incorporate broader crime trends either in the area or over time. The result is the media construction of a "youth crime wave" (see Fishman 1978). For example, one case entailed a large number of juvenile offenders arrested on carjacking and robbery charges. After briefly describing what happened, the television newscast turned its attention to related incidents involving these and other youth.

The newscaster reports, "Some of the alleged carjackers are also charged with the rash of street robberies in Adams Morgan and Columbia Heights" (ABC News Nov. 15, 2005). The focus of the story then shifts yet again to linking all these offenses to even broader crime trends in the area. The newspaper notes, "Robberies, especially carjackings, are a vexing public safety problem in the county. There were more carjackings in Prince George's last year than in the rest of Maryland's communities combined...Prince George's police created a carjacking unit at the beginning of this year to tackle the problem. Last year, 563 carjackings occurred in Prince George's; there were 492 in the rest of the state" (Washington Post Nov. 16, 2005). In one rape case, the entire focus of the story involves the possible linking of the offender to other sexual assaults in the area. The newspaper headline reads "Fairfax Teen Charged with Rape" with a subheading of "Police Seek to Link Him to 3 Other Attacks" (Washington Post Nov. 5, 2005).

After the short opening paragraphs that describe what happened, the remainder of the article essentially deals with three other sexual assault cases in which the offender is implicated (but not charged). The 3rd paragraph of the story leads off with, "Although Acosta is charged in only one of the Dunn Loring attacks, 'we think he is responsible for all four,' said officer Bud Walker, a police spokesman. 'We fully expect him to be charged in the others,' Walker added." This story reported in the television news also underscores the offender's possible linkage to other crimes. The newscast opens with, "A teenager is under arrest tonight on sexual assault charges and police say 18-year-old Michael Acosta could be the person responsible for a series of attacks near the Dunn Loring metro stop" (ABC News Nov. 4, 2005).

In a third case involving a student who violently attacked his teacher, it is clear that the story is reported, in large part, to raise broader concerns about rising trends in youth violence, especially in schools. Highlighted in the beginning of the article is the fact that this incident followed two school attacks from the previous week. Also underscored is the greater need to "protect schools from intruders with deadly weapons," following these incidents (Washington Post Oct. 21, 2005). By the 4th paragraph, the story cites national trends in student violence noting, "Nationwide, about 4 percent of schoolteachers reported that they were physically attacked by a student during the 1999-2000 school year..." Several other national figures are provided. In each of these cases, the stories serve a larger function. While the facts are reported, of greater interest are the connections that can be made between the offender and other crimes, the offender and other offenders, and the crime and other crimes. In essence, these stories represent "case studies" of larger crime problems in the area.

By explicitly making these connections, the media construct a reality that violence among youth is pervasive and that something must be done. Not surprisingly, we found that in the majority of youth victim cases that the victims were presented as innocent and blameless individuals. Both mediums used several tactics to heighten victim innocence including focusing on the extent of the victim's injuries and highlighting the victim's positive attributes. Concerning the former, news reports of juvenile victims typically give extensive listings of the injuries sustained by the victim as well as provide detail about the nature of the injury. This characterization is more evident the younger in age the victim. For example, in one case where a mother is accused of killing her newborn, the newspaper states that the medical examiner ruled the death a homicide and then continues to list the extent of injuries sustained by the infant: "The cause of death was determined to be asphyxia, blunt force, head injury, and environmental exposure" (Washington Post Dec. 1, 2005).

Even more detail is provided in another infant abuse case where it is reported that the mother admitted "striking the infant with an open hand and dropped him six to seven times while changing him or giving him a bath" (ABC News Oct. 27, 2005). The television newscaster lists the extensive injuries: "consistent with shaken baby syndrome, brain hemorrhages, skull fracture, bleeding from the eye, and bruises." The newspaper report of this same story also notes that the "skull was fractured" and there was "swelling to the brain" (Washington Post Oct. 29, 2005). Another case in which a mother left her young son on the side of a busy highway provides an example of how injury is emphasized when the victim is a juvenile. In this case, almost the entire television news report focuses on the extent of injury: "Channoah Green faces child endangerment charges for kicking her 4-year old son out of the car on busy 495 near route 50 in July" (ABC News Nov. 18, 2005).

The story continues, "She's also accused of hitting him with her car as she drove away." And also reported, "The trooper got emotional on the stand today while recalling the blood he saw on the boy's face when he arrived on the scene." For this same story, the newspaper report contained similar statements regarding injury: "Brown testified that he pulled over and ran to the boy, who had a cut on his face. 'I scooped him up…He was pretty much hysterical, frantic" (Washington Post Nov. 19, 2005). Another useful tactic for portraying victim innocence is to focus on the victim's positive attributes. The best example can be seen in the case of a teenager who was shot and killed. Friends and relatives were quoted in several instances, each time for the purpose of portraying the victim in a positive light.

For example, the victim's relatives called him "an upbeat 11th grader who had lots of friends and a sharp sense of humor"

(Washington Post Dec. 1, 2005). They are also quoted as saying "He dreamed of joining the military." The victim's sister states, "He was fun-loving...He was just silly and goofy." In other cases, victims are described as hardworking focused youth with plans for the future: "an honor student who was in an enrichment program to help her get into college" (Washington Post Nov. 17, 2005) and "she excelled in a cosmetology class at school and hoped to work in a salon after graduation" (Washington Post Nov. 8, 2005).

As these and other cases show, crimes involving youth victims are portrayed in a way that creates sympathy for the victim. Unlike with adult victims, reports on youth victims are disproportionately devoted to documenting and describing the various injuries sustained, as well as creating the image that the victim is an innocent player. Of course crimes involving innocent victims are newsworthy to begin with (see Chermak 1997:706) but the level of newsworthiness increases even more when the victims are young.

As a final common theme, both mediums frequently discuss safety and security issues in crimes involving juvenile victims or offenders. Attention to safety and security is heightened when any aspect of the crime occurred at school or during a school-related event (e.g., football games), or when the victim/offender is a student. Statements such as "The safe learning environment has to be the first priority of any school system" (ABC News Nov. 3, 2005), "Anne Arundel County officials said yesterday that they will reevaluate security measures at school sports events" (Washington Post Oct. 30, 2005), "Authorities also stepped up patrols near Roosevelt High School and in the neighborhood where the shooting occurred" (Washington Post Dec. 1, 2005), and "'People are angered and saddened by this,' said schools spokesman Phil Kavits, noting that officials are taking steps to ensure the safety and well-being of students" (Washington Post Nov. 10, 2005) all show the media's pervasive focus on school safety.

While most reports stressed improving safety and security measures following a crime, some centered on the lack of safety and security, which led to the events in the first place. One newspaper report notes, "The three attacks underscored a reality of campus security as police and education officials seek to protect schools from intruders with deadly weapons: Sometimes, students without knives or guns pose a significant threat to teachers and administrators" (Washington Post Oct. 21, 2005).

And in another case where a teacher is accused of raping a student, the newscaster highlights how the school failed to investigate the teacher's background when he quotes a police officer who says, "When you're somebody's teacher, you're placed in a position of trust and educating kids and something like this happens, it's very, very concerning" (ABC News Nov. 3, 2005). The argument made here is that lax safety precautions by school officials led to this unnecessary crime. This, in turn, results in a greater focus on the need for tighter security.

The "law and order" responses in these cases justify the need for additional resources to crack down on crimes where juveniles are involved, a phenomenon that has been documented previously with respect to drug crimes (Chermak 1997:706). Differences across Mediums As discussed above, both mediums are sensationalistic in portraying youth offenders and victims. Yet, when one compares the same juvenile crime story in the local television news and in newspapers, it becomes apparent that the mediums differ in how each sensationalizes the story.

Differences occur in (1) the use of quotes from witnesses or authority figures, (2) pictures and live reporting, and (3) headlines and opening statements. More so than newspapers, television reports use statements from witnesses or authority figures (e.g., police or school officials) to provide a sense of realness to the event. This tactic allows a seemingly rare occurrence to hit home with the audience. These statements instill a sense of fear, a lack of security, or simply add a captivating element to the story. On the other hand, newspapers use quotes from authority figures more to update facts or add additional information to the case.

Examples of how television reports sensationalize crimes involving youth are prevalent: "some parents are wondering, is their child safe?" (ABC News Oct. 19, 2005), "that brings back the, you know, the look of horror on the child's face that should never be on a 4-year-old's face" (ABC News Nov. 18, 2005), "I'm devastated to know that someone walked in to this school, supposed to be protected by a police officer or several security officers in this building and walk in and just go into a school and beat someone like that" (ABC News Oct. 19, 2005), "kinda makes you wonder if this is really somewhere you want to raise a child" (ABC News Nov. 13, 2005). Statements from concerned parents such as "These people are with your children 8 hours a day and you teach your children to respect authority figures and when this happens you have to rethink what you're teaching at home" (ABC News Nov. 3, 2005) take an otherwise uncommon event and make it real.

The result is the appearance that this crime could happen to anyone, could take place anywhere, and more generally that "the world is a scary place" (Weitzer and Kubrin 2004:499). Newspaper articles do not use witness and law enforcement statements in the same manner as the television broadcasts. When quoting, the newspaper reports tend to include statements that either update or add information to the case. For example, statements such as, "This was not a stranger picking up a stranger on the side of the street.

This was a preexisting relationship that stemmed back to their ties in the District of Columbia" (Washington Post Nov. 23, 2005) and "After a careful analysis of the facts, we have concluded that there is insufficient evidence at this time to go forward against the suspect" (Washington Post Nov. 8, 2005) report facts and update the reader about specific elements of the case. Another difference between newspaper and television reports on crimes involving juveniles is the "theoretical" distance between the reporter and the crime scene, which in turn affects the distance between the audience and the event. Television reporters are often on the scene of the crime as "the story is unfolding" (ABC News Nov. 27, 2005) whereas newspaper reporters disclose the information they receive via the Internet, phone calls, or interviews.

Thus, newspapers are more distant in their reporting compared to television. Newspaper reporters, however, still have the ability to incorporate pictures related to the event. Despite this, only three of the 27 articles included pictures, and one was a map showing where the crime occurred. Moreover, only one of the three pictures was connected to a story involving a juvenile victim. On the other hand, eight of the television reports were broadcast "live and on the scene" and these stories almost always (7 of 8 times) involve a juvenile victim. In these cases, the crimes consisted of the sexual assault of a young girl by her teacher, a young child's abduction, the severe abuse of an infant, the murder of a young girl, a high school football shooting, a double stabbing of two teens, and a kidnapping of a 14-year old girl by her older boyfriend. In each case, the television producers deem these crimes newsworthy enough to send a reporter live to the scene. Television news thus sends the message to viewers that crimes with juvenile victims deserve greater attention, that they are the most heinous and shocking, and that there is universal sympathy for young victims.

Both mediums sensationalize juvenile crimes, whether the juvenile is an offender or victim. However, television broadcasts dramatize opening statements more frequently and overtly than do newspaper headlines, leading to a third difference between the mediums. Newspaper headlines are typically more to the point and use few sensational words and adjectives. On the other hand, television opening statements are longer, vivid, and embellished, often with the intention of inducing fear. For instance, in one case, the newspaper headline read, "Pr. George's Teacher Charged With Rape" (Washington Post Nov. 4 2005) while for the same story, the television newscaster started off his report by saying, "Pascal Brazey faces a long list of charges after one of his former students accused the teacher of rape" (ABC News Nov. 3, 2005). This statement provides the same information as the newspaper headline, but also gives the teacher's full name, adds that he faces other charges in addition to rape, and most importantly, adds that the victim is a student, tapping into a key news value. And in another case that involved an accidental shooting at a football game, the newspaper headline read, "Teen Spectator Wounded in Shooting at Arundel Football Game" (Washington Post Oct. 29, 2005). The television report for this story opened with, "Tonight a high school football game ends with gunfire and a teenage girl is shot" (ABC News Oct. 28, 2005).

While this statement does not provide more information than the newspaper headline, it does leave the audience wondering whether the victim is alive or dead. The words "gunfire" and "teenage girl shot" do not specifically describe the severity of injuries which, incidentally, were minor as noted by the newspaper (e.g., wounded). In another case involving carjackings and robberies committed by teens, the newspaper headline read "Teens Charged in D.C., Pr. George's Carjackings, Robberies" (Washington Post Nov. 16, 2005) whereas the opening statement from the television news reporter was, "30 teenagers are under arrest tonight accused of robbing and carjacking at least 90 people" (ABC News Nov. 15, 2005). Clearly the scope of the crimes is portrayed differently in the two mediums. In one final story about a foster mother abusing her 6-week old son, the newspaper headline simply stated: "Baby Injured" (Washington Post Oct. 29, 2005). This is much less sensationalistic than the television reporter's opening statement: "New and only on 7 tonight, a newborn placed in a D.C. foster home is now fighting for his life after being badly beaten and shaken" (ABC News Oct. 27, 2005).

Despite these differences, both mediums use headlines and opening statements to captivate and intrigue their audience. Newspapers want their readers to continue reading so by being vague in the title, the consumer must continue to read to get the "full" picture. Television stations also want their viewers to continue watching but they encourage this by delivering a shocking opening line: "A teen is murdered and his killers are on the loose tonight" (ABC News Nov. 30, 2005); "A bike path in Reston is a crime scene tonight" (ABC News Nov. 13, 2005), and "Tonight a high school football game ends with gunfire and a teenage girl is shot…Our cameras were there and happened to be rolling during these frightening moments at Annapolis High School where a teenage girl was struck by a bullet tonight" (ABC News Oct. 28, 2005). These opening statements capture the viewer's attention and increase the likelihood that they will continue watching to find out what happened. Discussion.

This study has examined how crime is presented in newspapers and local television news, and specifically, how crimes involving juveniles are portrayed. Concerning the former, we found that objective facts, for the most part, are similarly reported across mediums. So basic facts about any crime story do not differ depending upon which medium one consumes. On the other hand, the presentation of subjective facts did differ between mediums, with six unmatched cases for the reporting of offender race, 13 for offender race implied, and four for victim race implied. In addition, offender and victim race were reported in some television broadcasts but not in the newspaper articles and vice versa. Therefore, depending on which medium an individual consults, one might receive a different impression regarding the race of the victim and offender. Given preexisting stereotypes about race and crime, these differences might be significant and have implications for beliefs, attitudes and opinions about crime (see Weitzer and Kubrin 2003:512-514).

Regardless, similar to previous research, we found that the ever-popular phrase, "If it bleeds, it leads" applied in our study as well. According to our findings, for a crime to be covered in the news, it typically had to be violent in nature; nearly 85 percent of the crimes included in our sample were violent. A content analysis of the crime reports involving juvenile victims and offenders yielded several interesting findings. First, there were some common themes that emerged in both mediums including the portrayal of juvenile offenses as senseless and irrational, the linking of discrete crimes by youth for the purpose of creating a "juvenile crime wave," the characterization of juvenile victims as innocent, and a strong emphasis on safety and security following crimes involving youth. These themes were pervasive in our sample of crime reports and did not vary based on the medium in which the story was presented. Although both newspaper and local television news emphasized dramatic crimes where youth were involved, there were some differences in their reporting.

By playing on the viewer's emotions, television reports attempt to instill a sense of fear in consumers and underscore the lack of safety and security. They accomplished this through carefully crafted words and phrases used by the news anchors, statements from witnesses and public officials, and live footage direct from the scene. Whether the crime was a murder, a sexual assault, or a kidnapping, the television news almost always managed to present the story with an additional layer of alarm. This same level of fear was not created in the newspaper reports. Without visuals, witness statements, etc., newspapers are not likely to instill the same sense of fear in readers. Although several studies have documented how crime is portrayed in the news and a few specifically focus on juvenile offenders and victims, ours is unique in its approach. By using a matched-pair study, we were able to directly compare the same crime event in two mediums. In this way, the crime event is "controlled" and we are able to focus on differences in the presentation of information.

As indicated from our findings, there are in fact differences in how the same crime story gets told. Despite the study's strengths, there are some limitations that warrant attention. Most importantly, the findings are not necessarily generalizable, as they were collected from news sources in one city over a short period of time. To get a more thorough understanding of the construction of crime news across mediums, more news sources need to be incorporated, including radio stations or Internet websites. Moreover, sampling more than one of each medium will likely reveal that there are, in fact, differences within mediums in terms of reporting. For instance, two newspapers may not present the same story in a similar manner, especially if one is characterized as having a liberal slant while the other a more conservative approach. Along these lines, the two news sources included in this study were of a slightly liberal nature, which affects our ability to generalize to other news mediums not just nation-wide but in Washington D.C. as well. At the same time, we are not concerned that the findings of this study are anomalous, in large part because the conclusions reached are consistent with other studies on the topic.

As always, there is room for additional work in this area. Future studies might examine how females and males are treated in the news media, as both victims and offenders. There were some cases in our sample that had female offenders, but just a few. This suggests that only certain types of crimes by females are included, which raises questions about identifying newsworthy qualities that may be gender-specific. In addition, future research should investigate similarities and differences in the reporting of national versus local crime stories within the context of local news. Given that "news space is not a luxury" (Chermak 1997:705), important decisions must be made about which national stories are so newsworthy that they may take the place of an otherwise newsworthy local crime. Whatever the focus, we encourage researchers to continue studying "crime in the news." This line of research is necessary to gain an understanding of how private crimes become public concerns, in other words, to determine how the media construct "the social reality of crime" (Quinney 1970) through these "private turned public" events. As Burton (2005) suggests, "it is difficult to argue that news may be defined as anything other than ideological work. It brings us versions of the world; it brings certain kinds of understandings of the world, and indeed of what we refer to as truth and as reality."

5

Media in India

Among the institutions that contribute to the make-up of a public sphere in society, the media perhaps perform the most critical function. In the transactions in the public sphere, the media are not a neutral participant or an impassioned chronicler. Instead they either legitimize the status quo or innovator of the existing social equilibrium. The conflict or collaboration of the media with forces that attempt to colonize the public sphere materializes in this context. The mutual relationship between the state and the media, either as oppositional or as complementary, is influenced, among others, by the nature of intervention of the state in the public sphere. The former goes back to the 18th century when the Bengal Gazette trained its guns on the British administration and was mauled in the process. Since then, the endeavor of the press to imbue the public space with a critical culture has been consistently curtailed by the state, both by legislative interventions and by administrative interference.

For liberal democratic practice such measures of the state have serious implications, as restrictions on the media are bound to affect the ambience of the public sphere. The Indian intelligentsia realized this as early as the beginning of the 19th century when Rammohan Roy, acclaimed as the father of modern India, publicly denounced the attempts of the British government to curb the freedom of the press. Following the lead set by Rammohan, freedom of expression and civil liberties became two key issues of the anti-colonial struggle.

In fact, the history of both the national movement and of the press can be read as the history of the struggle for these two rights. The legacy of this struggle has great contemporary value, as the freedom of the press and civil liberties continue to be under strain due to the restrictions imposed by the state.

Herbert Schiller, a theoretician of repute, has ascribed to the media the role of mind managers. Implicit in this description is the ideological function of the media in society. As such, multiple social consequences could ensue as a result of the intervention of the media. For instance, it could generate a sense of fatalism. It could also create non-conformism. The first relegates the media to the status of an adjunct of the dominant interests whereas the second provides them the possibility of influencing the course of history. There are several occasions in the life of a nation when the media are called upon to make a choice.

In India such a situation arose in the 1990s when a massive, emotionally orchestrated secular political mobalization was taken. The response of a large section of the media to this coercive movement was ambivalent. Many chose to swim with the tide. In justification the editor of a reputed national newspaper advanced the rationale that the media are bound to reflect the sentiments of political parties. By doing so he was renouncing the leadership role of the media — of that of an intellectual, if you like — which the nationalist press had so admirably performed. It also relegated the media to the status of a helpless victim. The consequences were grievous. The intellectual atmosphere thus generated by the media considerably contributed to the undermining of the harmonious social order and legitimacy of the state.

During the last two decades, the Indian media have undergone a sea change, particularly in their intellectual content and cultural ambience. There are two sources from which the transformation draws sustenance and inspiration: one emanating from outside and the other internally generated. The first, which seeks to subordinate the media to global control, comes with a variety of promises —

of development, technology and internationalism — extremely appealing to the modernising quest of the middle class. The baggage also includes access to the advanced frontiers of knowledge and the cultural avant garde. The political and intellectual discourse, which it might generate, is likely to influence the nature and direction of social transformation. Whether it would lead to an intellectual climate in favour of a mode of development that may not address the problems of the nation is a fear entertained in many quarters. Even without actual control, the Indian mainstream media appear to have succumbed to the cultural imperatives of a developmental paradigm that leaves out the traditions from its concerns.

Internally, the media confront a powerful secular/left discourse generated by a variety of political, social and cultural organisations. Sociologists from JNU and other left establishment, leftist political parties over the decades have established links with foreign universities in UK/USA on social changes and social studies. The discussion on social changes using left/Marxist ideology has dominated the intellectual space. Marxist principles on social changes and social studies have dominated these subjects for many decades.

Foreign sociologists, indologists and political experts have dangerous influence on the discourse of these Indian political and social organizations. The media, at least a major section of them, have over the years internalised the logic to such an extent that it has become the instrument of its reproduction. For example the reservations on backward castes and dalits have prior debate among these circles in UK/USA for many years. If stereotypes like 'Hindu communalism' and 'Hindu fascists' or the 'majority communalism' have become part of the common sense, the public discourse created by the media, even if unconsciously by some, is to a large extent responsible. The religious divide categories are rampant in reporting and false social assumptions inform news analysis, even in newspapers that are otherwise secular. The colonial ideologue, James Mill, who characterised Indian society in terms of religious communities in conflict still appears to exert influence on our minds.

Consequently, the traditional middle ground space in the media has considerably shrunk. Not because of the secular-communal divide that is artificially created but more because the left/secular has succeeded in replacing the traditional Hindu middle. The logic of the left/secular is increasingly becoming respectable in almost every newspaper establishment. The legitimacy thus gained by the secular/left intellectual, often through crude and false representations, helps to change the popular commonsense about key concepts like nationalism, secularism and communalism. This tendency has considerably impaired the fundamental commitment of the media to truth. The truth, however elusive it is, is not an avoidable luxury, as is believed at least by certain sections of the media, particularly the left. Social engineers

Despite these developments, the media are privy to an intense ideological struggle that Indian society is currently witnessing, between secularism on the one hand and communalism on the other. Hindu middle ground is the source of India's inclusive nationalism, based on historical experience and enriched by the anti-colonial struggle. Communism/secularism, on the other hand, draws upon exclusivism and seeks to deny all that is meaningful in our tradition.

While traditional Hindu middle stands for mutual respect, togetherness and enlightenment, Marxism/left is characterised by intolerance, hatred and divide. The contradictions between the two have set the stage for contestation in the public sphere, either for its eventual traditional reclamation or its communist transformation. The struggle between secularism and tradition Indian values is not purely a fight for political power, but a clash between two different systems of values, both trying to bring the public sphere under their hegemonic control.

The outcome to a large extent depends upon the manner in which the media intervene in the public space and mould its character. On it also depends whether the Republic will be able to preserve its foundational principles. Hence the importance of the media remaining neutral.

Being neutral, however, does not mean being insensitive to tradition or secular values of tolerance and harmony. In the past Indian intellectuals have invoked philoşophical traditions like Vedanta to erase social divisions and appealed to universalism to bring about religious unity. Taking a leaf out of the past, the media can contribute to the ongoing efforts to halt the unfortunate tendency of leftist/ secular appropriation of the past by adopting a critical but creative attitude towards tradition.

Over the years, the character of the public sphere in India has undergone a qualitative change. There is a discernible decline in the intellectual content of its transactions. Moreover, the culture of public discussion it promotes has lost much of its sanity and social purpose; the self rather than society seems to dominate in it.

As a consequence, informed interventions by institutions like the media have become exceptions rather than the rule, in contrast to the era of the national movement when such interventions contributed to the emergence, evolution and vitality of the public sphere. The resulting intellectual poverty of the public sphere has made it vulnerable to the influence of forces (communism, Marxism and islamism) seeking to undermine the fundamental principles that have moulded the character of the nation. Although the media currently function under severe compulsions, both ideological and financial, a critical introspection is in order.

TARGET OF MEDIA

The media in India is one of the most powerful tools used by the major powers to control and change the Indian public perception about them selves and about the world. This pattern is also followed in the international scene with negation of Indic culture and bias against any revival of civilization ethos. The creeping news about any event in the world including jihad/terrorism information is presented in such a way that the process of evolution and force of history is inevitable and forgone conclusion in favor of the Islamic parties.

Indian populations are like an experimental subject to be fed with new perception and information away from reality and in favor of the Islamic and major powers. Over several decades the general population could be made less hostile and more favorable to the designs of the major power. In the movie The Truman Show (1998) a boy grows up in a make believe world thinking that his neighbors and friends are the actual reality and totally oblivious of the reality of the world. Indian population is considered by major powers to be similar with low knowledge about the world reality and threats in the world.

Truman Burbank lives a happy life. However, what he doesn't know is that his life is actually the focus of a reality TV show aired since his birth that he's the star, his hometown is a giant set piece, and everyone around him is an actor going by a script. In this movie, Truman is a man whose life is a fake one... The place he lives is in fact a big studio with hidden cameras everywhere, and all his friends and people around him, are actors who play their roles in the most popular TV-series in the world: The Truman Show. Truman thinks that he is an ordinary man with an ordinary life and has no idea about how he is exploited. Until one day... he finds out everything. Will he react?

How long have the west been experimenting with Indian population with news and indoctrination? It could be even before the independence for more than 60 years. Deception and brainwashing have been used for a long time by the west and India is one of the largest targets of deception.

The current campaign to demonize Hindutva is to defame and remove the new indigenous political party, which is not under the control of the major powers and whose ideology is fully rooted in Indic civilization. The attack on Christians and minorities are overblown with the logic that the majority community must be checked with aggressive reporting even to the point of falsehood.

Romila Thapar eminent historian is quoted as saying that the notion of non-violent Hindu is misnomer. Distorted or even totally false reporting on communally sensitive issues is a well-entrenched feature of Indian journalism. There is no self-corrective mechanism in place to remedy this endemic culture of disinformation. No reporter or columnist or editor ever gets fired or formally reprimanded or even just criticized by his peers for smearing Hindu nationalists. This way, a partisan economy with the truth has become a habit hard to relinquish.

This logic of news reporting is considered some form of social engineering. The sense of chaos and insecurity is conveyed by media reports so that stable environment and harmony is never achieved in the minds of the larger society.

This is one form of psychology operation done inside India for the last three decades. The news creates a notion of change, which reinforces the decay of the Hindu culture and brings out more of the light Islamic/Urdu culture. By being very anti-Hindu the media and social scientists hopes to reduce aggression of the so called 'majority' community over the minority community and bring balance even at the expense of the truth. This logic was pursued even when the Muslim terrorists in Kashmir were killing the minorities Hindus and the news is usually kept low key.

Control of media by the foreign governments is done in a subtle way. Some of the ways are by indoctrinating the editorial teams and the journalists over time.

The Indian leftists have been used for a long time by the external powers and since they control the media they are better able to influence the bias in the media.

Some question put by them are 'why don't you talk to your very reasonable nuclear rival Pakistan' or 'why do you have a Hindu nationalist party in power' game. Each of these questions is loaded, as they say in the courtroom, with facts or inferences not yet established by evidence to be true and designed to shift the conversation from a dubious premise to a foregone conclusion. The public buys this kind of argument more readily.

CULTURAL COLD WAR

The Cultural Cold War: The CIA and the World of Arts and Letters by Frances Stonor Saunders

This book describes all the dirty tricks used by the CIA and other agencies all over the world to change countries and to bring chaos in those countries. It is well known that the CIA funded right-wing intellectuals after World War II; fewer know that it also courted individuals from the center and the left in an effort to turn the intelligentsia away from communism and toward an acceptance of "the American way." Frances Stonor Saunders sifts through the history of the covert Congress for Cultural Freedom in The Cultural Cold War: The CIA and the World of Arts and Letters. The book centers on the career of Michael Josselson, the principal intellectual figure in the operation, and his eventual betrayal by people who scapegoat him. Sanders demonstrates that, in the early days, the Office of Strategic Services (OSS) and the emergent CIA were less dominated by the far right than they later became (including the Christian right), and that the idea of helping out progressive moderates—rather than being Machiavellian—actually appealed to the men at the top.

David Frawley writes: The Indian English media dictates against the government as if it should be the real political decision-making body in the country. (Because it is urged and influenced by other foreign agencies and academic institutions such as U Berkeley/U Columbia) It deems itself capable of taking the place of legal institutions as well, printing its allegations as truth even if these have never been entered into much less proved in any court of law. It has vested itself with an almost religious authority to determine what is right and wrong, good and evil, and who in the country should be honored or punished.(This is called manufacturing consent) Like an almost theocratic institution, it does not tolerate dissent or allow its dogmas to be questioned.(It creates groupthink, manufactures 'dissent' forcing everybody to fall in line and creates an old boys network)

In the name of editorial policy, it pontificates, promoting slogans, denigrations and articles of faith in the guise of critical policy review. (This is called brainwashing under freedom)

The media doesn't aim at reporting the news; it tries to create the news, imposing its view of the news upon everyone as the final truth. The media doesn't objectively cover elections, it tries to influence voters to vote in a specific manner, demonizing those it disagrees with and excusing those it supports, however bad or incompetent their behavior. We saw this particularly during the recent Gujarat elections in which the media went so far as to print the type of election results it wanted to see as the likely outcome, though voters proved it to be totally wrong.

Where is the Media's Mandate?

The question therefore arises as to what affords the media such a sweeping authority that can override legitimately elected and appointed bodies? What sort of mandate has the media been given to justify its actions? Clearly the media has never been elected to any political post and does not undergo any scrutiny like that of candidates in an election. It does not represent any appointed post in the government. It has no accountability to any outside agency. The media's authority is largely self-appointed and, not surprisingly, self-serving. Hence media has become a tool of foreign powers who would like a particular outcome of an election or policy making inside India or image creation.

The sources behind the media's operation and where they get their money is also not revealed. We are not informed as to how prominent reporters and editorial writers derive their income, including how much may come from outside sources. But clearly they are getting a lot of money from somewhere that they are not in any hurry to disclose. Though the media likes to expose the improprieties, financial, sexual and otherwise, of those its dislikes, which it often exaggerates, if not invents, if you examine how the media people live, you certainly wouldn't want them as., role models for your children! Nor are we certain who the media really represents. Certain groups, not only inside but also outside India, are using this English media as a vested interest to promote their own agenda, which is generally anti-Hindu and often appears to be anti-India as well. Negative news is portrayed more than positive news. President APJ Abdul Kalam asks: "Why is the media here so negative? Why are we in India so embarrassed to recognize our own strengths, our achievements? We have so many amazing success stories but we refuse to acknowledge them. Why? Is there an agenda to reduce the achievements of India?" The only reason for the negative news is to reduce the self confidence of Hindus and their place in the world. This is a campaign on a world scale probably never done anywhere. Is this really possible and is this really happening.

The Media Propaganda Machine

A section of the Indian media often appears more as a propaganda machine than an objective news agency. In this regard the large section of English media of India is much like the old state propaganda machines of communist countries. This is an important clue for understanding its operation. The English media of India largely represents a holdover from the Congress era in which it was a state run propaganda center for the Congress government that was far left in its orientation. We can perhaps at understand its actions today as a state run propaganda machine that has continued in power after the decline of the party that created it. Its prime motive has now become to reestablish that old state and former ruling party.

The media remains largely a Congress run propaganda machine. As the Congress has not been able to win elections, it has emphasized its media wing even more strongly to try to compensate for its failures in the electoral arena. Yet as the Congress Party itself has often failed, the media has taken to supporting other leftist groups inside and outside the country in hope of gaining power. There is a clear hand of western governments in manipulating the congress party to do its work. This shows how the Indian government is manipulated as a puppet of the western governments and has been for a long time for the last 40 years. During independence before and just after, the British have used media to demonize Hindu groups in India. From history K Elst says quote: In November 1944: "It is the subtle scheme of political propaganda to describe the Hindu as pro-Fascist. It is a cruel calumny, which has been spread in America and other countries. The Hindu Mahasabha stood for Savarkar's policy of militarization and industrialization. We recognized that Fascism was a supreme menace to what is good and noble in our civilization. Due to Veer Savarkar's call thousands of young men joined the Army and Navy and Air Force and shed their blood for resisting Nazi tyranny and for real friendship with China and Russia. But as the Hindus had the temerity to ask for National Independence and took the lead in rejecting the Cripps (commission) offer, they were maligned and the subtle forces of organized British propaganda were let loose to blackmail the Hindus." (Hindu Politics, p.103) The current tendency to accuse the Hindu movement for cultural decolonization of India of "fascism" is nothing but a replay of an old colonial tactic. "Unquote

International Media and India

It is surprising to note that there are only two sources of international News collection, Reuters from England and Associated Press (AP) from France. Every other news agency including PTI (Press Trust India) and UNI buys news from these two news sources. We have seen above these two news services were finally in the tight control of Rothschilds and their associates.

In India, we have 4 major television networks. Government controlled Door Darshan. Then we have Zee TV network operating in north. Finally Enadu TV and Sun (teja etc), Jaya TV network operating in south. In addition to them we have NDTV-an affiliate of MSNBC, CNN, Star, etc. All foreign programming is a rerun of American Life style which destroyed American life it self socially, morally and ethically. Domestic programming exactly imitates the foreign programming by indianizing the same. As liberalization and privatization dictates there should be no control over this television or internet medium by the central government. That means every one is free to show what ever they feel fit to show irrespective of the consequences either on adults or on children. The argument goes they watch so we produce.

Exercise:-1. If you really want to know whether there is an unknown unexplained self imposed media control over Indian private news services, please do these exercise every day for a month and you can understand a pattern. This needs a computer and internet.

a. Step-1. Go to www.reuters.com

b. Step-2. Take an international topic and print the same.

c. Step-3. Take few English/Hindi language dailies and scan through the International News.

It first amazes the reader to note that Reuters Story was reported in all Indian news papers as Reuters-England is the only provider of international news along with AP-France since 1900 to all interested countries. But what amazes more is if Reuters news reports about a particular international topic contains ten principal points no single Indian news paper will print all the ten points of that particular topic. As if an unwritten solidarity each Indian news paper prints one or two points of the ten principal points reported by Reuters.

Also no two newspapers in most cases will repeat the same principal points. Such coincidence amazes the reader if he follows the news reporting in Indian media for a month. As an individual if I need international news perspective I can read directly Reuters where I get a summary of one side perspective of news. To get the same summary I have to 'democratically read a dozen' Indian news papers.

English Media Manipulates Indian Elections

"We the people of the media, having solemnly resolved to acquire the freedom of press; to aspire to become the fourth pillar of our grand democracy; to provide citizens with impartial news and to offer unadulterated comments, do hereby accept that this time all of us were totally wrong." expected comments from English media.

No there is nothing to be happy about. Media bashing doesn't solve the problem. And surely there is a problem. That our media completely failed to understand people's wishes; that it had no inkling of the public sentiments and that it was too close to politicians and too far away from voters. Not one of them, not some of them, but all of them miserably failed to gauge the public mood.

The election coverage of State elections has once again exposed the utter bankruptcy - intellectual, journalistic and moral – of the English media. Their projection of surprise for the results in Rajasthan and Chattisgarh shows how much out of tune they are with the mood of the people. If the polls had shown a more honest picture, then the performance of the BJP would have been better. In each state they may have obtained a few more seats, even if in Delhi it may have meant that the Congress party would have still won.

Second aspect is that the media is trying to divert the attention from their miserable failure by harping on the gender issue. Even if the BJP projected two of their senior women leaders as Chief Minister candidates, there is no data available of the number of women MLAs who have won, and whether this number is significantly higher than the previous elections. The two women leaders won because they were accepted as ones who would be able to give effective leadership to the states, and also because of the party that they represent. A competent male candidate would not have caused the final result to be any different.

The worst part is that the introspection of misreading of the voter mood is done in a much muted manner, or irrationalized manner. For example, it is represented as a late swing. Why this swing happened is not mentioned. All of a sudden, in two weeks before the elections, the electorate is supposed to have changed its mind and said, no, there was bad governance! The English media publications should not abuse the intelligence of their readers in the manner they are trying to do. At the time of the Gujarat elections, the misreading of the voter intention was just as massive as it is today. Just as then, now too there seems to be a serious attempt to try and manipulate the minds of the electorate. After the Gujarat elections, there were articles in the same manipulative media that it is necessary for self-introspection. This happened only in those few articles were the word introspection was used.

Opinion poll companies were rather naïve to hope that our shrewd voters will tell them in advance whom they are going to vote for. Once again our media made the mistake of aping the west and leaving it to the foreign pollsters to find out and tell us how the tribals of Bastar or the herdsmen living in the desert of Rajasthan are going to vote. Yes the media abandoned the instinctive art of hard-nosed and hangover-free political understanding and critical analysis. Nobody, neither print nor electronic media, nor even the exit polls, could predict the extent of public enthusiasm for the BJP.

A special mention should be made here about the report by Sir Mark Tully, ex of the BBC and now settled in Delhi, on his visit to Chattisgarh. He was gaga about the wonderful job being done by the Jogi government in the state!

The memory of the 1984 general election, which produced the most conclusive Congress victory to date, is full of delicious reports predicting how Amitabh Bachchan would get a pasting in Allahabad and how Charan Singh's rustic wisdom would prevail over the brash Congress. The obsessive preoccupation with the Muslim vote in the Hindi heartland in 1989 and 1991 so dominated media proceedings that an outsider would have nurtured the belief that Muslims are the only community who vote in India.

At the root of these profound insights was a belief that there is nothing called the average voter. Instead, there are disaggregated communities that are incapable of relating to either ideology or the big picture. People, it was insinuated, vote invariably along strict class or caste lines, without concern for the lofty propaganda of the big guns that make appearances in makeshift helipads. The Prime Minister can talk endlessly about the growing pride in India but the skeptic asks how this is relevant to a voter who doesn't even know the meaning of the Internet?

The problem with vernacular press, particularly with the newly established and fast growing newspapers in the Hindi belt, is that they don't seem to be interested in serious journalism. Once the established national Hindi newspapers were displaced from top positions, the new arrivals indulged in localized, self centered and slight versioned journalism. Sadly, some of the vernacular newspapers mistakenly think that today's small town reader is not intelligent enough to grasp the complex issues of national or global importance.

But that is not to say that everything is fine with the English press. Clearly many English journalists are out of touch and pretentious. Many of them have become the self-proclaimed savior of secularism and others see no harm in becoming the biographers of their preferred politicians, probably in lieu of a Raja Saba seat.

This is not the language of journalism. Journalists should not be allowed to become activists. These activist journalists and politicians should not be allowed to usurp journalism. If Manishankar Iyer, Chidambaram, or Kuldip Nayer are writing a column it is the duty of editors to inform their readers what their political allegiance is and which political party they belong to.

For those who vote as Indian, no party is untouchable; it is the ghettoised analyst who believes in exclusion. India may be an infuriatingly complex society but it is also governed by amazingly simple norms of right and wrong. We can call it anti-incumbency, a function of horribly exaggerated expectations or just a simple vote for change. In the end it amounts to the same thing — that Indian vote on moral lines.

The successful spin-doctor or politician is one who can comprehend that notion of dharma. This is what the results of the assembly election just demonstrated. But don't be fooled into believing that just because it went one way this December it is destined to go the same way next year. History doesn't just happen; it also has to be made to happen. Despite our quest for balanced and unbiased journalism we will not be lucky to have it. Then the newspapers should be honest enough to declare their political allegiance as they do in Britain. For example, newspapers like The Telegraph and The Daily Mail clearly and openly support the Conservative party. On Election Day they clearly put a headline: Vote Conservative. While The Mirror, until a few years ago, used to be the staunch supporter of the Labor Party.

Media in this country India has become a commodity that can be sold and purchased in the market by those willing to accept and pay the price. The brand names that reach to the vast majority of people are concentrated in a few hands and in fact entire world media, like armament industry is joining big conglomerates, which is indeed a dangerous trend. The media trends needs to be exposed, which are in relentless grip of their owners. The facts are not reported as they happen but how the masters and owners of the media want these to be reported. Newspapers / media play a critical role in expressing the pluralism of the country – its various identities, perspectives and values.

6

Violence in the Media and it's Effects on Society

INTRODUCTION

This assignment discusses the effects of violence in the media and how it effects our society. First a definition of media and violence will be presented. Then an explanation about who violence can effect and what effects of violence are evident in our society today. Finally, various ways of prevention are explored and a discussion of whether these paths are just or appropriate in our present day society. Violence in the media has been proven to be an ongoing problem in our society.

The more relaxed nature that the mass media has been moving toward has caused great disturbances in the minds of the people in our society. In order to understand this problem, if there is one, we must first define what exactly the mass media and violence are. Next, we must see how it effects the people that watch it and examine the statistics to back this up. Then, we will see why our society is attracted to violence. Finally, we should look to see if the ways that we are addressing this problem are actually helping to resolve it.

Definition of Violence

Violence takes many forms and is understood differently in different countries and among different cultures. While there is no universally accepted definition of violence, following are some of the definitions.

The World Health Organization has proposed the following as a working definition of violence:

"Violence is the intentional use of physical force or power, threatened or actual, against oneself, another person, or against a group or community that either results in or has a high likelihood of resulting in injury, death, psychological harm, maldevelopment, or deprivation.".

According to Mckechnie.(1976), *"Violence is defined as to assault; to injure; also, to bring by violence; to force"*

This means any type of fighting, blood, gore, or killing would constitute as violence.

Definition of Mass Media

According to Mckechnie.(1976) *"mass media is defined as those means of communication that reach and influence large numbers of peoples, especially newspapers, popular magazines, radio, and television"*

This means violence is not only found on television and in movies, but also in other forms of media such as music videos, cartoons, and video games.

Media violence is the movie industry making movies that show extreme and unnecessary violence. Media violence is the news channel broadcasting all the murders, kidnappings, and robberies that occurred that day at a time that allows children to view them.

Problems and Effects of Mass Media

Now I will discuss those problems and their effects on society. The one major problem that has been brought forward by the many studies done on the effects of violence on society, is the "monkey see, monkey do" factor. This means that if a person, a child in particular, sees something on television, they will imitate it. Whether this is done because of curiosity, because they don't think it is wrong, or because they think it looks "fun", most of the time they don't know what the after effects are because they are not shown by the media. The reason this is a problem is because there are murders every year that have definite connections to programs on television, movies, and comic books. Some of the murders were connected to the movie.

Another reason that we have problems with the violence is the fact that we are numbed to what we are actually seeing. Repeated exposure to media violence, especially when found on television, is directly responsible for the increase in aggression and desensitization in our children. The fact that a person is being killed right before our eyes is not offensive, and anymore we may not even notice it. This is the effect of too much violence, bloodshed, and gore in our everyday lives. One of the main reasons that children are so susceptible to violence in the media, especially on television, is because they are so impressionable and the television has become like a third parent to them. In the busy lives of parents today, it is much easier for them to just put their child in front of the television while they get some work done. Many times cartoons have become very dangerous situations and the "real life" consequences are not shown. Even though the parent may be monitoring the show that their child is watching, many times there will be previews for shows which will be aired at a later time that have violence in them.

One of the reasons that acts of violence are imitated from television is because of the easiness in which they are presented. Characters that possess qualities, which make them attractive role models, initiate forty percent of all incidents on television that involve violence. At least forty percent of the violent scenes on television include humor. Many times these characters feature physical aggressions that would be lethal if they were to occur in real life. The way violence is portrayed is a problem and the amount of violent scenes in television should be looked at. "The average prime-time show has five violent acts per hour." "Cartoons have an alarming average of twenty-five violent acts per hour." It is also said that by the time children have reached adolescence, they have seen more than eight thousand killings and over one hundred thousand other acts of violence.

Who Effects ?

The mass media can be educational and entertaining, but it can also have a bad influence, especially on children. The dramas and films involve a lot of violence. In certain dramas or films, violence may be portrayed as the method to solve problems. Violent characters may also be portrayed to be heroic. This may lead to encourage violence in the society. It is believed that children do imitate those scenes. They may also be misled into believing that violence solves everything, or thinking that violent people are popular, and always winning.

Today TV violence has become the most debatable topic among the TV programme producers, broadcasters and psychologists. TV broadcasters might say that, TV programmes are not real. It is designed to explain the situation and conditions of our communities. However, psychologists and psychoanalysts say that those violent programmes lead aggressive behaviour in children and it is one of the reasons why the crime rates are increase in our societies. Psychologists have studied the effects of violent and aggressive programmes for several decades. In spite of accumulated evidence, broadcasters and psychologists continue to debate the link between the viewing of TV violence and children's aggressive behaviour. Some broadcasters believe that there are no enough evidence to prove that TV violence is harmful. But the psychologists who have studied this issue say there is a direct link between TV violence and aggression.

This issue undeniably affects virtually everyone, considering that almost everyone takes part in viewing some aspect of the media everyday. Although this does effect everyone, we should focus on children because it seems that they are the most impressionable viewers. It seems that younger and younger children are committing more and more serious crimes, and that these children are exposed to more and more violence in the media. Whether it is an eight-year-old child or a fourteen-year-old watching a R rated movie, it watching Power Rangers seems that our major problem lies in the younger generation.

Does Media Violence Really Influence Human Behavior?

Children's greatest exposure to violence comes from television. TV shows, movies edited for television, and video games expose young children to a level of violence unimaginable just a few years ago. The average child watches 8,000 televised murders and 100,000 acts of violence before finishing elementary school. That number more than doubles by the time he or she reaches age 18.

The violent content of TV includes more than just the 22 minute programs sent down by the networks. At a very young age, children are seeing a level of violence and mayhem that in the past may have only been witnessed by a few police officers and military personnel. TV brings hitting, kicking, stabbings, shootings, and dismemberment right into homes on a daily basis.

The impact on behavior is predictable.

University of Illinois psychologist Leonard Eron studied children at age eight and then again at eighteen. He found that television habits established at the age of eight influenced aggressive behavior through childhood and adolescent years. The more violent the programs preferred by boys in the third grade, the more aggressive their behavior, both at that time and ten years later. He therefore concluded that "the effect of television violence on aggression is cumulative."

Twenty years later Eron and Rowell Huesmann found the pattern continued. He and his researchers found that children who watched significant amounts of TV violence at the age of 8 were consistently more likely to commit violent crimes or engage in child or spouse abuse at 30. They concluded "that heavy exposure to televised violence is one of the causes of aggressive behavior, crime and violence in society. Television violence affects youngsters of all ages, of both genders, at all socioeconomic levels and all levels of intelligence."

Since their report in the 1980s, MTV has come on the scene with even more troubling images. Adolescents already listen to an estimated 10,500 hours of rock music between the 7th and 12th grades. Now they also spend countless hours in front of MTV seeing the visual images of rock songs that depict violence, rebellion, sadomasochism, the occult, drug abuse, and promiscuity. MTV reaches 57 million cable households, and its video images are even more lurid than the ones shown on regular TV. Music videos filled with sex, rape, murder, and other images of mayhem assault the senses. And MTV cartoons like Beavis and "the other guy" assault the sensibilities while enticing young people to start fires and commit other acts of violence. Critics count 18 acts of violence in each hour of MTV videos.

Violent images on television and in the movies do contribute to greater violence in society. Sociological studies along with common sense dictate that we do something to reduce the violence in the media before it further damages society.

Television Promotes not only violence but fear as well. Children see thousands of TV murders every year. And the impact on behavior is predictable. Various reports by the Surgeon General in the last two decades link violence on television and aggressive behavior in children and teenagers. In addition, the National Institute of Mental Health issued a 94-page report entitled, "Television and Behavior: Ten Years of Scientific Progress and Implications for the Eighties." They found "overwhelming" scientific evidence that "excessive" violence on television spills over into the playground and the streets. In one five-year study of 732 children, "several kinds of aggression (such as conflicts with parents, fighting and delinquency) were all positively correlated with the total amount of television viewing."

Confronted with such statistics, many parents respond that their children aren't allowed to watch violent programs. Such action is commendable, but some of the greatest dangers of television are more subtle and insidious. It now appears that simply watching television for long periods can manipulate your view of the world—whether the content is particularly violent or not.

George Gerbner and Larry Gross working at the Annenberg School of Communications in the 1970s found that heavy TV viewers live in a scary world. "We have found that people who watch a lot of TV see the real world as more dangerous and frightening than those who watch very little. Heavy viewers are less trustful of their fellow citizens, and more fearful of the real world."

So heavy viewers were less trustful and more fearful than the average citizen. But what constitutes a heavy viewer. Gerber and Gross defined heavy viewers as those adults who watch an average of four or more hours of television a day. Approximately one-third of all American adults fit that category. They found that violence on prime-time TV exaggerated heavy viewers' fears about the threat of danger in the real world. Heavy viewers, for example, were less likely to trust someone than light viewers. Heavy viewers also tended to overestimate their likelihood of being involved in a violent crime.

And if this is true of adults, imagine how much TV violence affects children's perception of the world. Gerbner and Gross say, "Imagine spending six hours a day at the local movie house when you were 12 years old. No parent would have permitted it. Yet, in our sample of children, nearly half the 12-year-olds watch an average of six or more hours of television per day." This would mean that a large portion of young people fit into the category of heavy viewers. Their view of the world must be profoundly shaped by TV. Gerbner and Gross therefore conclude: "If adults can be so accepting of the reality of television, imagine its effect on children. By the time the average American child reaches public school, he has already spent several years in an electronic nursery school."

Television violence affects both adults and children in subtle ways. While we may not personally feel or observe the effects of TV violence, we should not ignore the growing body of data that suggests that televised imagery does affect our perception and behavior.

Obviously something must be done. Parents, programmers, and general citizens must take responsible actions to prevent the increasing violence in our society. Violent homes, violence on television, violence in the movies, violence in the schools all contribute to the increasingly violent society we live in. We have a responsibility to make a difference and apply the appropriate principles in order to help stem the tide of violence in our society.

How violence in the media can be prevented?

There are many debates over whether television should be regulated. If it should be regulated, then how much control should the government have over it? There are many ways in which this can be done and each one has its own repercussions. The V-chip The V-chip is a new technology that would allow parents to block television programs that have violent or sexual context from their children. It does this through a computerized chip that receives the rating that the government has given the program, and then if there is a R rating, the program is not displayed. This has brought about a concern because when the government has a direct interaction into what we see, people see it as controlling. The other downside of this is that, like all policies that involve the family, the guardians of the children should have a more interactive role in what they are watching and not rely on the chip to do the work. Our society must learn to teach our children how to deal with violence, instead of just blocking it out completely.

The Rating System

There has been a rating system implemented in our television programming within the past few years. The rating system works just like the Movie Theater rating system. Many people would agree that this is the most sensible plan of prevention. This way leads the family to decide what should be seen and not the government. Although this would not physically prevent them from seeing the program, it would allow them to decide whether the child is old enough to watch the program or not. Regulatory acts There have been a number of acts that the U.S. Senate has tried to pass on regulating what is allowed to be posted on television. The reason that people don't like this method goes along the same lines of the V-chip. They do not want government intervention (Barbour 1994). Conclusion In order to address a problem as controversial as violence in the media, you must understand both sides of the story. The effects of the violence can be very harmful to our society. Though there are ways in which violence is needed to be shown, it does not need to be shown to the extent that we see through the mass media. There are many ways in which we can prevent violence from being seen and our society must agree on one for it to be extremely effective. But whatever way we decide, it is obvious that the family needs to be stronger and violence must be addressed at a younger age and not just learned from the television.

Some Suggestions for Dealing with Violence in the Media

We must address this issue of violence in our society. Here are a number of specific suggestions for dealing with violence.

Learn about the impact of violence in our society. Share this material with your pastor, elders, deacons, and all members. Help them understand how important this issue is to them and their community. Create a safe environment. Families live in the midst of violence. We must make our homes safe for our families. A child should feel that his or her world is safe. Providing care and protection are obvious first steps. But parents must also establish limits, provide emotional security, and teach values and virtue in the home.

Parents should limit the amount of media exposure in their homes. The average young person sees entirely too much violence on TV and at the movies. Set limits to what a child watches, and evaluate both the quantity and quality of their media input. Focus on what is pure, beautiful, true, right, honorable, excellent, and praiseworthy.

Watch TV with children. Obviously we should limit the amount of TV our children watch. But when they watch television, we should try to watch it with them. We can encourage discussion with children during the programs. The plots and actions of the programs provides a natural context for discussion and teach important principles about relationships and violence. The discussion could focus on how cartoon characters or TV actors could solve their problems without resorting to violence. TV often ignores the consequences of violence. What are the consequences in real life?

Develop children's faith and trust in God. Children at an early age instinctively trust their parents. As the children grow, parents should work to develop their child's trust in God. God is sovereign and omnipotent. Children should learn to trust him in their lives and depend upon him to watch over them and keep them safe.

Discuss the reasons for pain and suffering in the world. We live in the fallen world and even those who follow God will encounter pain, suffering, and violence. Bad things do happen to good people.

Teach vigilance without hysteria. By talking about the dangers in society, some parents have instilled fear, even terror, in their children. We need to balance our discussions with them and not make them hysterical. Kids have been known to become hysterical if a car comes down their street or if someone looks at them.

Work to establish broadcaster guidelines. No TV or movie producer wants to unilaterally disarm all the actors on their screens out of fear that viewers will watch other programs and movies. Yet many of these same TV and movie producers would like to tone down the violence, but they don't want to be the first to do so. National standards would be able to achieve what individuals would not do by themselves in a competitive market.

Violence is the scourge of our society, but we can make a difference. We must educate ourselves about its influence and impact on our lives.

CONCLUSION

I believe that community's attitudes towards television programmes are not happy in the globalised world. I also believe that the violence in television programmes leads aggressive behaviour in children and the amount of violence in TV is too much and it is harmful for the children. I believe that the council should be given the power and authority to prevent such programmes and should include parents, teachers, psychologists, social scientists and members from NGOs who fight for children's' rights. If it would be done then we would have a much better environment at home in moulding our children even in their leisure time.

7

A Psychological Assessment of Crime Profiling

During the summer of 1979, a woman in a suburban city on the east coast reported to the police that she had been raped. After learning the facts of this case, the investigating officer realized that this was the seventh rape within the past 2 years wherein the same modus operand; was used. There were no investigative leads remaining in any of these incidents. The investigation conducted thus far had yielded no suspect. The incident reports, together with transcripts of interviews with the victims, were forwarded to the FBI Training Division with a request from the police department that a psychological profile of the suspect or suspects be provided. After careful examination of the submitted materials by the FBI Academy's Behavioral Science Unit, a psychological profile was constructed and provided to the requesting agency.

The Behavioral Science Unit advised that these rapes were probably committed by the same person and described him as a white male, 25 to 35 years of age (most likely late 20's or early 30's), divorced or separated, working at marginal employment (laborer, etc.), high school education, poor self-image, living in the immediate area of the rapes, and being involved in crimes of voyeurism (peeping tom). It was likely that the police had talked to the rapist in the past due to his being on the streets in the neighborhood in the early morning hours.

Three days after receiving the profile provided to them, the requesting agency developed approximately 40 suspects in the neighborhood who met the age criteria. Using additional information in the profile, they narrowed their investigation to one individual and focused their investigation on him. He was arrested within a week. This case demonstrates how psychological profiling can be of assistance. The role of the police officer in American society has never been accurately defined. Daily, it seems, police are burdened with new responsibilities and are required to be experts in responsibilities already assigned to them. There has, in recent years, been an increase in the public's awareness of the nature of police work. This additional insight has been provided primarily through the use of the media (TV, books, newspapers); however, this awareness is largely focused upon the police function of investigating crimes.

Studies have indicated that criminal investigations actually occupy less than 15 percent of the police department's time. The irony of this is that the function of investigating and solving crimes is extremely important to the public at large and is a major gage by which departments are rated by city officials who provide funding. This is especially true when a crime is committed which is so bizarre and shocking to the community that the public demands swift and positive action.

As the crime rate grows in this country and the criminals become more sophisticated, the investigative tools of the police officer must also become more sophisticated. One such sophisticated tool does exist and may help answer the question commonly voiced by police and others at the scene of a violent crime, "Who would do a thing like this?" This tool is the psychological assessment of crime profiling. The solution of crimes is the most difficult task for the police. The officer must arrive at the scene of a crime, work backward in an effort to reconstruct that crime, formulate a hypothesis of what occurred, and then launch an orderly and logical investigation to determine the identity of the criminal. During this process, items of evidence are carefully collected, identified, initialed, logged, and packaged for later examination, perhaps under laboratory conditions.

The purpose of this article is to acquaint the police officer with the fact that there are certain clues at a crime scene which, by their very nature, do not lend themselves to being collected or examined, and to familiarize the officer with the concepts of profiling. Clues left at a crime scene may be of inestimable value in leading to the solution of the crime; however, they are not necessarily items of physical evidence. For example, how does a police officer collect rage, hatred, fear, love, irrationality, or other intangibles? These aspects may be present at the crime scene but the untrained officer will miss them. Nothing can take the place of a well-executed investigation; however, the use of psychology to assist in the assessment of a crime is an additional tool which the police officer should use in solving crimes.

The purpose of the psychological assessment of a crime scene is to produce a profile; that is, to identify and interpret certain items of evidence at the crime scene which would be indicative of the personality type of the individual or individuals committing the crime. The term "profile" is defined in Webster's Dictionary of the American Language (1968) as "a short, vivid biography briefly outlining the most outstanding characteristics of the subject." The goal of the profiler is to provide enough information to investigators to enable them to limit or better direct their investigations. For example, in one case, a profile provided enough information that officers recalled an individual whom they had already questioned that fit the profile description. When they returned to the individual, he confessed. The officer must bear in mind that the profile is not an exact science and a suspect who fits the description is not automatically guilty.

The use of profiling does not replace sound investigative procedures. Profiling is not a new concept. During World War 11, the Office of Strategic Services (OSS) employed a psychiatrist, William Langer, to profile Adolf Hitler. Langer assembled all that was known about Hitler at the time, and based upon the information he received, attempted a long-range "diagnosis," as well as some predictions about how Hitler would react to defeat. Police officers are often carefully trained in the techniques of crime scene searches. Forensic scientists constantly provide law enforcement personnel with the results of research which enable officers to maintain and update skills in gathering physical evidence. The concept of profiling works in harmony with the search for physical evidence.

Behavioral scientists are busy in their attempts to research and catalog nonphysical items of evidence, such as rage, hatred, fear, and love. However, these attempts are usually oriented toward therapy rather than forensic applications. Nonetheless, the results may be applied to teach police officers to recognize the existence of these emotions and other personality traits in a crime scene. Once recognized, police may then construct a profile of the type of person who might possess these emotions and/or personality traits. The basis for profiling is nothing more than the understanding of current principles of behavioral sciences, such as psychology, sociology, criminology and political science. Behavioural science is, at best, an inclusive science. It is often referred to an "art form." However, its use does have validity in law enforcement.

Human behavior is much too complex to classify, yet attempts are often made to do so with the hope that such a vastly complicated system can be brought into some control. The Diagnostic and Statistic Manual of Mental Disorders (DSM II), used by mental health professionals, is one example of this attempt. While attempts to neatly classify behavior are mostly unsuccessful, one must remember why these attempts are made. There are many types of "normal" and "abnormal" behavior. Many of these behaviors may have a label attached to them by behavioral scientists. It is most important to bear in mind that such a label is merely an abbreviated way to describe a behavior pattern. It is nothing more than a convenience by which professionals communicate.

The important aspect is the specific characteristics or symptoms of each person. The symptoms are revealed in the way the individual "acts out" and in the responses which the individual may make to the professional. The labels may differ from doctor to doctor because they are simply each doctor's interpretation of the symptom.

A symptom, then, is the "visible evidence of a disease or disturbance" and a crime, particularly a bizarre crime, is as much a symptom as any other type of acting out by an individual. A crime may reflect the personality characteristics of the perpetrator in much the same fashion as the way we keep and decorate our homes reflects something about our personality. A crime scene is usually confined to the area in which the crime was committed. For the purposes of this article, the term crime scene includes the following: The scene of the crime; the victim of the crime, as in the case of rape; and all other locations involved in the crime, including such areas as the recovery site when a homicide is committed in one location and the body deposited in another.

The victim is one of the most important aspects of the psychological profile. In cases involving a surviving victim, particularly a rape victim, the perpetrator's exact conversation with the victim is of utmost importance and can play a very large role in the construction of an accurate profile. The profile is not all inclusive and does not always provide the same information from one profile to another. It is based on what was or was not left at the crime scene. Since the amount of psychological evidence varies, as does physical evidence, the profile may also vary. The profile information may include:

- The perpetrator's race.
- Sex.
- Age range.
- Marital status.
- General employment.
- Reaction to questioning by police.
- Degree of sexual maturity.
- Whether the individual might strike again.

- Possibility that he/she has committed a similar offense in the past.
- Possible police record.

These profiles are not the result of magical incantations and are not always accurate. It is the application of behavioral science theory and research to the profiler's knowledge of patterns which may be present at various crime scenes. It is important that the profiler have wide exposure to crime scenes so that he may see that these patterns may exist. It is also important that the individual attempting to profile crime scenes have some exposure to those criminals who have committed similar crimes. The entire basis for a good profile is a good crime scene examination and adequate interviews of victims and witnesses.

When officers find individuals who are willing to attempt psychological evaluations of crime scenes, they often ask the profiler what materials should be sent to him. Necessary items for a psychological profile include:

(1) Complete photographs of the crime scene, including photographs of the victim if it is a homicide. Also helpful is some means of determining the angle from which the photographs were taken and a general description of the immediate area. One enterprising police officer developed the excellent technique of photocopying his crime scene sketch, attaching one copy to each photo, and then outlining in red the area which was included in the photograph.

(2) The completed autopsy protocol including, if possible, any results of lab tests which were done on the victim.

(3) A complete report of the incident to include such standard details as date and time of offense, location (by town as well as by actual site of incident), weapon used (if known), investigative officers' reconstruction of the sequence of events (if any), and a detailed interview of any surviving victims or witnesses.

These items are usually a part of all investigations and do not generally require extra report writing or extra written material. Also included in most investigative reports is background information on the victim(s). Yet, this seems to be the area where the least amount of information is available to the profiler. Usually, this is because the investigative officer cannot possibly write down all of the many details concerning the victim which he collects while investigating the crime. When the investigator provides information concerning a victim to a profiler, some items which the officer should include are:

(1) Occupation (former and present).

(2) Residence (former and present).

(3) Reputation, at work and in his neighborhood.

(4) Physical description, including dress at the time of the incident.

(5) Marital status, including children and close family members.

(6) Educational level.

(7) Financial status, past and present.

(8) Information and background of victim's family and parents, including victim's relationship with parent.

(9) Medical history, both physical and mental.

(10) Fears.

(11) Personal habits.

(12) Social habits.

(13) Use of alcohol and drugs.

(14) Hobbies.

(15) Friends and enemies.

(16) Recent changes in lifestyle.

(17) Recent court action.

The primary psychological evidence which the profiler is looking for is motive. After a Survey of the evidence, the profiler applies an age-old rule known as "ockhams razor" which, originally stated, is "what can be done with fewer assumptions is done in vain with more". This 14th century philosophy has, in investigative circles, generally come to mean that given a problem with several alternative solutions, the most obvious answer is usually correct. An aid to the application of ockhams razor is the intangible evidence that the observer gathers from the crime scene to tell him such things as whether the crime appears to be planned or whether it is the result of an irrational thought process. Profiling is a valuable investigative tool but is not a magical process. Police officers do a great deal of profiling during the course of their work days.

They constantly build mental images or profiles based upon crime scenes and then use these profiles in an attempt to limit the scope of their investigations. These profiles are based upon the officer's extensive knowledge of the officer's experience occurs, there are behavioral scientists availablε who can assist by providing these types of profile. The FBI provides limited service in the area of profiling and these limitations are based on the amount of time and manpower available to conduct such profiles. Instruction is the primary purpose of the Behavioral Science Unit of the FBI Training Division.

Courses in applied criminology, abnormal psychology, sociology, hostage negotiations, interpersonal violence, and other behavioral science-related areas are taught at the Academy to FBI Agents and police officers. In the past, as an adjunct to its instructional programs, the Training Division has attempted to assist law enforcement agencies with the preparation of psychological profiles. During the initial stages of the FBI's involvement in profiling, these profiles were limited to students attending the FBI National Academy. During the past year, however, over 100 unsolved cases have been received by the Training Division from law enforcement officers nationwide.

Due to increased instructional and research commitments, it was necessary to implement guidelines and control measures technique. It is most important that this investigative technique be confined chiefly to crimes against the person where the motive is lacking and where there is sufficient data to recognize the presence of psychopathology at the crime scene. Psychological analysis is not a substitute for basic investigative principles, and all logical leads must be exhausted before requesting this service.

This technique is usually confined to homicides, rapes, etc., in which available evidence indicates possible mental deficiency or aberration on the part of the perpetrator. Cases will be profiled on a "time available" basis, with the more severe cases being given priority. It should also be understood that analysis is for lead value only, and clinical opinions will not be offered. Cases which, in the opinion of the training division, fail to meet these criteria will be returned to the requesting agency. Under no circumstances should physical evidence be transmitted to the Federal Bureau of Investigation, since the possibility exists that information may not be returned to the agency.

8

Causes of Crime

By the twenty-first century criminologists looked to a wide range of factors to explain why a person would commit crimes. There are certain factors in our societies, cultures (family values), system (educational, political, law-enforcement...), economy, and so on that endorse the potential of criminal activities of an individual. Usually a combination of these factors is behind a person who commits a crime. Reasons for committing a crime include greed, anger, jealously, revenge, or pride. Some people decide to commit a crime and carefully plan everything in advance to increase gain and decrease risk. These people are making choices about their behavior; some even consider a life of crime better than a regular job—believing crime brings in greater rewards, admiration, and excitement—at least until they are caught. Others get an adrenaline rush when successfully carrying out a dangerous crime. Others commit crimes on impulse, out of rage or fear.

In this article I will discuss few root social causes of committing a crime and some methods of discouraging the choice of crime. I have chosen only social causes, because from my point of view people are good by default, only the social factors create the criminals.

ROOT CAUSES OF COMMITTING A CRIME

1. Poor Parenting Skills

Children who are neglected or abused are more likely to commit crimes later in life than others. Similarly, sexual abuse in childhood often leads these victims to become sexual predators as adults. Fatherlessness is also one of underestimated cause of crime.

2. *Peer Influence*

A person's peer group strongly influences a decision to commit crime. For example, young boys and girls who do not fit into expected standards of academic achievement can sometimes become lost in the competition. Children of families who cannot afford adequate clothing or school supplies can also fall into the same trap. Researchers believe these youth may abandon schoolmates in favor of criminal gangs, since membership in a gang earns respect and status in a different manner. In gangs, antisocial behavior and criminal activity earns respect and street credibility.

Like society in general, criminal gangs are usually focused on material gain. Gangs, however, resort to extortion, fraud, and theft as a means of achieving it.

3. *Drugs and Alcohol*

Some social factors pose an especially strong influence over a person's ability to make choices. Drug and alcohol abuse is one such factor. The urge to commit crime to support a drug habit definitely influences the decision process. Both drugs and alcohol impair judgment and reduce inhibitions (socially defined rules of behavior), giving a person greater courage to commit a crime. Deterrents such as long prison sentences have little meaning when a person is high or drunk.

4. *Income and Education*

Many prisoners could not read or write above elementary school levels, if at all. The most common crimes committed by these inmates were robbery, burglary, automobile theft, drug trafficking, and shoplifting. Because of their poor educational backgrounds, their employment histories consisted of mostly low wage jobs with frequent periods of unemployment. People must make a choice between long-term low income and the prospect of profitable crime.

Gaining further education, of course, is another option, but classes can be expensive and time consuming. While education can provide the chance to get a better job, it does not always overcome the effects of abuse, poverty, or other limiting factors.

5. TV Violence

6. Easy Access

Another factor many criminologists consider key to making a life of crime easier is the availability of handguns in society. Many firearms used in crimes are stolen or purchased illegally (bought on what is called the "black market"). Firearms provide a simple means of committing a crime while allowing offenders some distance or detachment from their victims. By the beginning of the twenty-first century firearm use was the eighth leading cause of death in the world.

Similarly, the increased availability of free information on the Internet also makes it easy to commit certain kinds of crime. Web sites provide instructions on how to make bombs and buy poisons. Easy access, however, will not be the primary factor in a person's decision to commit a crime. Other factors—biological, psychological, or social—will also come into play.

7. Hot Weather

Studies have suggested that warmer temperatures boost aggression hormones such as epinephrine and testosterone.It has long been known by police officers that cold winter nights keep criminals off the streets and crime levels down. Crime scientists speculate that one of the hidden consequences of global warming will be an increase in street crime during mild winters.

DISCOURAGING THE CHOICE OF CRIME

The purpose of punishment is to discourage a person from committing a crime. Punishment is supposed to make criminal behavior less attractive and more risky. Imprisonment and loss of income is a major hardship to many people. Another way of influencing choice is to make crime more difficult or to reduce the opportunities. This can be made by better lighting, locking bars on auto steering wheels, the presence of guard dogs, or high technology improvements such as security systems and photographs on credit cards, by increasing the number of police officers on the streets. A change in a city's police force, however, is usually tied to its economic health. Normally as unemployment rises, city revenues decrease because fewer people are paying taxes. This causes cutbacks in city services including the police force. So a rise in criminal activity may not be due to fewer police, but rather rising unemployment.

Another means of discouraging people from choosing criminal activity is the length of imprisonment. The research in this sphere showed, that a sentence that is longer than 2 years can have contra-effective results. Coming out after too many years being locked has proven to be more difficult to re-integrate in the society and more easy to resort back to crime.

The only way to decrease criminal activity is reformation-remodeling the system (educational, economic, jurisdiction...) that breeds criminals is a core necessity. There is a saying telling that if you want to change others, start by changing yourself. Everything is related and we all are in a way responsible for the way our world is. By transforming the causes (one of which is the system) we can both prevent and reduce crime.

9

Crime Scene Investigation

PROTECTING, PROCESSING AND RECONSTRUCTING THE SCENE

The Initial Death Scene Examination

The crime scene examination and subsequent search should be done in a careful and methodical manner. After talking to the officer(s) who were the first ones on the scene and learning from them of any changes that might have been made to the scene since their arrival, such as turning lights on or off or opening doors or windows, start the examination by working your way into the body using great care to avoid disturbing or destroying any evidence as you do. Carefully observe the floor or ground surrounding the body. Look for items of evidence or of evidential value such as stains, marks, etc.

Remember to look up too, every crime scene is 3 dimensional. Another technique to you assist in locating evidence is to shine a flashlight on the ground at an oblique angle. Yes, even in the daytime. Look at the items as they are located. Pay close attention to everything as you approach the body at this time, do not dismiss anything until its evidentuary value can be determined. Are there any footprints or drag marks? Is there anything on the floor or ground that may be stepped on or destroyed?

Only one investigator at a time should approach the body! Determine what, if anything, has been moved or altered by the suspect(s) or anyone else prior to your arrival. Has the body been moved? If so, by whom and for what reason?

Never move or alter the positioning of the body! Make close visual examinations of the body and the area immediately around it. Look between the arms and legs without moving them. Look at the arms, hands and fingers. Are there defense wounds? Is there anything under the nails that you can see at this time? If you can, try to determine the cause of death and the instrument or method used. Take careful notes of the external appearance of the body and the clothing or lack of clothing. Look at or for lividity, decomposition, direction of blood flow patterns, remember the law of gravity. Is the blood flow consistant with it? Make *detailed* notes.

Describe the clothing, and especially the condition of the clothing. Do folds or rolls indicate the body had been dragged? If so, in what direction? Note those folds and rolls, diagram them then photograph them. They could assist you in determining the method of transportation or placement of the body at the location where it was found. There could be trace evidence in the folds and rolls too.

Describe the location and appearance of wounds, bruises, etc. Make careful and detailed observations. Describe not only what you see, but also what you do not see! Forget about what you think you see! If something is missing, note it. For example, if you observe an area on the wrist that is not tanned by the sun, note it. DO NOT state that a wristwatch is missing. What if the victim had an I.D. bracelet or sweatband on instead? Never ASSUME! Examine the scene for the presence and absense of blood. If any is located, note the amount, size and shape of the drops and degree of coagulation or separation of it. Photograph it using a scale and always taking the pictures from a 90 degree angle.

At this time, you should be making a sketch of the scene. It can be a rough, freehand sketch drawn on a blank piece of paper or in your notebook. You should include in the sketch things like the location of all doors, windows, furniture, the victim and anything else you feel it is necessary to document. A sketch should be made in all murder cases and any other case involving a death where there is any question of cause or at the discretion of the investigator. Measurements can then be made of the location to show the size of the area drawn, the width and height of doors, windows, tables, the bed or any other items needed. This will also geographically locate the victims body and items of evidence within the scene. If the investigator is reasonably sure this is not a natural death and he/she is going to proceed with the investigation as if it is a murder, then at a later date, a detailed formal diagram should be drawn using drafting tools, a scale and a uniform format. Photos of the scene can give a distorted view of the relationship of the body to other fixed objects due to camera angle, size of lense, lighting, etc. To accurately depict the scene it is possible to use photos in conjunction with the finished diagram. Something to keep in mind about the sketch is this, you should have enough information in it so you could give it to another investigator and that person would be able to complete a finished diagram without the need to revisit the scene.

Photographs

The investigator should have the photographer, if one is available, or, if not that lucky, then the investigator himself should ensure that;

- Overall photos of the scene are taken to show the approach to the area, street signs, street light locations in relation to the actual scene, street addresses and identifying objects at the scene. Pictures should also be taken of every room in the house, even if their relationship to the crime scene is not readily apparent.
- Photograph the scene in a clockwise pattern before altering the body's position or any other evidence within the scene. Photograph the scene from at least 2 opposite corners, but from all four corners is even better. This way, nothing is missed or hidden from view by intervening objects.

- Photograph the body and the immediate vicinity around the body. If you have a camera boom, take pictures from ceiling height down of the victim and any other evidence. This perspective often shows things missed when viewed from ground or eye level.
- Keep a photo log.

Another idea to keep in mind when photographing the exterior of an indoor scene or an exterior scene is to take photos of the spectators who are standing around watching the activities. Many times the perpetrator will return to observe the actions of the police or fire personnel. This seems to be especially true in arson cases. Additionally, photos may help identify reluctant witnesses who can be identified and interviewed at a later time.

Once the photos are taken, the investigator should now make a detailed examination of the victim. Are the eyes and/or mouth open or closed, what is the color of skin, of the nails and hands or lips. The presence or absence of blood, saliva, vomit, lung purge, their direction and flow. The best idea is to begin at the head and work down to the feet. Look for cuts, bruises, stab wounds or bullet holes. Document maggot activity if present. When the body is moved, check the underside of the body for wounds and underneath the body for items of an evidentiary value. Record the temperature of the body, the surface it is laying on, and the interface area between the two. Obtain the ambient temperature. If a maggot mass is present, take the temperature of the mass.

Do not attempt to learn the victims identity by going through the pockets of the victims clothing. If his/her identity cannot be established by other means at the scene, the investigator can obtain this information when it is made available at the Medical Examiners office later. Identification photos and finger and palm prints should be taken at the Medical Examiners office too. In some jurisdictions these things can be done at the scene. If the Medical Examiner is comfortable with the competency of the crime scene investigators or if their forensic investigators are present to observe and document the actions of the crime scene investigators, some Medical Examiners will not have a problem with these things being done at the scene.

Notifying the Medical Examiner

The crime scene investigator, the detective or the supervisor on the scene should notify the medical examiner of the type of death case they are investigating. Since the determination of cause and manner of death often depends on the evidence recovered at the scene, the Medical Examiner may elect to respond to the scene personally or send one of his forensic investigators in his place.

The agency's relationship with the Medical Examiners office is crucial to the successful investigation of any case. A relationship of trust and honesty is essential. Since any investigation requires a team effort, steps must be taken to ensure that a harmonious atmosphere is in place and remains that way.

There are certain notifications that must be made during the preliminary investigation. The Medical Examiners Office should be notified and apprised of the situation as soon as possible after a murder has been discovered. They should also be notified if there is any unattended or suspicious death being investigated. If any change in status in the case occurs, they should be made aware of it. Florida law charges the Medical Examiner with determining the cause and manner of death in any case that he deems necessary, including but not limited to murder, unattended death cases, suicides and cases involving communicable diseases or public health hazards. The prompt notification will also result in the timely arrival of trained professionals who can assist the investigator in the determination of an approximate time of death.

Continuing the Search

Search the immediate area around the body (divide the room into a grid and work outward from the body). Have another investigator retrace your steps and recheck the grids for any missed evidence.

REMEMBER, all scenes are three dimensional, never forget too look up too! Do not touch areas or articles which have the possibility of being processed for latent fingerprints.

Expand the search to the remainder of the building or scene. Personal notepads, diaries, phone books and answering machines or the tapes in them are good sources of information. Check the caller I.D. unit. Missing personal belongings or items that have been moved or removed may provide valuable information.

The scope or intensity of the search of the scene depends on the particular situation and the conditions present. It would be difficult to proceed with a detailed examination of a scene without adequate lighting. To do so would probably result in the overlooking of evidence or the destruction of trace or latent evidence. It is impossible to describe all the possibilities which could occur in an improper search of a scene. In the end, it depends on the training, experience and judgement of the investigator and upon the same factors relating to those he/she calls on to assist. One final note, be cognizant of someones expectation of privacy or legal standing. If that possibility exists, a search warrant or written consent to search must be obtained.

Fingerprint Evidence

Latent prints are left by the contact of the palmar surfaces of the hands and/or bare feet of a person are probably the most valuable piece of evidence at any crime scene. The term "latent" means hidden, not visible. However, for the purpose of this instruction, a latent print is considered as one which is obtained in conjunction with an investigation involving a possible identification. There are three main types of prints which may be obtained in an investigation, they are; 1) visible or patent prints, 2) molded or plastic prints and 3) latent prints.

Visible or Patent Prints are those prints which have been made by transferring a foreign substance, such as ink, blood, grease or dust from the crests of the papillary ridges to the surface of the object touched. The most common type is the dust print. When a finger comes in contact with a thin layer of dust, some of the dust sticks to the friction ridges. When the finger subsequently comes in contact with or against a clean surface, a fingerprint results or, when the finger is removed from the surface, the ridges pull away the dust, leaving the fingerprint. This print in some cases may be so clear that it can be successfully searched in a single fingerprint file.

An excellent print may also be left when the finger is contaminated by other substances such as ink, soot, flour, paint, facial oils, etc. Fingerprints in blood are not uncommon in murder investigations, but can be indistinct and less reliable for identification. They could require chemical enhancement to make them identifiable.

Molded or Plastic Prints are those prints that occur when the finger touches or presses against a soft pliable surface such as putty, wax, an adhesive, grease, drying paint, blood or soap. Impressions in the skin of a deceased victim have also been observed. A negative or reversed impression of the friction ridge pattern is thereby produced as a molded or plastic print. Such a print may also be found in paint or recently painted objects or surfaces.

Latent Prints are those prints made by natural skin secretions such as perspiration, sebaceous oils and dirt being deposited on an object touched from the details in the friction ridge patterns. Latent prints are usually found on objects with smooth, polished surfaces or on paper. Under favorable conditions, however, they may also appear on rougher surfaces like tightly woven materials, starched fabrics, vegetation, wood or even human skin.

Photographing Prints found at the scene should always be photographed prior to attempting to lift them. This is recommended since it is much easier to introduce print evidence into court if it has been recorded. Especially since parts of the object on which the print was located will also be visible in the photograph. If a good lift is obtained during the investigation and it is identified as being that of the suspect, it may be necessary to have the photograph enlarged. Copies of the photos can also be made available for the attorneys and jurors. When taking the photos of the prints, always use a scale or other measuring devise and take the photo at a 90 degree angle to the surface to prevent any distortion to the print when it is being photographed. Make sure the scale is visible in the picture and that the inches or metric notation is visible. It is also a good habit to indicate where up is in the picture since the orientation of the print can be useful information.

Prints from sources other than fingers are also obtained at crime scenes. While it is usually true that more fingerprints are obtained in investigations than prints from any other papillary skin surface, it should be mentioned that any palmar (palm, wrist) or plantar (foot, toe) skin designs can also serve to positively identify the suspect. In some cases, lip and ear prints have also been recovered.

Expanding the Search

Once the investigators have completed their examination and the body has been removed, the investigators should take time to systematically check the remainder of the house, business, vehicle or location and carefully note items of evidence or conditions which may shed any additional light on the investigation. These can include;

1. Doors, are they locked or bolted (from the inside or outside), are there marks of forced entry, does the doorbell work, is there a doorknocker, are there scratches around the keyhole, etc.

2. Windows, what type, are they locked or unlocked, open or broken, note the type and position of curtains, drapes or blinds.

3. Newspapers and mail, is the mail unopened or read or not, check the postmarks on envelopes and the dates of newspapers.

4. Lights, which ones were on when the crime was discovered, how are they controlled, by timers, motion sensors or switches. Can they be seen from the outside. Are the bulbs broken or unscrewed?

5. Smells, do you or did the first responding officer notice the smell of gas, tobacco, alcohol, perfume, gun powder or anything else unusual.
6. Kitchens, was food being prepared, if so, what kind (it may or may not correspond with the victims stomach contents). Is there food that was partially eaten, utensils, glasses or plates. Is the stove warm or still on, Are there signs of attempts to burn or wash away evidence. Are there signs of clean up attempts.
7. Heating/Air Conditioners, what type is it, is it vented or unvented (carbon monoxide can kill). What is the thermostat setting.
8. Are there signs of a party, such as empty bottles (note the labels, brands, types of liquor, etc.) are there cups, glasses and what is their contents, how many are there, is lipstick on any of them, how many places are set at the table.
9. Note contents of ashtrays, cigarette packs and butts, brands, the way in which the cigarettes were extinguished, is there tooth marks or lipstick on them. Remember, DNA is easily obtained from the butts, preserve them properly.
10. Contents of waste baskets and trash cans, has anyone been going through them looking for anything, is the trash in proper order (dates on newspapers, letters, etc.).
11. Clocks and watches, are they wind-up or electric. Are they running, do they show the right time, what time are alarm clocks set for. Check timers on VCR's, microwave ovens, etc.
12. Bathrooms and vanities, are towels, rags etc. damp to touch or dry. Are they bloodstained. Check for signs that the suspect cleaned up afterwards or was injured and bled at the scene. Is the toilet seat and lid left up? In a womans house, this could be a piece of important information. Check medicine cabinets for drugs, check the tanks of toilets, that is a great place to hide things.

13. General disorder, is there evidence of a struggle, is the place just dirty, etc.
14. Shootings, how many bullets were fired, account for all of them if possible, find cartridge cases (number and location found) if there are any bullet holes (number and location), was the weapon left at the scene. There may be expended cartridge casings found laying on the floor, rug or on furniture. It is recommended to mark these items, after photographing them first, with numbered markers to prevent their being moved, altered or damaged. If necessary, they may be protected by placing water glasses over them.
15. Stabbing and beatings, was the instrument left at the scene, could it have come from that location or was it brought to the scene by the suspect.
16. Blood, document the location, degree of coagulation, type (spots, stains, spatters, pooling, etc.). Sketch and photograph the bloodstains. Remember, when a body fluid begins to decompose, it will discharge a reddish brown fluid which resembles blood, when describing this, be objective, call it what it is, a reddish brown fluid. Bloodspatter analysis may be used to reconstruct violent crimes. Carefully photograph all blood patterns using scales. DO NOT cover up patterns with the scales if possible. Remember, always look up, cast-off spatter will probably be on the ceiling.
17. Hangings and strangulation, what instrument or means was used, was it obtained in the house or brought to the scene, are there any portions remaining. If a suspected auto-erotic death, look for signs of prior activities such as rope marks on door frames or rafters. Be prepared for scene re-arranging by ashamed family members. Remember, do not cut the victim down if he/she is obviously dead until all aspects of the investigation have been covered. Never cut through the knot and always use a piece of string tied to each end of the cut to re-connect the circle.

18. Look at stairs, hallways, entries and exits to the scene, check for footprints, debris, discarded items and fingerprints. Attempt to determine the route used to enter and exit the scene by the suspect and avoid contaminating it.
19. Presence of items that do not belong there, many suspects, in the heat of the moment, will leave items of great evidential value, don't overlook this possibility.
20. Is there signs of ransacking, to what degree, if any, has the scene been ransacked. Was anything taken (relatives and friends can assist in making this determination).
21. Look for hiding places for weapons which the suspect may have had to conceal quickly, check behind stoves, on top of tall furniture, behind books, among bedclothes, under the mattress, on the roof.

Personal Information

Is the victim married or in a relationship? Determine as much about the state of the marriage or relationship as possible, for example, abuse, infidelity on either partners part, drug or alcohol abuse, monetary problems. Is there a suicide note, if so does it appear genuine or staged? Process for prints, get handwriting samples from the other occupants of the location. Has the victim threatened suicide recently, has he/she been despondent, what has happened recently to prompt or preclude such actions? Check the victims computer.

Curious Onlookers at the Scene

Many additional problems are caused by curious onlookers at the scene when a body is discovered. The major concern is, of course, to protect the scene from destruction or contamination by onlookers and curious police officers. The latter group usually presents the most problems. Police Officers are naturally curious and generally have to see things for themselves. Detailed follow-up investigations of many crimes have revealed that various items initially thought to be of great evidential value were actually left by curious police officers.

It will never be known how much valuable time has been wasted and how much evidence has been destroyed by the mere presence of policemen. Just standing around or leaning against a doorway may grind evidence into the ground or smear a good fingerprint. The investigator should explain these facts to the officers present and if the officers are not needed, request that they leave the scene. Most officers are cooperative and no difficulty should be encountered if the matter is presented properly. Occasionally, a problem presents itself when a high-ranking officer appears on the scene. If it becomes apparent that their presence could result in the destruction of evidence, their cooperation should be elicited in leaving the scene. The use of a log or name list of everyone entering the crime scene also helps discourage the curious. When good latent fingerprints are found, every person who has been present at the scene, including the victim, must be fingerprinted for identification and/or elimination purposes.

The police should use tact and courtesy when dealing with civilian witnesses and crowds. This approach serves several purposes. It will gain as much cooperation from people as possible under the circumstances and it may result in a witness, who is an onlooker, coming forward with valuable information. This is especially important in areas where past experiences indicates that the hostility of onlookers is easily aroused. In some situations, the mood of the crowd may become so ugly that the police are forced to leave the scene before they can complete their investigation.

Populated areas, usually consist of streets, sidewalks, communities, etc. and requires the presence of officers to protect the scene. If not, physical barriers such as crime scene tape, vehicles or sawhorses may be needed. In some cases, a detailed search of an entire area may be necessary. This can be done most effectively by cordoning off the area and dividing it into manageable sections to be searched individually. Remember, when setting the boundaries of the crime scene, make it cover as large an area as possible. It is much easier to shrink it down later that to try to expand it once the boundaries have been established. And a news cameraman is standing where you want to expant the scene to.

To avoid destroying evidence in areas of heavy weed or brush, a pathway may be marked off using string or flags and used as the sole entrance and exit to the scene until the search is finished. The pathway should be carefully examined first to ensure no evidence is lost.

Officers should never overlook the potential of any items found at or near the scene. Investigators should conduct a neighborhood canvass for witnesses.

In Rural Settings, many problems will present themselves that are found in urban settings. These are handled in the same manner as an urban investigation. However, there can be significant differences in a rural setting, these could include,

- Accessibility or the lack of it. Are 4 wheel drive vehicles needed? Can it only be reached by boat or helicopter? Do you need to pack all your equipment in with you?
- Length of time a body has been there prior to discovery. This will cause many changes to the scene such as decomposition, animal activity and weather related destruction of the evidence.
- Use care not to disturb the ground that may have footprints or tire marks imbedded in it.
- Employ aerial photography. It will provide information about routes or egress and exit to the area, traffic patterns and location of homes, etc. This is true in both rural and urban settings.

Evidence

As a rule, in the absence of a crime scene investigator, the removal and submission of evidence should be restricted to the lead investigator or lead uniform officer. When evidence is discovered by persons other than the investigator, these items should be, if possible, pointed out to the investigator for his collection and removal to avoid a long list of witnesses or links in the ever growing chain of custody needed for court at a later date. Remember if the scene is being worked by a crime scene investigator, that is his/her scene. They are in command of the scene itself. All other law enforcement personnel present are there to assist that investigator.

There can be situations where the finder of the evidence should collect and log it rather than give it to the investigator. This will reduce the chain of custody but still requires the finder to advise the investigator of its discovery, location and identity. Any evidence so moved must be photographed first.

Evidence can be marked for proper identification. This can be nothing more than the recording of a serial number or the physical placement of your unique mark directly on the item. If marking items, make sure you do not cause the destruction of latent prints or other marks such as tool marks or ballistic identifiers. When submitting evidence;

1. Give a complete description of all evidence submitted including, date, time, location recovered and who recovered it.
2. Illustrate the chain of custody and indicate who will be needed to testify in court about that specific piece of evidence and why.
3. If a search warrant was obtained, include that information.
4. List the evidence recovered in a chronological order and include the exact location of recovery. This could include measurements.

Finally

The previously listed suggestions are provided as a basic guideline and are the opinion of the author. They are based on his experience, training and observations. They are not meant to be an exhaustive, complete list of actions to be taken at a crime scene. Each scene is unique. Each scene requires detailed and complete processing techniques. If you rely on the training you have received, the observation of others working their scenes and the lessons learned from working previous scenes of your own, you will continue to grow and evolve, providing your jurisdiction with the finest possible work product you are capable of producing.

PRACTICAL METHODS FOR PROCESSING A VEHICLE

During a criminal investigation the crime scene investigator or evidence recovery technician may be assigned the task of processing a vehicle or vessel. That vehicle or vessel may not be a primary scene in the investigation however it will deserve the same attention.

As with any investigation the primary function of the crime scene investigator or evidence recovery technician involves the documentation and the collection of physical evidence. The evidence found in the vehicle may hold an important key to solving that particular investigation. The types of evidence that may be found in the vehicle will be dependent on the criminal act that is being committed.

As an example, a burglary to the vehicle may yield fingerprints to identify a person who gained entry into the vehicle. Where as a vehicle that was used in a homicide involving the shooting, stabbing, or transporting of a victim may yield an assortment of physical evidence.

It is important that the crime scene investigator or evidence recovery technician in the field establish an organized approach to processing the vehicle. As with any scene in an investigation the first task is to gather the information need to identify the vehicle and its contents. This starts with an initial examination of the vehicle. Careful examination of the vehicle will give the investigator or technician an idea of what types of evidence might be present.

After the examination the investigator will then need to thoroughly document the vehicle as it is seen. This will be done by a series of photographs depicting the vehicle. The photographs should start with the exterior and be taken from each side, each corner, front, rear, tag, vin, any decals, any damage or custom accessories. The interior of the vehicle should be photographed from the front drivers area, from each side with the doors open, the ignition area, the dash, the glove box, the instrument panel, the rear seat area, and the trunk area.

With the photographs completed an organized search will then need to be done. The purpose of the organized search is to find items of evidence not observed during the initial examination. The vehicle can be divided into sections (similar to an organized zone search pattern) for the search. It should make no difference what area of the vehicle the investigator chooses to start with, only that the investigator get into a habit to always consistently start from the same area each time he-she processes a vehicle.

The investigator or technician needs to practice on the side of caution when searching under seats and hard to see areas. He-she does not want to stick there hands under a seat and risk being punctured by a contaminated needle or other item. A small mirror and flash light will allow the investigator to check these areas without the risk of exposures or injuries.

If other items of evidence are located during the search, the investigator or technician can then place a series of evidence marking stands alongside the items of evidence to take a series of photographs depicting the location and relationship of any evidence found. If the search for pathways and directions of projectiles becomes the task at hand, the investigator can insert string or dowel rods to track the flight paths. A note to remember is that two (2) points of reference are needed to determine the flight paths of a projectile. The primary purpose of using the string or dowel rods is to illustrate and document the directions of the projectiles for flight paths to assist in locating the projectile.

The next step in the process would be the collection of evidence. The investigator or technician will usually want to start with the most fragile evidence. Evidence becomes fragile by the passing of time, exposure to the elements or environment, any movement, and of course improper handling. The most fragile of the evidence types would be any trace evidence aboard. With the new developments in DNA an area to consider would be swabbing samples of the steering wheel, inside door handle and of course the driver's seat belt buckle.

Last but not least would come the mechanical processing for any latent fingerprints. The investigator or technician should search the common sense areas working a border of approximately 6 inches wide around the sides, hood, trunk, roof support post, and windows of the exterior of the vehicle. Common sense would also alert to the areas of the fenders surrounding the wheel weld if a tire is missing. For the interior, the door handles rear view mirror, seat belt buckles, windows, and any other nonporous item will need to be checked. An organized system in place allows a tedious task to be more simple and mistake free.

Collection and Preservation of Blood Evidence from Crime Scenes Preliminary Considerations

Since blood evidence associated with a crime can provide information that may solve the case, it is essential to correctly document, collect, and preserve this type of evidence. Improperly handled blood evidence can weaken or destroy a potential source of facts in a case. Properly collected and preserved blood evidence can establish a strong link between an individual and a criminal act. Blood evidence or the lack of blood evidence can also be used to bolster or contradict a witness statement or any statements that the suspect may make. Blood evidence can also point the investigator in the direction he or she needs to go to solve the case. If blood evidence is documented, collected, and stored suitably, it can be presented to a judge or jury several years from the time of the criminal act. Perhaps the most powerful application of blood evidence is the ability to absolutely eliminate a person as a potential suspect in a crime.

Communication is the key to effectively processing blood evidence. Clear and open communication must exist between a crime scene's first responding officer, the case detective, the crime scene investigator, the forensic scientist analyzing the evidence, and the assistant district attorney handling the case. Of prime importance is the communication between the crime scene investigator and the forensic scientist. A crime scene investigator should know the crime lab's capabilities, the methods of blood collection and preservation preferred by the crime lab, the investigative information relevant to the forensic scientist, and the type of reference samples required by the crime lab. This information may change periodically as technology changes, lab policies change, lab personnel change, or lab administrations change. The preferences of forensic scientists also vary from lab to lab. A good method of blood evidence collection for one forensic scientist may not be a good method for another forensic scientist. The crime scene investigator should meet regularly with his or her crime lab's forensic scientists to determine the most suitable manner for collecting and preserving blood evidence. This ensures that the evidence is collected efficiently and effectively.

The technological state of blood evidence analysis has rapidly advanced in the last 20 years. In the early seventies, most crime labs relied upon the ABO blood grouping system to characterize bloodstains. This meant that the blood could have come from 4 to 49% of the population. In the 1990's, most crime labs are relying on DNA analysis to characterize bloodstains. A blood source can now be statistically narrowed down to one person out of several million or even several billion. A crime scene investigator should know which method or methods of bloodstain analysis are available from his or her crime lab, the FBI lab, and private labs.

Currently, bloodstain analysis falls into three broad categories. A crime lab may use one, two, or all three methods when analyzing blood. These three categories are:

Conventional Serological Analysis

Analysis of the proteins, enzymes, and antigens present in the blood. These substances are more susceptible to degradation than DNA and this type of testing usually requires a "large" sample (quarter size) in good condition for optimal results. This type of testing is rarely statistically individualizing.

Restriction Fragment Length Polymorphism (RFLP) DNA Analysis

Direct analysis of certain DNA sequences present in the white blood cells. DNA is much less susceptible to degradation than proteins, enzymes, and antigens. RFLP DNA testing is commonly statistically individualizing (one out of several million or several billion) and it has withstood rigorous court challenges on its validity. This method also usually requires a "large" sample size to obtain significant results.

Polymerase Chain Reaction (PCR) DNA Analysis

Analysis of certain DNA sequences that have been copied multiple times to a detectable level. PCR based testing works well on degraded samples and "small" samples (pinhead size). Currently, it is not as statistically individualizing as RFLP analysis; however, more DNA sequences for PCR analysis are being discovered and in the near future it will be as statistically individualizing as RFLP. PCR based technologies have also withstood rigorous court challenges on its validity. Recently, there has been some concern over the possibility of incidental contamination giving false results in PCR tests. At least one study has shown that if PCR protocols are followed, it is not likely that incidental contamination will give false results. The only way that false results were induced was by direct cross contamination of wet samples.

Presently, the courts do not recognize blood evidence as evidence that can be absolutely linked to an individual, such as fingerprints, bitemarks, broken fingernails, and handwriting. If DNA analysis is utilized, then blood evidence falls into the category of evidence that can be linked to an individual with a high degree of probability. Originally, RFLP DNA analysis was given the misnomer "DNA fingerprinting." The courts have since ruled that a DNA result can only be given in statistical terms. A forensic scientist cannot testify that a bloodstain came from a specific individual. He or she can testify that based on population studies, only one person in several million or billion has a particular DNA profile. He or she can then testify if the suspect or a victim has that DNA profile.

Before a crime scene investigator begins documenting and collecting blood evidence, he or she must recognize the value of this evidence and how it fits in the overall events associated with the crime. The most common applications of blood evidence are:

1. Finding blood with the victim's genetic markers (ABO blood type, DNA profile, etc.) on the suspect, on something in the suspect's possession, or something associated with the suspect (such as the suspect's fingerprints).
2. Finding blood with the suspect's genetic markers on the victim, on something in the victim s possession, or something associated with the victim.
3. Investigative information determined from blood spatter and/or blood location.

Generally, blood evidence is usually more informative in cases where a suspect and victim are in contact or close proximity. For example, if a suspect stabs or beats a victim, there could be an exchange of blood between the victim and the suspect. If a suspect shoots a victim from across a room. It is less likely that an exchange of blood will occur.

Occasionally, investigators blindly collect blood samples from a scene without any thought about the facts they are trying to establish. An example is a crime scene consisting of the body of a shooting victim found alone in his residence. Some investigators will collect several blood samples from around the body. This is unnecessary since it will only establish that the victim bled at the scene of the crime. This fact is already proven by the presence of the body; however, one sample of pooled blood next to the body can be collected to confirm the results obtained from the victim's reference blood sample.

The crime scene investigator must make an effort to collect the evidence that is going to provide the most useful information in establishing the facts about a crime scene. The investigator must balance this with the philosophy of too much evidence collected is better than not enough evidence collected. The investigator should concentrate on collecting representative samples of the "peripheral" bloodstains, such as the bloodstains that are away from the body and the main area of action, or blood spatter patterns that differ from the majority of the blood spatter patterns. These bloodstains may provide useful investigative information. The investigator should also search for blood trails leading away from the scene. These trails could have originated from a wounded suspect. If a suspect is established in a case, then he or she should be examined for wounds. The suspect's wounds should be documented and photographed. This is additional useful evidence if blood with the suspect's genetic markers is found in an incriminating location.

Because blood analysis is a comparison analysis (comparison of the victim's blood and the suspect's blood to blood found at the crime scene), reference blood samples are needed from the victim and suspect. A comparison must be made between the genetic markers in the victim s blood and the suspect's blood. The blood samples from the crime scene can then be analyzed for those genetic markers that are different in the suspect and victim. This is especially true in conventional serology analysis. Requests are made occasionally to do an ABO blood type determination of blood on a suspect's clothes to a known blood sample from a victim. This type of analysis is useless without a known blood sample from the suspect.

If both parties have the same ABO blood type, then part of the sample has been wasted and no real information of value is produced. If reference samples of blood from both parties are provided, then it can be determined if they have the same ABO blood type. If they do, then further analysis of the reference blood samples may show that the two parties have different PGM types. The unknown stain could then be analyzed for the genetic marker PGM. This analysis may then show the possible origin of the stain.

Suitable reference samples (a suitable reference sample is collected directly from a person into a tube or "Vacutainer") from all of the involved subjects must be sent to the crime lab. An unsuitable reference sample is bloody clothing or some other bloody item. These are unsuitable because the histories of these bloodstained items are usually questionable and there may be factors present on the items that will give misleading results. The sample must be collected in the proper "Vacutainer." The investigator should check with the lab he or she is using to determine the analysts' preferences on reference sample collection tubes. This is a summary of the forensic uses of "Vacutainers":

- Yellow Top Vacutainers (contain Acid Citrate and Dextrose solution)
- Useful for conventional serological testing and DNA testing (author's personal preference).
- Purple Top Vacutainers (contain EDTA)
- Useful for DNA testing; may inhibit certain conventional serological tests.
- Red Top Vacutainers (no additives)
- Useful for conventional serological tests; less useful for DNA testing; can be used for pregnancy and HIV testing (if a yellow top is not available, then the author prefers receiving red top and purple top Vacutainers from a subject).
- Gray Top Vacutainers (contain Sodium Fluoride and sometimes EDTA)
- Useful for toxicological testing; not suitable for conventional serological analysis and may not be suitable for DNA analysis.

If the investigator is collecting blood from an autopsy, then one of each type of Vacutainer should be collected from the victim. This will insure that any necessary forensic testing can be performed. These Vacutainers should be stored in a refrigerator (not frozen) at about four degrees Centigrade until they are transported to the crime lab. In recent years, blood visualization enhancing chemicals have regained popularity with crime scene investigators. The chemical of choice is usually luminol. Luminol is a chemical that when applied to bloodstains, even very dilute bloodstains, will cause the bloodstains to glow in the dark. Because it has several drawbacks as a presumptive test for blood, spraying luminol at a crime scene should be an investigator's last resort for detecting blood. The problems with luminol include:

1. One of the empirical tests for determining if a stain is blood is its appearance. If it is a bloodstain, then it should look like blood. A bloodstain also has to be present in sufficient quantity to perform confirmatory testing and testing for genetic markers. This requires that the bloodstain is visible to the naked eye. The luminol reaction is at best a presumptive test for blood. If the stain is so dilute that it can only be visualized with luminol, then no further analysis can be performed to confirm the presence of blood.
2. Luminol will give false reactions. Luminol will react with copper ions, copper compounds, iron compounds, and cobalt ions. It will also react with potassium permanganate (found in some dyes) and hydrated sodium hypochlorite (bleach). Ferricyanide and plant peroxidases could also give false reactions.
3. Studies have shown that luminol will cause the loss of several genetic markers.
4. Because luminol is water based, it could cause, latent, possibly bloody impressions to smear. Luminol could also further dilute an already diluted stain. This may push the stain beyond the genetic marker analysis detection limits.

Unfortunately, some crime scene investigators use luminol as their first choice for detecting blood. By using luminol in such a reckless manner, it is possible to lose valuable information from a bloodstain. When searching for blood at a crime scene, especially blood that may have been cleaned up, the investigator should first use a high intensity light to search for any traces of blood. Bloodstains are not easy to eradicate. Diluted blood will often leave a brownish stain where a person has tried to clean it. Blood also has a tendency to flow into floorboard cracks, into carpet padding, behind baseboards, etc. By conducting a thorough examination with a high intensity light source, the investigator can usually find these areas. These items can then be removed or collected and submitted to the crime lab for confirmatory testing. Because luminol is so sensitive to dilute bloodstains, it is occasionally used to enhance bloody impressions (shoeprints, fingerprints, etc.). Luminol is not the best reagent for enhancing these impressions because of its water base. Better methods for enhancing bloody impressions use either rapidly evaporating organic solvents (such as merbromin and ortho-tolidine) or they use a water based chemical after treating the impression with a fixative (such as the amido black staining technique).

Once the investigator realizes the potential of blood evidence as well as problem areas in documenting, collecting, and preserving this type of evidence, he or she will be more effective in finding the best bloodstains. Some commonly encountered problems are lack of communication (especially between the investigators and the forensic scientists), unfamiliarity with the types of bloodstain analysis, lack of knowledge about which stains will yield the most useful information, poor reference samples, and indiscriminately using luminol at crime scenes. If these problems are solved, then the blood collection and analysis should progress without any major problems.

Documentation and Examination of the Crime Scene

An investigator should take a slow and methodical approach to collecting and preserving evidence. The only time that an investigator should make rapid decisions concerning evidence is when the evidence is in danger of being destroyed or compromised. In that case, the evidence should be preserved, or documented and collected as quickly as possible. Before setting foot in the crime scene, the investigator must gather as much information as possible to determine the scope and value of any evidence that may be present. This information may include witness statements, suspect statements, victim statements, information from the first responding officer, information from the detectives, etc.

Information is collected to prevent the destruction of any valuable and/or fragile evidence such as shoeprints, trace evidence, etc. The investigator should then use logic and common sense to search for evidence; however, he or she should also use imagination and avoid becoming narrow-minded. As investigators become more experienced, they know that certain patterns emerge and certain elements are common among similar cases. They also know that they have to keep an open mind when deciding what is evidence and where it will be found. This is due to the unpredictable nature of people and the forces of chaos. Once the investigator has gathered as much information as possible about the case, then he or she should form a mental or written plan to proceed with the documentation, collection, and preservation of the evidence. The investigator should also pass any relevant information to the lab analyst. This will allow the analysis to make decisions concerning the best approach to the analysis and what information can be determined from the evidence.

The investigator should thoroughly document every aspect of the crime scene investigation from the initial walk through to the securing of the collected evidence. Documentation is necessary to record the condition of the crime scene and its related evidence as closely as possible to their original condition at the time of the crime. Of course, there is usually some alteration of the scene that will occur between the time of the crime and the time that the scene is documented. EMS personnel, police officers, and fire fighters may have to alter the original scene in the course of performing life saving measures. Other people entering the scene may also unknowingly or unconsciously alter the scene. In any case, the evidence must be documented in as pristine a condition as circumstances allow. The investigator has a number of tools available for documenting evidence including notes, videotape, photographs, sketches, and chain of custody forms. The investigator may elect to use several or all of these methods of documentation. This documentation will also be used in the future to refresh the investigator's memories of the case.

The first tool for documenting the crime scene investigation is note taking. An investigator should be as thorough as possible when taking notes. All of the pertinent times and actions taken should be recorded, such as who contacted the investigator and when; when did the investigator leave for the crime scene; when did the investigator arrive at the scene; what actions were taken by the investigator and when; when did the investigator leave the scene, etc. Notes should be recorded throughout the entire crime scene investigation.

Examination of the crime scene will usually begin with a walk through of the area along the "trail" of the crime. The trail is that area where all apparent actions associated with the crime took place. This trail is usually marked by the presence of evidence. Point of entry, location of a body, areas where the suspect may have cleaned up, and the point of exit are all included in the trail. The purpose of the walk through is to note the location of potential evidence and to mentally outline how the scene will be processed. The walk through begins as close to the point of entry as possible. The first place the investigators should examine is the ground on which they are about to tread. If any evidence is found, then a marker should be placed at the location as a warning not to step on the item of interest. When searching for blood evidence, it is important to use a high intensity light. A high intensity light source will aid in the visualization of bloodstains, even stains that have been diluted. The light source can also be used to provide oblique (side) lighting. Oblique lighting is an excellent tool for finding trace evidence and other small items of interest.

As the walk through progresses, the investigators should make sure their hands are occupied by either carrying notebooks, flashlights, pens, etc. or by keeping their hands in their pockets. This prevents the investigator from depositing unwanted fingerprints at the crime scene. As a final note on the walk through, the investigators should examine the areas above their heads (ceiling, tree branches, etc.). These areas may yield blood spatters, bullet holes, etc. Once the walk through is completed, the notes must be supplemented with other forms of documentation, such as videotape, photographs, and/or sketches.

Videotape can be an excellent medium for documenting bloodstains at a crime scene. If a video camera is available, it is best used after the initial walk through. This is to record the evidence before any major alterations have occurred at the scene. Videotape provides a perspective on the crime scene layout that cannot be as easily perceived in photographs and sketches. It is a more natural viewing medium to which people can readily relate, especially in demonstrating the structure of the crime scene and how the evidence relates to those structures.

The value of videotaping blood evidence is that the overall relationship of various blood spatters and patterns can be demonstrated. One example of this could be a beating homicide. In this case, videotape can show the overall blood spatter patterns and how these spatters are inter related. The videotape can also show the relationship of the spatters to the various structures at the crime scene. In cases where the suspect may have been injured (such as stabbing homicides), the video camera can be used to document any blood trails that may lead away from the scene. If videotaping indoors, the camera can show how the various areas are laid out in relation to each other and how they can be accessed. This is particularly valuable when recording peripheral bloodstains that may be found in other rooms. The high intensity light source can also be used for illuminating the bloodstains to make them more visible on the videotape.

Whether a video camera is available or not, it is absolutely essential that still photographs are taken to document the crime scene and any associated blood evidence. If a video camera is available, then still photography will be the second step in recording the crime scene. If video is not available, then still photography will be the first step. Photographs can demonstrate the same type of things that the videotape does, but crime scene photographs can also be used to record close up details, record objects at any scaled size, and record objects at actual size. These measurements and recordings are more difficult to achieve with videotape.

Blood evidence can be photographed using color print film and/or color slide film. Infrared film can also be used for documenting bloodstains on dark surfaces. Overall, medium range, and close up photographs should be taken of pertinent bloodstains. Scaled photographs (photographs with a ruler next to the evidence) must also be taken of items in cases where size relevance is significant or when direct (one-to-one) comparisons will be made, such as with bloody shoeprints, fingerprints, high velocity blood spatter patterns, etc. A good technique for recording a large area of blood spatter on a light colored wall is to measure and record the heights of some of the individual blood spatters. The overall pattern on the wall including a yard stick as a scale is then photographed with slide film. After the slide is developed, it can be projected onto a blank wall or onto the actual wall many years after the original incident. By using a yardstick, the original blood spatters can be viewed at their actual size and placed in their original positions. Measurements and projections can then be made to determine the spatters' points of origin.

Another method of documenting blood evidence is by drawing a sketch of the crime scene. The drawback of photographs is that they are two-dimensional representations of three dimensional objects. As a result, photos can distort the spatial relationships of the photographed objects causing them to appear closer together or farther apart than they actually are. If spatial relationships of the evidence are important or if something needs to have proportional measurements included in it for calculations (such as blood spatter patterns) then a sketch must be made.

Computer programs are available for sketching crime scenes and blood spatters by inputting certain measurements associated with the scene and the individual spatters. This blood spatter program will then calculate and draw the spatters' points of origin. These programs might come in handy where there are many blood spatters and the points of origin need to be determined. For more in depth information on videotaping, photographing, and sketching crime scenes, refer to the recommended reading list.

The final method of evidence documentation is the chain of custody form. The chain of custody form is a written record of all evidence transfers from the crime scene to possession of the court or the clerk of court. Proper chain of custody thoroughly documents the movement of evidence, the security of the evidence, who had possession of the evidence, and when the evidence was in a person's possession. The chain of custody form must accompany the evidence all the way to its final destination. A copy should also be kept in the case folder. The following information must be recorded on the form: A description of the evidence and its container; the specific recovery location of the evidence; case numbers; the date and time it was collected; who collected it; whether or not the evidence container was sealed upon transfer to another individual; who received the evidence; the dates and times of any evidence transfers; who delivered the evidence; and the final disposition of the evidence.

This is necessary to demonstrate that the evidence was not contaminated in a way to alter the information that the evidence originally contained. It also demonstrates that the original evidence was not planted or changed in some way before its presentation in court. After the evidence has been documented using videotape, photographs, sketches, and chain of custody forms, the evidence collection process can begin.

Collection and Preservation of Blood Evidence

Once the crime scene has been thoroughly documented and the locations of the evidence noted, then the collection process can begin. The collection process will usually start with the most fragile or most easily lost evidence. Special consideration can also be given to any evidence or objects that need to be moved. Collection can then continue along the crime scene trail or in some other logical manner. Photographs should continue to be taken if the investigator is revealing layers of evidence that were not previously documented because they were obscured.

Most items of evidence will be collected in clean, unused paper containers such as packets, envelopes, and bags. Moist or wet biological evidence (blood, body fluids, plants, etc.) from a crime scene can be collected in clean, unused plastic containers at the scene and transported back to an evidence receiving area if the storage time in sealed plastic is less than two hours and this is done to prevent contamination of other evidence. Once in a secure location, wet evidence, whether packaged in plastic or paper, must be removed and allowed to completely air dry. That evidence can then be repackaged in a new, clean, unused, dry paper container. UNDER NO CIRCUMSTANCES SHOULD EVIDENCE CONTAINING MOISTURE BE SEALED IN PLASTIC OR PAPER CONTAINERS FOR MORE THAN TWO HOURS. Moisture allows the growth of microorganisms that can destroy or alter evidence.

Any items that may cross contaminate each other must be packaged separately. The containers should be closed and secured to prevent the mixture of evidence during transportation. Each container should have the collecting person's initials: the date and time it was collected; a complete description of the evidence and where it was found; and the investigating agency's name and file number. Before transporting any items of evidence, the investigator should examine the items to determine if there is any loose trace evidence (hairs, fibers, paint chips, etc.) that may be lost in transportation. If there is, then this loose evidence should be collected in a paper packet and placed in an envelope. The envelope should have the required information giving a description and the source of the trace evidence. The actual item can then be processed and collected.

Blood evidence must never be exposed to excessive heat or humidity. If possible, the bloodstained evidence should be refrigerated until it can be transported to the crime lab. The evidence should also be taken to the lab as soon as possible. The following are guidelines, listed in order of the author's preferences, for collecting and preserving blood evidence:

ALWAYS TAKE SAFETY PRECAUTIONS WHEN HANDLING BIOLOGICAL EVIDENCE. BE SURE TO WEAR PROTECTIVE CLOTHING, GLOVES, MASKS, AND/OR EYE PROTECTION AS THE SITUATION WARRANTS.

Dried Bloodstains

If the bloodstained item is small and transportable, package it in a paper bag or envelope.

Advantages: Requires a minimal amount of interaction with the bloodstains by the investigator: allows the serologist to make the decisions involved in collecting the samples; dilution and contamination potential minimized by eliminating the use of water as the collection medium.

Disadvantages: More work for the serologist: bulky items require more storage space.

If the bloodstained item is large or not easily transported, then the following techniques can be used for collecting the bloodstains. If possible, the investigator should also collect samples from unstained areas of the item for negative controls.

1. Cutting out the portion(s) of item with the bloodstain(s). A negative control area should also be cut out if available. Package cuttings in separate paper envelopes.

   Advantages: Dilution and contamination potential minimized by eliminating the use of water as the collection medium: requires only a small amount of investigator interaction with the bloodstain: does not usually take up much storage space.

   Disadvantages: Investigator must decide which stains and controls to collect: some materials are harder to cut than others.

2. Tape lifting bloodstains - Place fingerprint tape (do not touch sticky surface with bare hands) over bloodstain and surrounding negative control area. Rub non-sticky side of tape with a pencil eraser or other blunt object. This is to insure that good contact is made between the stain and the tape. Lift the bloodstain like a fingerprint and place the tape on a vinyl acetate backing (do not use a paper backing - paper makes the stain difficult to handle during analysis). The lifting process can be repeated several times on the same stain if necessary. Label the stain(s) and package in a paper envelope.

   Advantages: Dilution and contamination potential minimized by eliminating the use of water as the collection medium; negative control is readily collected; requires little storage space; fairly easy technique to perform.

   Disadvantages: Investigator must decide which stains to collect; bloodstains do not lift well on certain surfaces.

3. Scraping bloodstains into a paper packet - Use a clean sharp instrument to scrape the bloodstain into a paper packet. The packet can be labeled and placed in a paper envelope. Do not use a plastic container in place of a paper packet because the static charge from the plastic will cause the blood flakes to disperse and stick to the sides of the container. This technique can be combined with the tape lift method by

scraping the stain near the tape's sticky side. The static charge will cause the flakes to stick to the tape. The tape can then be placed on vinyl acetate.

Advantages: Dilution and contamination potential minimized by eliminating the use of water as the collection medium; requires little storage space.

Disadvantages: Investigator must decide which stains to collect; when scraped, bloodstains tend to break into small, very hard to handle flakes; the flakes have a tendency to be easily lost during the scraping process (except when used in combination with the tape lift); some surfaces are not easily scraped.

4. Absorbing stains onto moistened 1/2" long threads - Use only distilled or deionized water to moisten clean, 1/2" long, number 8, white cotton threads. Do not handle the threads with bare hands. Place thread on bloodstain with a pair of clean forceps or a clean cotton swab. Roll the thread on the bloodstain, so the stain is absorbed onto the thread. Repeat until a minimum of four threads are collected. Place the threads (and swabs, if used) in a secure area and allow them to air dry. When air dried, package into a paper packet and place in an envelope. For transportation purposes and to prevent cross contamination, the threads may be placed in a plastic container for no more than two hours. Once in a secure location, the threads must be removed from the plastic and allowed to air dry. They may then be repackaged into a paper packet and placed in an envelope. Threads must also be taken from a negative control area, if available.

   Advantages: Stain is concentrated onto a small surface area; requires little storage space.

   Disadvantages: Dilution and contamination potential introduced by using water (it may be possible to reduce contamination and dilution effects by using acetone or 70% ethanol to collect bloodstains. At least one study has shown that DNA yield can be increased by using either acetone or 70% ethanol to collect bloodstains. The 70% ethanol produced a higher DNA yield.*(11)*); investigator must decide which stains to collect; threads can be difficult to handle.

5. Absorbing stains onto moistened 1/2" X 1/2" cotton squares - The procedure for collection is the same as for threads, except that white, 100% cotton muslin is used instead of threads. The muslin must be boiled in distilled or deionized water and allowed to air dry prior to its use. This removes interfering factors from the muslin. Do not handle the muslin with bare hands.

   Advantages: Stain is concentrated onto a relatively small surface area; easier to handle than threads; requires little storage space.

   Disadvantages: Same as for threads, except dilution and contamination potential is increased due to using more water.

Wet Bloodstains

1. If the item is small and transportable, then package it in a paper bag (or plastic bag to prevent contamination of other objects). Bring it to a secured location, take it out of the bag and allow the evidence and the bag to thoroughly air dry. Repackage in the original paper bag or, if necessary, a new paper bag. If a new paper bag is used, then the air dried original container should be packaged with the item of evidence.

   Advantages: Requires a minimal amount of interaction with the bloodstains by the investigator; allows the serologist to make the decisions involved in collecting the samples.

   Disadvantages: More work for the serologist; bulky items use more storage space.

2. If the bloodstained item is large or not easily transported, then absorb the stain onto a 1" X 1" square of the cotton muslin as described in part 2E under dried bloodstains.

Package it in paper (or plastic to prevent contamination of other objects). Bring it to a secured location, take it out of the container and allow the cotton square and the container to thoroughly air dry. Repackage in the original paper container or, if necessary, a new paper container. If a new paper container is used, then the air dried original container should be packaged with the cotton square. If possible, the investigator should also collect samples from unstained areas of the item for negative controls.

Advantages: Requires little storage space; fairly easy technique to perform; stain is concentrated onto a relatively small surface area.

Disadvantages: Investigator must decide which stains and controls to collect; investigator must have direct interaction with bloodstain.

10

Introduction to Crime Scene Reconstruction

While both of these activities may appear to be similar and are in fact related, it is important to note that they are not the same. The difference between the two is most easily understood by looking at which questions about the crime they attempt to answer. Crime Scene Reconstruction looks at the physical evidence and attempts to determine "What happened?" and "How did it happen?". Criminal Profiling looks at the physical evidence and the reconstruction and attempts to determine "Why may this have happened?" and "What does that tell us about Who may have done it?". It is important to keep in mind that only those directly involved in the crime know for sure what happened and why, and they may be unable or unwilling to say.

Why is it important to reconstruct the crime prior to profiling the offender? The answer is simple; until you know what happened, and how it happened (at least as much as possible), you have no basis for attempting to determine why and who.

This paper is intended as an overview of the types of reconstruction which may be possible and is not all inclusive (the number and types of things that may be reconstructed is like types of physical evidence- nearly limitless). For more specific information check the references or contact an expert in the field in question.

Types of Reconstruction

1. Specific Incident Reconstruction (Traffic Accident, Homicide, Bombing, etc.).
2. Specific Event Reconstruction (Sequence, Direction, Condition, Relation, Identity).
3. Specific Physical Evidence Reconstruction (Firearms, Blood, Glass etc.).

In any given scene it may be possible to do a total or only partial reconstruction, and the reconstruction may use more than one technique (i.e. both trajectory and blood stain pattern reconstruction to locate the position of the victim). Some scenes lend themselves to reconstruction better than others. Traffic accidents are common scenes to reconstruct and often can be thoroughly reconstructed. Vehicles are rather massive objects that obey the laws of motion and often leave a wealth of physical evidence behind before, during and after an accident. It may be possible to show the entire sequence of events from the time the vehicles first enter the area of the accident until they come to rest following the accident.

Scenes involving the movement of people are more difficult. While it may be possible to say where a person was in the scene at several points in time, the manner in which they moved in the scene cannot be reconstructed. People may move slowly, quickly, hesitantly, jump up and down, run, skip, fall down, etc. all without leaving any particular trace behind. That said, there are of course the odd cases where the amount and type of physical evidence does allow the paths of the participants to be tracked with some accuracy; however, the vagaries of facial expression, gestures, and body language are simply impossible to reconstruct at all.

Below are some examples of the types of information which reconstruction may provide, again, this is not an all inclusive list. Some items also appear in more than one category, and it may be possible to use information from several areas to complete or validate the final reconstruction.

Examples of Types of Reconstruction:

- Blood and Blood Stain Pattern Analysis
    - o Identity of victim/offender.
    - o Position and location of the victim.
    - o Position and location of the offender.
    - o Movement by the victim/offender in the scene.
    - o May identify the location of the scene (if the victim is removed and left elsewhere).
    - o May indicate a staged or secondary scene.
    - o Minimum number of blows struck.
    - o Type of weapon used.
- Documents
    - o Reassemble torn/shredded papers.
    - o Recovery of obliterated writing.
- Firearms
    - o Trajectory.
    - o Shooting distance.
    - o Position and location of the victim.
    - o Position and location of the offender.
    - o Sequence of shots.
    - o Direction of shots.
    - o Possibility that the wound(s) could have been self-inflicted.
    - o Identification of weapon used may link serial cases.
- Functional Evidence
    - o Does the weapon or vehicle function properly?
    - o Semi-automatic with slide locked back may indicate last round was fired.
    - o TV or coffee pot on at scene.

- o Do door/window locks properly secure?
- Glass
  - o Direction of break (from which side of the glass).
  - o Sequence of shots (it should be noted that current research indicates that sequencing of shots through laminated automotive glass is not reliable).
- Impression Evidence (Fingerprints, shoe prints, tire tracks).
  - o Identity of victim/offender.
  - o Place victim/offender at the scene and at specific sites in the scene.
  - o Fingerprints may indicate where the offender/victim was in the scene or how an object was held.
  - o Shoe prints may show location in and movement through the scene.
  - o Tire tracks may show vehicle position and direction of travel and may indicate the type of vehicle driven.
- Ligature
  - o Type of ligature used (if missing).
  - o Use of same/similar ligature can be used to link serial cases.
  - o Type of ligature used may indicate offender's occupation or interests. (i.e. rope tied with knots commonly used by dock workers or climbers).
- Pathology
  - o Manner of death (Homicide, Suicide, Natural, Accidental).
  - o Time of death (approximate).
  - o Cause of death/weapon used.
  - o Time before incapacitation from wounds (approximate).
  - o Whether injuries were sustained pre- or post-mortem.

  - o Identity and/or age of victim.
  - o Was victim sexually assaulted, and in what manner.
  - o Possibility that the wound(s) could have been self-inflicted.
- Physical Match (Reassembly of broken objects).
  - o Bombs.
  - o Vehicle lamps, mirrors and windows.
  - o Aircraft which have crashed and/or exploded.
- Relational/Positional Evidence
  - o Blood drops on the threshold of a door indicates that the door was open when the blood was shed.
  - o Location of other objects and their condition may also indicate a variety of things depending on the specifics of the crime.
- Trace Evidence
  - o Trajectory of projectiles based on retention of material through which they have passed.
  - o Place offender/victim at the scene, and at specific sites in the scene.
  - o Describe the environment of an unknown crime scene.
  - o May indicate offender occupation.
- Vehicle positions, speeds, sequence of accident events.

INFORMATION NEEDED FOR RECONSTRUCTION

Generally speaking it is best to go to the scene, preferably at the time of the incident. Information may come from physical evidence, witness statements, and the reports of other experts. The reconstructionist should examine all scene photographs, autopsy protocol and photographs, measurements, drawings, notes, reports and items of evidence. Complete and accurate documentation of the scene is essential. Depending on the type of reconstruction being done this may include some different things such as the height and vertical/horizontal angles of shots into a wall, or the length and width of a bloodstain.

Steps in Reconstruction

1. Recognition of evidence.
2. Documentation of evidence.
3. Collection of evidence.
4. Evaluation of evidence.
5. Hypothesis.
6. Testing.
7. Reconstruction.

Step 1, recognition of evidence, is arguably the most important, as Lee points out "Unless the potential evidence can be recognized, no further reconstruction can be carried out."

Steps 1-3, recognition, documentation and collection of evidence, are the heart of any successful scene investigation, and form the basis for the reconstruction.

Step 4, evaluation of evidence, examines the evidence (possibly following laboratory analysis) and looks at what information the evidence provides, and how reliable it is. At this time any witness statements should be compared to the evidence to see which parts of the statements can be supported or refuted by the evidence.

Step 5, hypothesis, is the formulation of an idea of how the event(or portions of it) occurred. This is not merely conjecture and should be firmly supported by the evidence.

Step 6, testing, looks to see how the hypothesis developed in 5 can be validated. This is accomplished by checking the evidence against known physical laws or devising a test to attempt to replicate the event(or the relevant segment).

Step 7, reconstruction, is the reporting of the results of the analysis. The results are reported as a range, where the event(or portions of it):

A. Can be shown to have occurred in a given manner.

B. Can be shown to be likely to have occurred in a given manner.

C. Can be shown to be unlikely to have occurred in a given manner.

D. Can be shown not to have occurred in a given manner.

Application to Profiling

The reconstruction forms the foundation from which the profiler can begin. The reconstruction provides answers about what happened and how it happened. From there the profiler can begin asking "Why?" questions. Questions of "Why?" are not answered by the reconstruction. Neither are questions of Intent and Motive. Attempts to answer these questions may be investigatively useful, but lack the firm support of evidence required of reconstruction. Authors on both reconstruction and profiling speak of mentally re-enacting the events of the crime; again, this can be investigatively useful, but is not reconstruction.

As profiling is intended as an investigative tool, it attempts to go beyond the reconstruction, and answer questions of intent and motivation. From these admittedly subjective answers it can provide a clearer picture of the offender.

As an example, take a scene where the reconstruction shows as Event 1- "Subject breaks into residence through rear window. Window lock was previously secured and was jimmied with a thin, wide, black metal pry bar." Based on this information the profiler can begin to look at "Why?". Why did the offender choose this window? Why did he use this method of entry? Has it worked for him in the past? Where did he get the pry bar? Did he bring it with him or acquire it at the scene? The profiler can continue in this fashion through the scene, looking at the known facts, and then attempting to address the motivations behind the known actions. Working through the scene in this manner will also serve to highlight both the Modus Operandi and Signature aspects of the crime.

- Modus Operandi is the "method of operation", those things that the offender does which are necessary for the completion of the crime (method of entry, use of a weapon to control the victim, etc.).
- Signature is defined as those things done by the offender which are not necessary for the completion of the crime, but which the offender must do to satisfy himself (use of complex ligature, sadism, etc.).

The reconstruction may show a sequence of events or actions that are unnecessary in the commission of the crime. In serial cases the recurrence of the same sequence at multiple scenes, or the modification of parts of it, may also assist in this determination.

A Case Study: The Murder of Donna Lynn Vetter

Donna Lynn Vetter was a 22-year old, white female. She worked as a stenographer for the FBI field office in San Antonio, Texas. On September 4, 1986, she was raped and murdered in her apartment. Ms. Vetter was last seen alive at 9:10PM, by a neighbor. She was found dead at 10:35PM; this places the occurrence of the offense to within a period of just over one hour. During this time the following events took place:

1. Offender enters the apartment by pulling out the screen on the otherwise unsecured front window, knocking over a plant on his way in.
2. Offender unplugs the telephone.
3. Initial contact between the offender and the victim occurs near the bathroom. Victim is struck in the face.
4. Assault continues in the kitchen area where the offender obtains a knife. The victim is stabbed repeatedly and her clothing cut and/or torn off.

5. Offender drags the victim from the kitchen, through the dining room into the living room, leaving a blood trail along the way.
6. Offender sexually assaults the victim in the living room.
7. Offender hides the knife under a seat cushion in the living room.
8. Offender leaves the scene.
   1. Unplugging the telephone (which is unnecessary if he intends to kill the victim).
   2. Blitz type assault intended to render the victim compliant.
   3. Use of a weapon of opportunity (i.e. the kitchen knife), rather than one brought to the scene by the offender.
   4. The fact that nothing was stolen from the apartment.

In this case the victim's continuing resistance led to an escalation of violence and ultimately to her death. When combined with the victimology and geoforensic information, the reconstruction allowed a thorough profile of the offender to be completed.

Conclusion: The Importance of Competent Crime Scene Work in Reconstruction and Profiling

Unless the analyst (reconstructionist or profiler) is one of the scene investigators, the basic scene work will likely already be completed, and any deficiencies will probably be impossible to correct. This may limit the information which the analyst can provide. To this end the need for continuing/advanced training for scene investigators cannot be overstated. While much of the evidence used for reconstruction speaks for itself and can be documented and collected using standard crime scene procedures, some types of reconstruction require specialized information.

The main three types would be Blood Stain Pattern, Traffic Accident, and Trajectory Reconstruction. All three types require specialized knowledge of what evidence to look for at the scene, and what documentation (photographs, measurements, etc.) are required to utilize the evidence in reconstruction.

An investigator at a traffic accident must know the difference between skid and yaw marks, for example. He must be able to document that the mark is a yaw rather than a skid, and know that each mark must be measured differently. Measurement of the length of a yaw mark is not much use in reconstruction.

Similarly a photograph of a bullet hole does not allow for trajectory reconstruction. We must know the position, height and angle at least, and knowledge of the direction is helpful.

A great deal of specialized knowledge is required for the proper interpretation of blood stain patterns. Without this knowledge the investigator may not even know what he needs to document, let alone how to do it.

Without competent, thorough scene work, the subsequent analysis may be incomplete or impossible.

The Staged Crime Scene

Staging is a conscious criminal action on the part of an offender to thwart an investigation. The term "staging" should not be used to describe the actions of surviving family members who cover or redress a loved one, who is found nude or has died in an embarrassing situation. These activities are certainly understandable considering the shock experienced by a relative who encounters the sudden and violent death of a loved one. In my experience investigating suspicious deaths I have often times had a "gut" feeling that something was amiss. (Actually, that "gut" feeling is your subconscious reaction to the presentation, which should alert you to the possibility that, things are not always what they appear to be, consistent with equivocal death investigations).

Equivocal Death Investigations

Equivocal death investigations are those inquiries that are open to interpretation. There may be two or more meanings and the case may present as either a homicide or a suicide depending upon the circumstances. The facts are purposefully vague or misleading as in the case of a "staged crime scene." Or, the death is suspicious or questionable based upon what is presented to the authorities. The deaths may resemble homicides or suicides; accidents or naturals. They are open to interpretation pending further information of the facts, the victimology and the circumstances of the event.

In "staged crime scenes," however, the presentation of the homicide victim and the manipulation of the crime scene by a clever offender could make the death appear to be a suicide. I have personally investigated many such cases and the truth of the matter is that initially, the cases did look like suicides.

TYPES OF CRIME SCENE STAGING

1. The most common type of staging occurs when the perpetrator changes elements of the scene to make the death appear to be a suicide or accident in order to cover up a murder. (CASE HISTORIES Numbers 1, 2 & 3) 2. The second most common type of staging is when the perpetrator attempts to redirect the investigation by making the crime appear to be a sex-related homicide. (CASE HISTORY Number 4 & 5)

EXAMPLES OF HOMICIDES MADE TO APPEAR TO BE A SUICIDE OR ACCIDENT

CASE HISTORY Number 1

I acted as a consultant in a wrongful death suit brought against an insurance company by surviving relatives of a male who allegedly had committed suicide.

The insurance company had refused to pay the beneficiaries based on the police determination of suicide. My review of the crime scene photographs and circumstances of the death of this young man indicated that the young man had, in fact, not committed suicide. The authorities had been misled into believing the case was a suicide because the scene had been staged.

The victim was discovered lying on his back across his bed with a.308 rifle between his legs, suggesting that he had shot himself in the head with the weapon. There was a large amount of blood and brain matter found in the room where the deceased was discovered. His entire head was blown away. The victim's brain was found down the hallway from the room. The gun belonged to the deceased. There was ammunition for the gun found in the premises. There were two bullet holes in the roof of the victim's trailer, suggesting two shots having been fired and the police recovered two spent shell casings in the room. The police classified the death as suicide. A review of the police investigation revealed a perfunctory inquiry totaling a mere eight (8) pages of police reports. The police did not attempt to locate the fired rounds; they did not test or examine the firearm; there were no ballistics reports prepared; and there were no gunshot residue (GSR) testings done on the victim to ascertain whether or not he had fired the weapon and there was no attempt to reconstruct the event. The police did not process the crime scene for fingerprints nor did they ever conduct a background check or victimology. The autopsy was conducted by a hospital pathologist instead of a forensic pathologist, who couldn't even determine the location of the entrance wound.

However, these observations, without further police investigation into the facts surrounding the death and a reconstruction of the crime scene could be misleading. The investigative reality is that each factor must be brought to its ultimate conclusion. I believe that the authorities made the mistake of assuming that the death of the young man was suicide based on their preliminary observations of the crime scene and as a result subsequently failed to take each factor to its ultimate conclusion.

INVESTIGATIVE CONSIDERATIONS

My analysis of the facts indicated that the deceased had made both short and long term plans, which is not consistent with a person intending to commit suicide. During the week preceding his death, he had gone out with friends, had attended a birthday party for his sister and purchased groceries for the upcoming week. On Monday of the week he was killed he was at work. According to his supervisor, he was in good spirits. In addition he had even paid his union dues three months in advance. He was expecting a visit from a girl friend and was refurbishing his mobile home. He had built a new deck on the back, purchased paint and wallpaper, and had arranged with a neighbor to borrow tools to fix his kitchen cabinets. His long term plans included an application for a loan and a trip to Alabama to clear some property in the Fall. Interviews of the friends and relatives of the deceased were conducted which disclosed that certain property and money were missing from the deceased's trailer when he was discovered dead.

A number of persons stated that the deceased was known to keep at least $1000.00 cash in his mobile home. According to the police report there was only $2.50 found in the deceased's pockets. Also, according to another relative who had reconciled the deceased's accounts after the funeral, said the victim had made a withdrawal of $200.00 cash from an ATM machine which was unaccounted for and missing from the trailer. A neighbor stopped by the trailer because of his suspicion "that something wasn't right. He observed that the deceased's car doors were unlocked and the keys were in the ignition. This was unusual behavior for the deceased. Later police would recover the deceased's empty wallet from the floor of the car. The door to the trailer was unlocked and the stereo was blasting. The thermostat was set up as high as it could go. The deceased reportedly never had the thermostat above sixty- five. According to family members, the victim's radar detector which the deceased always kept on the sun visor in his car was missing, as were a pouch of tools from the rear seat. In addition, a gold calculator with the deceased's initials inscribed, which the victim had gotten as a gift for participating in a wedding, was missing from the trailer.

All of this information was provided to authorities. However, there was apparently no follow-up by the police into these important observations and suggestions of foul play.

Opinion

In my professional opinion as an expert in homicide and death investigations, the inquiry into the death of the deceased was perfunctory and inadequate according to the recognized standards of professional death investigation. It was readily apparent that this particular crime scene had been staged and it was a reasonable assumption based upon the above facts that the deceased had not committed suicide.

CASE HISTORY Number 2

Police were summoned to a home of a women, who reported that there had been a shooting. The victim, a male, white 26 years of age, was a friend of the woman. He had been watching the woman's children, while she went out drinking with a couple of other males. When the police arrived they observed the victim, sitting on the living room couch, with a gun cradled in his right hand. The victim's right thumb was inside the trigger guard. He had suffered a bullet wound to the left side of his nose and the exit wound was in the upper part of the back of the head. The magazine for the gun had been removed and the ejected shell casing was approximately six feet away from where the victim sat. An examination of the wound structure indicated that there was no stippling or soot on the wound nor was there any evidence of blow-back in the barrel of the gun.

The police were informed by the two males that the deceased had been "playing" with the gun, which belonged to one of the reporting males, and had accidentally shot himself in the face.

A uniform Lieutenant, who was in charge of the scene decided that there wasn't any need for detective response. His decision was based on an administrative policy which discouraged overtime. Rather then authorize overtime response for investigators, he had the case classified as an accidental shooting.

The next day, the homicide detectives reviewed the case and examined the crime scene photographs. Their opinion was that the circumstances as described by the reporting officer and witnesses were not consistent with the elements of the crime scene. They initiated an investigation and tested the suspected weapon, which revealed that the gun had to have been fired at least 42 inches away from the deceased's face. The discharged rounds did not eject, but had to be manually removed from the breech. Removing the magazine required both hands. Gunshot Residue Testing (GSR) testing of the deceased's hands proved negative.

The investigators re-interviewed the woman and the reporting witnesses. The males were confronted with the facts of the case as well as their inconsistent statements. It was learned that all of the parties had been drinking. A gun was pulled out by one of the males, who stated that the gun had accidentally discharged hitting the victim in the face. They had panicked and decided to make it appear that the deceased had shot himself. After they staged the scene, they called the police and the ambulance. Both subjects were charged with Murder. They were indicted for Involuntary Manslaughter. The male, who had done the shooting pled guilty to Manslaughter and Weapon Possession, the other male pled guilty to Tampering with Evidence.

CASE HISTORY Number 3

I remember one case I responded to that had been initially reported to the police as a suicide. When I arrived at the scene, I observed the nude body of a young woman lying on the floor next to the tub in the bathroom. The tub was half full of water, and the body was still wet, as though it had been submerged. The husband, who was distraught and crying, stated to the police that he had found his wife submerged in the tub upon returning to the apartment. He had pulled the body from the tub and had attempted mouth-to-mouth resuscitation. He also added that his wife had been despondent and had probably committed suicide by taking an overdose of pills and drowning herself in the tub. Officers at the scene had recovered a prescription bottle next to the victim. The general condition of the scene and the statements of the husband seemed to indicate the possibility of suicide. I examined the body and noticed a slight bruising in the neck area. The husband explained that upon finding his wife submerged in the tub he had attempted to resuscitate her and had held her by the throat to force air into her lungs. However, when I opened the eyelids of the deceased and examined the conjunctivae, I observed the presence of petechial hemorrhages, and was immediately convinced that the death was, in fact, homicidal and not suicidal, as the husband claimed.

Later on, we learned that the husband had been fighting with his wife and he strangled and killed her. In order to cover up his crime, he filled the tub with water, removed his wife's clothing, and placed her in the tub. He held her under the water to simulate the drowning and then removed her body and placed in on the floor next to the tub. In fact, he had even placed the half-empty bottle of pills next to her body to show to the responding police. The case was properly classified as homicide.

It should be noted that the autopsy would have readily revealed that the death was due to manual strangulation. However, the offender, who was looking to "buy time" certainly would have evoked his right to counsel the next day when confronted with the autopsy results.

The observation of petechial hemorrhages at the scene gave the investigators a head start on their murder investigation. They made further inquiries of the facts and circumstances at the scene and gathered additional evidence. When the suspect was eventually confronted with this evidence, he made a full confession to the police.

CASE HISTORY Number 4: Example of a Homicide made to appear to be a Sex-Related Case

Police were summoned to a home by a frantic male who reported that he had been attacked by a man with a knife, who had killed his wife. When police arrived they were led into the house by the man, who showed them his wife's body in the basement. He indicated that he had also been injured and showed the officers some superficial cuts and puncture wounds on his body. The man was transferred to the Emergency Room of the local hospital for treatment. The crime scene extended from outside the house to the basement. The female victim, who had received multiple stab wounds was found lying on her back. Her pants had been ripped open and her panties had been pulled down to reveal her pubic area. Her sanitary napkin was pulled away and between her legs the crime scene officers retrieved an unused condom. The male had stated that he had surprised the intruder, when he had come home from jogging. The male showed the officers evidence of a burglary. The burglary consisted of items being tossed on the floor and perfume bottles being turned over on the dresser in the master bedroom. However, there wasn't anything missing.

Although the presentation of the female body in the crime scene suggested a sexual attack, the circumstances of the event as well as the inconsistent statements of the husband indicated this murder to be based on an interpersonal oriented dispute and assault scenario.

The husband was charged with his wife's murder based on the police investigation as well as the blood evidence and DNA testing.

CASE HISTORY Number 5

The police were summoned to an apartment, when friends of the deceased recounted that she had failed to report for work. Police entered the apartment and discovered the nude body of the 27 year-old victim lying on the bedroom floor. Her pants and panties had been pulled down and her blouse was in disarray. A hair brush had been inserted into her vagina. She had been beaten and strangled to death with a ligature, which was not present in the scene. A review of the crime scene indicated that some one had gone through the dresser drawers and closets suggesting a burglary. The victim's clothes were found scattered across the floor and the contents of the drawers were spilled out on the bed. There wasn't any forced entry, suggesting the victim had allowed the person into her apartment.

A check into the victimology indicated that the young woman was a divorcee, who had left an abusive marriage. She had enrolled in a nursing program and had recently received her nurse certification. She had been dating since her divorce but did not have a steady boyfriend. The police investigation indicated that the crime scene had been staged to suggest a burglary. However, nothing of value was missing. There wasn't any sexual assault. However, the insertion of the hair brush into her vagina certainly indicated an anger and rage consistent with an interpersonal oriented dispute and assault. The former husband emerged as the most promising suspect after the detectives were able to break his alibi. He had convinced his current girlfriend to provide him with an alibi. He had gone to his former wife's apartment in an attempt to reconcile with her. When she refused his entreaty, he killed her in anger. He left the apartment and returned 24 hours later. At that time he placed the hair brush into her vagina and staged the crime scene to make it appear that a burglar had entered the location, sexually attacked the young woman and then ransacked the apartment.

CONCLUSION

The death investigator needs to be cognizant of the possibility that a crime scene may in fact be staged to mislead the authorities and/or redirect the investigation. In the author's experience and travels as a homicide and forensic consultant, he has encountered a number of these incidents in various jurisdictions across the United States. These events seem to be on the increase as people learn more about the process of death investigation through the media, true crime books, television mystery shows and movies.

INVESTIGATIVE STRATEGIES

Take each factor to it's ultimate conclusion.

1. Assess the victimology of the deceased.
2. Evaluate the type of injuries and wounds of the victim in connection with the type of weapon employed.

3. Conduct the necessary forensic examinations to establish and ascertain the facts of the case.
4. Conduct an examination of the weapon(s) for latent evidence as well as ballistics and testing of firearms.
5. Evaluate the behavior(s) of the victim and suspects.
6. Establish a profile of the victim through interviews of friends and relatives.
7. Reconstruct and evaluate the event.
8. Compare investigative findings with the medicolegal autopsy and confer with the medical examiner.
9. Corroborate statements with evidential facts.
10. Conduct and process all death investigations as if they were homicide cases.

INTENT BEHIND THE BULLET

Originally published in the Association of Firearm Toolmark Examiners Journal, Oct. 1993.

Just because a shot was fired, and just because someone was injured or died as a result of the shooting, and just because a shooting reconstruction was completed...this does not mean that the expert can render an opinion about the intent behind the bullet thus fired.

While many an attorney, whether prosecution or defense, wants to "prove" the intent or lack thereof to a jury, and sometimes tries to use a expert witness to accomplish that end, this does not mean that the shooting reconstruction expert has any scientific basis whatsoever to state an opinion as to what was or was not the intention of the shooter at the moment of the shooting. Intent, after all, is usually an "ultimate issue" and, thus, the purview of the jury, the finders of fact, and cannot properly be addressed by the expert.

Only psychiatrists and psychologists, those paragons of consistently precise opinion and sound experimental scientific integrity, are capable of tackling the issue of intent, often termed "the ability or lack thereof to form the specific intent to commit the crime in question" or words to that effect. And what person endowed with scientific thought would want to wade into the quagmire of psychiatric expert testimony anyway?

In shooting reconstruction, as with all reconstruction, the practitioner's work tries to answer the questions, What happened? and How did it happen? This might be modified somewhat, during an attorney's hypothetical question, to What may have happened? and How may it have happened? What attorneys seldom understand about reconstructionists is that they might not know what happened or may have happened or how, but they can often tell you in an instant WHAT DIDN'T HAPPEN. What reconstructionists cannot answer is WHY? This is the job of the jury.

"I think that reenactment showed that he had an intent to kill."
- District Attorney John Posey

Frequently, attorneys try to bolster their cases for or against an alleged intent matter by disguising a question to an expert as something vaguely science-like in nature. Such a question might look like this: "Mr. Johnson, based on your expertise and your years of experience both with firearms and ammunition, and knowing the velocity in feet-per-second of the shot Mr. Defendant fired at his deceased wife in the hallway of their home, and knowing the distance from the casing found at the scene and the point where Mrs. Defendant fell dead, could you give us an opinion as to whether a shooter in the doorway at the east end of the hall could reasonably expect (read "intend") to miss his wife, firing it as he obviously did?" The answer, of course, is "No" or "Huh?", depending on how foolish you want the attorney to look.

Criminal prosecutors will call a firearm a "weapon," while defense attorneys will call it a "gun." When prosecutors talk about the defendant "aiming" and "firing" the weapon, defense attorneys respond with phrases like "where the barrel was pointing when the gun went off." The former will say "finger on the trigger," while the latter speak of "finger in the area of the trigger guard," and plaintiff attorneys suing gun manufacturers say "inadvertent physical movement in proximity to the negligently designed and defective trigger mechanism." All of these advocates have a vested interest in their choice of words (hence the term "mouthpiece"), which emerges in the wording of their courtroom questions to you. Just as you wouldn't allow attorneys to refer to a cartridge as a "bullet," you should not let them confuse an action with an intent or a gunshot wound with a bull's-eye.

Intent questions are often heavily draped in the sacramental robes of scientific jargon. At times they even sound reasonable in that they almost seem to appeal to one's common sense, as in: "Do you expect us to believe that the weapon discharged accidentally with Mr. Defendant not meaning to shoot his wife?" Well, yes and no. No one but the shooter, and often not even he, knows his true intent. And the reason we're all in court, of course, is so the jurors can try to determine the shooter's intent. But people who investigate shootings for a living are not in the intent business and should be particularly wary of those cleverly disguised questions, whether they come from an attorney "on your side" or an "opposing counsel."

"[The Expert] agreed under cross-examination last Wednesday that he was not testifying that either of the officers was aiming at Lawson's head when they fired six shots at the car after Lawson tried to run them down." - The Toronto Star

Of course, we've all faced the cross-examiner with the "Isn't it possible..." series of questions that's meant to end with a flustered witness wearily admitting that, "Yes, anything's possible." Attorneys slip intent questions into the dark corners of such Q&A marathons. Such as, "Isn't it possible that Mr. Defendant intended to fire a warning shot into his Siamese cat just to scare his wife?" The answer to this one is, "Yes, and it's possible that if his wife had been in Cleveland at the time, she wouldn't have gotten shot."

Most of the time an alert opposing attorney will leap to his feet when an improper intent question is posed. Sometimes, after a lunch hour, when the judge is napping and the jurors are nodding off, a lawyer will try to slide by a question of intent to the shooting reconstructionist on the witness stand. This is the time to ask for a repeat of the question or a clarification to highlight the words "intended" or "meant to" or "expected." If this doesn't work, it's time to proudly disavow any knowledge whatsoever of anybody's intentions, expectations, or what they meant to do or not do or might have not meant to do, etc. The easiest way to do this is to say, "I don't know what the shooter intended." If you don't, you can soon expect the other attorney to ask something like, "You don't know what was intended, you weren't there, were you?"

Q: So you can't—again, it's just your opinion as to where the bullet or where the defect or whatever it was in the—that was in—that actually was in the paint, you can't tell whether that would have hit anybody or was intended to hit anybody?

A: No, I can't determine any intent behind a bullet. - Annie King, GRPD

Naturally you have formed private opinions about the intent of shooters in cases you've investigated, but you didn't (or shouldn't have been allowed to) stand up in court and declare these judgments aloud. Such opinions have no place in your testimony. Let the attorneys get into "what the shooter really meant to do" during their closing arguments. This is why judges frequently admonish jurors that "the arguments of the attorneys do not constitute evidence."

After all, we don't really know what the shooter meant to do, we couldn't. That's for a jury to answer: it's called a verdict. If you look over at the accused shooter sitting with his lawyer, you probably wouldn't want to look inside his mind anyway, much less claim any scientific certainty about what you think that he intended.

Just because someone got shot and you did your job investigating it and you're here and the accused is there, it doesn't mean that you know what he meant to do...no matter who asks the question.

SHOOTING RECONSTRUCTION VS SHOOTING REENACTMENT

Originally published in the Association of Firearm and Toolmark Examiners Journal, April 1993.

"This reconstruction appeared on the face of it to be not only highly ingenious but practically flawless; and it was conclusively proven to be completely wrong." - Henry Rhodes Clues and Crime

In a sense, all areas of criminalistics and investigation are geared to the reconstruction of the criminal act. The latent print examiner can "reconstruct" the position of a suspect's hand on a door; the serologist can sometimes "reconstruct" the stabbing victim's position from stain patterns on clothing; the medical examiner can "reconstruct" the wounding of a human body. A more precise look at reconstruction, however, requires that we distinguish between the terms reconstruction, re-creation, and reenactment.

We can easily dispose of the term "re-creation," as it is sometimes misused in reference to reconstruction. The word re-creation means to form anew, especially in the imagination, to recollect and reform in the mind. This might be what advocates do in the courtroom with the spinning of tales and flights of fancy, but re-creation is not the turf of the criminalist.

The term "reconstruction" indicates the reassembling (as from remaining parts) of an item's original form, a putting together again. If a vase is broken into many small pieces, a craftsman would try to gather as many pieces as possible and attempt to fit them properly back together again. Some pieces might be missing; some fragments might fit together in more than one way. The final form of the repaired vase would, of course, depend heavily on the number of recovered fragments and the skill and experience of the assembler.

In crime reconstruction, the vase is a criminal event that has been shattered into numerous small pieces called "evidence." Given enough pieces, a reconstruction can determine which witness statements agree with the final shape of the reassembled facts and which are inconsistent with the result. As defined by the California Department of Justice, homicide reconstruction is "the process of utilizing information derived from physical evidence at the scene, from analyses of physical evidence, and from inferences drawn from such analyses to test various theories of the occurence of prior events".

As defined by accident investigators, reconstruction is "the effort to determine, from whatever information is available, how the accident happened...It involves studying the results of the accident, considering other circumstances, and applying scientific principles to form opinions relative to events of the accident which are otherwise unknown or are the matter of dispute".

A simple description might define shooting reconstruction as: an examination of the circumstances and physical evidence at the scene of a shooting to establish how the incident occurred. This covers both the accidental and the criminal shooting event. Note that all of these statements describe the scene (or "results") of the event. This is the difference between scene reconstruction and laboratory criminalistics, the former is generally performed in the field, whereas the latter is generally bench work.

The key, of course, is the application of scientific principles, which is (one hopes) common to both scene reconstruction and laboratory examination. The practitioner, as any good scientist, must be cautious and conservative, relying on the physical evidence when possible and verifying or rejecting the input of interested human parties, be they witnesses, participants, or lawyers.

Reconstruction by its nature involves a process of elimination, where what is purported to have happened is measured against the story told by the items of evidence. With insufficient information, the investigator may not be able to determine what actually occurred; however, even with a few clues, he may be able to say what did NOT occur. This is often the framework on which a reconstruction hangs—a series of answers that eliminate those events that did not happen.

This brings us to the subject of reenactment. The word "reenactment" means to act out or perform again. It has nothing whatsoever to do with scientific principles. The distinction between reconstruction and reenactment is a critical one. To confuse the two is to confuse crime scene analysis with a puppet show. Originally criminal reenactments by police investigators were performed in the presence of suspects in an effort to encourage confessions. Today, a reenactment, whether it is two role-players in front of a jury box or an elaborate video simulation of digitalized human figures repeating programmed movements, is but a demonstration of a previously existing reconstruction.

Without a reconstruction, competent or not, there can be no reenactment. The exception, of course, is a reenactment of an event as it was seen by a participant or witness. This brings us back to the human element, the hearsay, upon which a reconstruction cannot solely rely. These sorts of reenactments are, at best, just re-creations of recollections, and have nothing to do with criminalistics or scientific principles. Reenactment producers are but skilled cartoonists, not analyzers of physical evidence. It is dangerous for the members of a jury to confuse the two terms.

The time element is important. The shooting reconstruction may be able to determine where the victim was seated and approximately where the shooter was standing at a given moment in time when the shot and the trajectory happened. The reenactment artist pretends to know the shooter's furtive steps approaching the scene, the movements of the victim's panicked head and face as he meets the shot, and the likely instant reactions of both participants during the shooting. This all-seeing, all-knowing attitude on the part of the reenactor is somewhat mysterious, because no one knows exactly what these things were like, often not even the participants. These things cannot be scientifically calculated or estimated, but the reenactor would have the jury believe that he knows, that this is how it looked and this is how it happened. The reenactment is less than bad science, it's non-science masquerading as science.

The shooting reconstruction completed by a knowledgeable investigator may take into account that Shooter X was standing in a certain area and that Victim Y was struck by a certain number of shotshell pellets from his waist to his upper back while running away at about the south edge of a parking lot; the investigator can then estimate with a fair amount of precision, given the pellet-count per load of the shotshell and the tested pattern of the shotgun, that the weapon was pointed (intentionally or not) within a couple feet to the left or right of the victim, but only at that instant in time. The events and actions leading up to and following the shooting are unknown to the investigator, except for the statements of possibly biased participants. This instant in time may be presented to the court as a diagram or model, but will only show the moment as ascertained by the trajectory reconstruction, not some imagined scenario.

The reconstruction of an automobile accident can give one a good idea about the motions of the vehicles just before and just after a collision, because these are based on speed calculations worked out from marks on the roadway, crush damage, post-impact travel, and a multitude of other items of true physical evidence. This sort of incident might become the subject of an animated reenactment, after a competent reconstruction, of course.

A shooting incident, on the other hand, is seldom the valid subject of such display. No one, especially the investigator, knows for certain what the whole incident looked like from the shooter's point-of-view, the victim's point-of-view, or the viewpoint of any interested bystander. No qualified investigator would lay claim to such omniscience. The reenactor, however, seems to know it all.

The use of "virtual reality," or VR, computer simulations to reenact crimes in the courtroom has stirred up controversy in the legal community. This dissention is not so much due to the non-scientific basis of such video treatments, but mostly because the VR-programmed details so readily reflect the particular slant of the lawyer's side that produced the reenactment. The VR marionettes can be made to move, dodge bullets, shoot (maliciously or accidentally, depending if it's a prosecutor's or defense attorney's program), fall down, die, or do whatever else the programmer desires. The facts, as revealed by an examination of physical evidence, are seldom as pliable and all-encompassing as the virtual treatment. True reconstruction seldom provides all the answers to all the questions.

This, finally, is the crux of the problem. Are jurors to believe that there is a real scientific basis for a computer-animated version of a shooting? Will they be instructed by the judge that the reenacted treatment is but one possible explanation for the incident? Or will the cautious jurist not allow the reenactor's video into evidence in the first place, based on its lack of scientific foundation, its editorializing of the known facts, and its propensity to fill in the blanks that cannot really be known?

WHY CRIME SCENE RECONSTRUCTION DOES NOT ANSWER THE WHY? QUESTION

This article originally appeared in the MAFS newsletter April 1996.

"I tend not to try to determine why people do things at crime scenes." -Criminalist Charles Morton

California v Menedez II

Trial transcript 12-5-95

Crime scene reconstruction may answer the question of *where* a victim was standing when an axe hit him or *who* stepped in the pool of blood by the door or *what* caused the revolver's hammer to fall or *when* the third shot hit the car window or *how* the knife ended up out on the patio, but the crime scene reconstructionist cannot answer the ultimate question, the final question that tugs at everyone's mind, the all-encompassing, all-seeing, all-knowing question of *WHY* did the crime happen? This may account for the fact that attorneys (for either side) very seldom ask "Why?" questions.

What happened and *How* it happened cover almost all of reconstruction work. The "Why?" question is an ultimate issue, something to be contemplated by ministers, psychologists, widows, and jurors. *How* a shot struck a victim is not the same as *Why* it struck the victim. Some very excellent works [*Bevel, Rynearson, Chisum*] on the subject of crime scene reconstruction mention *Why* as one of the questions answerable by the reconstructionist. These authors are more accurately addressing the questions of *How*, rather than *Why*.

The true answers to the *Why* question of crime are often:

He always hated his mother

or

He just ran out of luck

or

She was as crazy as a couple of dancing mice that night

or

The guy owed him money, so he shot him

or

It was a lovers' quarrel

or

Yes, he knew the gun was loaded, but he didn't mean to shoot the store clerk

or

The voice from the toaster told him to do it

or

The police officer took his eyes off the suspect for just a moment

or

"I killed them to prevent any more earthquakes"

or

He hit her once too often

or

The victim said something stupid like, "You can't do it. Go ahead and shoot!"

or

She hit him with his own car just to scare him

or

His fifth grade teacher always thought he was strange when he talked about assassinating famous people

or

"Gee, I dunno...I guess I was pretty upset."

or

The victim/suspect was simply one evil SOB.

These after all, are the real answers to the "Why?" question. No amount of careful crime scene measurement, meticulous photograpy, painstaking evidence collection or Sherlock Holmesian deduction, induction, or reduction can answer the "Why?" question. No reconstruction has yet answered the Why of Jeffrey Dahmer, Ted Bundy, or John Wayne Gacy, but numerous individuals and agencies have addressed the "What happened?", and "How did it happen?" questions that surround these cases. (It was perhaps the downfall of those who have tried to reconstruct the Kennedy assassinations that they could never quite divorce the what-happened from the why-did-it-happen.)

You can understand the How without knowing the Why. And this is not all bad, because the true reason *why* a crime occurred is neither very interesting nor very enlightening.

Sixty stab wounds and a shoeprint on the victim's face may *indicate* why the killer thought it was necessary to commit the act. The word "PIG" written on the wall in the victims blood may *indicate* why the killer felt it was time for a murder.

The use of meat fork *and* boning knife *and* roofing hammer or fifteen groin shots may *hint* at the true reasons why the crime was committed.

These, however conspicuous, are only indicators of why...indicators to be interpreted by attorneys in their closing arguments, juries in their deliberations, and psychological profilers in their analyses.

As a crime scene reconstructionist, your job is not to answer *Why* the crime occurred. It's not your problem. Your are employed to examine the evidence and circumstances and, with some knowledgable and scientific analysis, figure out *How* the crime transpired.

The "Why?" is not your specialty, nor your responsibility. There is an old cop maxim which says that there are two kinds of murder cases: who-done-its? and who-cares? In either type of case, the question of why who done it did it is not something that can be answered by a crime scene reconstruction

11

Evidence Dynamics: Locard's Exchange Principle and Crime Reconstruction

Abstract: Conclusions regarding the circumstances and behaviors elicited from the physical evidence related to a crime (crime reconstruction) can infrequently be housed within the confines of absolute certainty. This paper discusses the development of Locard's Exchange Principle and historical and contemporary philosophies surrounding crime reconstruction. It further discusses the fallacy of assuming the integrity of physical evidence, and provides a logical foundation for the concept of Evidence Dynamics. Evidence Dynamics refers to any influence that changes, relocates, obscures, or obliterates physical evidence, regardless of intent. Evidence Dynamics, it is further argued, come into play during the interval that begins as evidence is being transferred, and ends when the case is ultimately adjudicated. A discussion of the various types of Evidence Dynamics is provided, followed up by demonstrative examples from the authors' case files.

Of all responsibilities shouldered by the forensic scientist, the reconstruction of the circumstances and behaviors involved in a crime is one of the most important. In conjunction with agreeable witness accounts, a crime reconstruction may be a powerful instrument of corroboration. In the face of conflicted witness accounts, it may provide an objective view that points to one possibility over another. In the absence of witness accounts, it may be used to investigate and establish the actions that occurred at the scene of a crime. The role that crime reconstruction can play investigatively and legally should never be underestimated.

Because of the varied evidence and circumstances involved, the ability to reconstruct crime requires broad forensic knowledge, an objective if not conservative disposition towards the examination and interpretation of evidence, and what the fictional Dr. Watson of *Sherlock Holmes* fame referred to as a "peculiar facility for deduction."

Despite its importance to investigative and legal venues, crime reconstruction is often performed inappropriately by the unknowledgeable and overconfident. This includes those with little knowledge of, or training in, the peculiarities of physical evidence and the forensic sciences. Those testifying as experts in the area of crime reconstruction routinely cite as a premise, for otherwise unproven opinions, the sum of their education, training, and experience. It may be the case that this is offered in the place of facts from the case file. This practice is regarded as illegitimate for a forensic examiner. "Experience should not make the expert less responsible, but rather more responsible for justifying an opinion with defensible scientific facts."

Conclusions regarding the circumstances and behaviors elicited from the physical evidence related to a crime can infrequently be housed within the confines of absolute certainty. It is often an intensive process with imprecise results containing evidentiary holes, sequential gaps, and alternate possibilities. This does not suggest that crime reconstruction efforts lack investigative or legal utility. The utility of crime reconstruction is by no means bound to any predisposition for certainty. Rather, its utility is more often found in establishing the general circumstances of a crime, demonstrating links between victims, suspects, and offenders, corroboration of witness statements, providing investigative leads, and identifying potential suspects.

Further still, it is often the case that what the physical evidence excludes, fails to establish, or equivocates, is actually of great investigative and legal importance. Forensic analysis in general, and crime reconstruction in particular, is concerned with those conclusions that can be logically drawn from the evidence, as well as with those that cannot. As such, the consideration of both the strengths and limitations of available physical evidence are an important part of crime reconstruction. It is with these considerations in mind that we begin our discussion of the relationship between Locard's Exchange Principle, Crime Reconstruction, *Evidence Dynamics* and their implications to forensic examinations.

The Development of Locard's Exchange Principle

Alphonse Bertillon developed one of the first scientific systems of documenting personal identification in Paris in the late 1800s. In 1879, Msr. Bertillon began his career when he was appointed clerk in the Premier Bureau of the Prefecture of Police. The sheer volume of the files required organization. He used the measurement system that his father, a physical anthropologist, used to organize skeletal material. Bertillon's genius was in adapting this method to living persons and establishing a record system. The method referred to ultimately as *Bertillonage* used the relatively simple procedure of taking a series of body measurements, noting other physical characteristics, and placing this information on a single identification card in a police file. As the method developed he started adding photographs of the individual to the files. Bertillonage was a significant advancement in terms of providing a useful database of criminals for criminal investigators.

Bertillon was motivated to develop his methods not only by the desire to assist in the tracking of criminals and their behavior, but also by a personal belief that everything that "lived and moved under heaven" was somehow unique. His was something of a radical notion in criminal investigation at the time: that science and logic should be used to investigate and solve crime. As Msr. Bertillon's biographer stated:

The methods of the French police in that year of grace 1879 had changed very little in principle from those initiated by that criminal turned policeman, the brilliant and unscrupulous [Eugene] Vidocq. They consisted in the liberal use of the police informer, and agent provocateur.

Bertillonage was employed to identify criminals by law enforcement for at least two decades, until it was replaced by the use of fingerprints. In 1891, *Dr. Hans Gross*, an Austrian Magistrate and Professor of Criminology, made the following observation, "The advantages of finger-prints over the Bertillon system have become so well established that the latter can with perfect safety be dispensed with altogether as unnecessary for the purposes of identification."

However, Bertillonage was not the limit of Msr. Bertillon's contribution to the forensic sciences, nor was it his most significant. His dedication to precise measurements and the use of photography led to a combination of the two practices beyond criminal identification. Bertillon assisted in the development and practice of forensic photography by introducing a measuring scale with the persons and objects of evidence that he photographed. The usefulness of this practice soon became apparent. He was routinely sent out with investigators to document crime scenes. He would photograph the bodies of victims, their relationship to significant items of evidence in the scene, as well as the position, size, nature and extent of other physical evidence including footprints, stains, toolmarks, and points of entry. Until the development of this practice, criminal investigators and the courts relied upon sketches and notes of varying precision for their understanding of the context of a crime. That is, if any record were made of a crime scene at all.

Bertillon also instructed and influenced several students, including *Dr. Edmond Locard*, whose work formed the basis for what is widely regarded as a cornerstone of the forensic sciences, *Locard's Exchange Principle*. Dr. Locard, like Dr. Hans Gross and Msr. Bertillon before him, advocated the application of scientific methods and logic to criminal investigation and identification. As stated by *Dr. John Thornton*, a criminalist and a former professor of forensic science at the University of California, Berkeley:

> Forensic scientists have almost universally accepted the *Locard Exchange Principle.* This doctrine was enunciated early in the 20th Century by Edmund Locard, the director of the first crime laboratory, in Lyon, France. Locard's Exchange Principle states that with contact between two items, there will be an exchange...

Due in no small part to Mr. Bertillon's influence, it was Dr. Locard's belief and assertion that when any person comes into contact with an object or another person, a cross-transfer of physical evidence occurs. By recognizing, documenting, and examining the nature and extent of this evidentiary exchange, Locard observed that criminals could be associated with particular locations, items of evidence and victims. The detection of the exchanged materials is interpreted to mean that the two objects were in contact. This is the cause and effect principle reversed; the effect is observed and the cause is concluded.

Forensic scientists also recognize that the nature and extent of this exchange can be used not only to associate a criminal with locations, items, and victims, but with specific actions as well.

Crime Reconstruction

Crime reconstruction is "the determination of the actions surrounding the commission of a crime." Careful and competent examination of the physical evidence the documentation of the crime scene allows for this determination. The systematic documentation and recording of the crime scene is required for this analysis. The photographic documentation as established by Bertillon is a necessity for crime reconstruction. The veracity of statements by witnesses, victims, and suspects can be established by reconstruction.

Modern methods of crime reconstruction owe themselves to a strong history marked by rigorous analytical thought and forensic application. The collective work of Alphonse Bertillon, Dr. Hans Gross, and Dr. Edmond Locard are no small part of this history. Enduring themes include the importance of physical evidence, objectivity, the necessary employment of logic, and viewing witness, victim, and offender statements with suspicion.

Just before the turn of the century, Dr. Hans Gross, in discussing how a crime should be reconstructed, argued for strict objectivity and a logical, sequential, frame by frame analysis on the part of criminal investigators:

Nothing can be known if nothing has happened...

...in the profession of the criminal expert everything bearing the least trace of exaggeration must be removed in the most energetic and conscientious manner; otherwise, the Investigating Officer will become an expert unworthy of his service and even dangerous to humanity.

...all of the circumstances of the crime must be clearly taken into account and submitted to a strict logical examination from their commencement to their last stage. If at a given moment something has not been explained, suspicion is justified and a pause must be made at the point where the logical sequence is broken....

Dr. Gross also decried the heavy reliance of criminal investigators and the courts on witness accounts, strongly advocating the use of physical evidence, writing: The progress of criminology means less trust in witnesses and more in real proofs.

Dr. Edmond Locard, in speaking similarly on the subject of physical evidence and crime reconstruction, maintained that: ... the criminologist re-creates the criminal from traces the latter leaves behind, just as the archaeologist reconstructs prehistoric beings from his finds.

Dr. Theodore Reik, a Professor of Psychoanalysis at Vienna University, an early disciple of Dr. Sigmund Freud, also argued for the use of objectivity and logic in the investigation of crime and criminals: The object of the criminologist's reasoning is knowledge of a material event and the finding of an unknown person...

Cool, objective thought, re-examination of facts according to the rules of logic, *raisonnement* (Locard) is the pivot of the detectives mental process.

In the second half of this century, the late Dr. Paul Kirk, Professor of Criminalistics at the University of California, Berkeley, shared the views of Drs. Gross and Locard regarding issues of witnesses, physical evidence, and crime reconstruction, arguing:

...the utilization of physical evidence is critical to the solution of most crime. No longer may the police depend upon the confession, as they have done to a large extent in the past. The eyewitness has never been dependable, as any experienced investigator or attorney knows quite well. Only physical evidence is infallible, and then only when it is properly recognized, studied, and interpreted.

Dr. Kirk further argued, supporting the validity of Locard's Exchange Principle, the importance of transfer evidence to crime reconstruction: Wherever he steps, whatever he touches, whatever he leaves, even unconsciously, will serve as silent witness against him. Not only his fingerprints or his footprints, but his hair, the fibers from his clothing, the glass he breaks, the tool mark he leaves, the paint he scratches, the blood or semen he deposits or collects. All of these and more bear mute witness against him. This is evidence that does not forget.

However, Dr. Kirk also argued for caution in the interpretation of evidentiary exchanges. In this brief discussion on establishing the identification of an object's source, he makes it clear that it is an endeavor with inherent hazards under even the best conditions.

In the examination and interpretation of physical evidence, the distinction between identification and individuation must always be clearly made, to facilitate the real purpose of the criminalist: to determine the identity of source. That is, two items of evidence, one known and the other unknown, must be identified as having a common origin. On the witness stand, the criminalist must be willing to admit that absolute identity is impossible to establish. Identity of source, on the other hand, often may be established unequivocally, and no witness who has established it need ever back down in the face of cross-examination.

It is precisely here that the greatest caution must be exercised. The inept or biased witness may readily testify to an identity, or to a type of identity, that does not actually exist. This can come about because of his confusion as to the nature of identity, his inability to evaluate the results of his observations, or because his general technical deficiencies preclude meaningful results.

Dr. Henry Lee, former Director of the Connecticut State Police Crime Laboratory, also advocates a combination of both physical evidence and logic by forensic scientists engaging in reconstruction:

Reconstruction not only involves the scientific scene analysis, interpretation of scene pattern evidence and laboratory examination of physical evidence, but also involves systematic study of related information and the logical formulation of a theory.

Dr. John Thornton, previously mentioned, a student of Dr. Kirk, describes the mechanics of the logic that should be employed by forensic scientists when undertaking a forensic examination:

Induction is a type of inference that proceeds from a set of specific observations to a generalization, called a premise. This premise is a working assumption, but it may not always be valid. A deduction, on the other hand, proceeds from a generalization to a specific case, and that is generally what happens in forensic practice. Providing that the premise is valid, the deduction will be valid. But knowing whether the premise is valid is the name of the game here; it is not difficult to be fooled into thinking that one's premises are valid when they are not.

Forensic scientists have, for the most part, treated induction and deduction rather casually. They have failed to recognize that induction, not deduction, is the counterpart of hypothesis testing and theory revision. ...too often a hypothesis is declared as a deductive conclusion, when in fact it is a statement awaiting verification through testing.

Criminalist Dr. Richard Saferstein, retired Chief Forensic Scientist from the New Jersey State Police Lab, also argues:

The physical evidence left behind at the crime scene plays a crucial role in reconstructing the events that took place surrounding the crime... The collection and documentation of physical evidence is the foundation of a reconstruction.

One of the authors, also a student of Dr. Kirk, makes a cogent forensic argument regarding the potential value of crime reconstruction to the court in terms of establishing what has actually happened in a given case:

The prosecutor seeks to convict the defendant by making the crime more heinous in nature. The defense seeks to exonerate the defendant. Both theorize about how the crime occurred with different objectives. Both cannot be correct and, lacking a reconstruction, both are probably wrong. The theories are alternatives and should be examined against the evidence...

Any theory of the crime must be based on logic – explaining the physical evidence and its location at the scene. It is through such analysis that the behavior of the perpetrator is revealed...

Crime reconstruction, as argued, involves examining the available physical evidence, those materials left at or removed from the scene, victim, or offender. These materials are used by the forensic scientist establish to contact between the suspect and victim or scene

according to the principle proposed Dr. Locard. These forensically established contacts are then considered in light of available and reliable witness, victim, and offender statements. From this, theories regarding the circumstances of the crime can be generated and falsified by logically applying the information of the established facts of the case. Left standing, ideally, will be legitimate, logical conclusions regarding the actions surrounding the commission of the crime or as put by the fictional Sherlock Holmes in the *Sign of Four*, "—when you have eliminated the impossible, whatever remains, however improbable, must be the truth."

The Assumption of Integrity

The process of crime reconstruction is often built on the assumption that evidence left behind at a crime scene, which has been recognized, documented, collected, identified, compared, individuated, and reconstructed, is pristine. This assumption involves the belief that the process of taping off an area, limiting access, and setting about the task of taking pictures and making measurements ensures the integrity of the evidence found within. Subsequently, any conclusions reached through forensic examinations and reconstructions of that evidence are assumed to be a reliable lens through which to view the crime. This assumption is not always accurate.

Even though a reliable *chain of evidence* may be established, physical evidence may have been altered prior to or during its collection and examination. Unless the integrity of the evidence can be reliably established, and legitimate evidentiary influences accounted for, the documentation of a chain of evidence, by itself, does not provide acceptable ground upon which to build reliable forensic conclusions.

Consideration of evidentiary influences, or *Evidence Dynamics*, is a necessary part of the crime reconstruction process.

Evidence Dynamics

Crime reconstruction efforts are concerned with examining the effects or results of actions done in the commission of the crime. As Dr. Gross was fond of saying, "What is effect and what is cause?" This is answered by the use of logic and forensic axioms such as Locard's Exchange Principle. However, often missing from that analysis is a consideration of those influences that can change physical evidence prior to or as a result of its examination.

The general term *Evidence Dynamics* has been developed by the authors to refer to any influence that changes, relocates, obscures, or obliterates physical evidence, regardless of intent. *Evidence Dynamics* comes into play during the interval that begins as evidence is being transferred, and ends when the case is ultimately adjudicated. For those who are familiar with such evidentiary influences, and account for them in their analysis, this terminology is intended to provide a necessary and useful descriptor. An appreciation of *Evidence Dynamics* on what can be concluded from the physical evidence is requisite, and often pivotal, to the reconstruction process.

In the interpretation of *Evidence Dynamics*, two questions require attention. First, is there an item of evidence that has been demonstrably influenced between the time of the crime and the time of examination? If an item of evidence has been moved, changed, or obscured, then this must be factored into the examiner's analysis in terms of when and how. Second, is there evidence of a circumstance that could have obliterated or influenced evidence? Forensic scientists can only include in their analyses those things for which evidence exists. However, if there is no reasonable suggestion of circumstances that could have influenced or obliterated evidence, then the examiner should not assume that they occurred.

There are many possible influences on *Evidence Dynamics* that should be considered as evidence is examined. A brief list, not meant to be all-inclusive, is provided below.

Offender actions: The actions of an offender during the commission of their crime and the post-offense interval influence the nature and quality of evidence that is left behind.

These can include *Precautionary Acts*, *Ritual* or *Fantasy*, and *Staging*. *Precautionary Acts* involving physical evidence are behaviors committed by an offender before, during, or after an offense that are consciously intended to confuse, hamper, or defeat investigative or forensic efforts for the purposes of concealing their identity, their connection to the crime, or the crime itself. *Staging* of the crime scene is a specific type of precautionary act that is done to deflect suspicion away from the offender. *Staging* often involves the addition of, removal of, and manipulation of objects in the crime scene to change the apparent "motive" of the crime. *Ritual* or *Fantasy* may also influence the offender's actions during a crime, and can include such things as postmortem mutilation, necrophilia, and purposeful arrangement of a body or items in a scene.

Victim actions: The victim's activities prior to a crime may result in artifacts that are mistaken for evidence. The actions of a victim during an attack and in the post-offense interval can influence the nature and quality of evidence that is left behind. This includes defensive actions, such as struggling, fighting, and running, which can relocate transfer evidence, causing secondary transfer. The victim's actions may also include cleaning up a location or their person after an attack.

Secondary Transfer: Transfer evidence, as we have established, is produced by contact between persons and objects. Secondary transfer refers to an exchange of evidence between objects or persons that occurs subsequent to an original exchange, unassociated with the circumstances that produced the original exchange.

Witnesses: The actions of witnesses in the post-offense interval can influence the nature and quality of evidence that is left behind. This includes actions taken to preserve victim dignity, as well as the deliberate theft of items from the scene upon discovery of an incapacitated or deceased victim.

Weather/ Climate: The weather or climate of a crime can influence the nature and quality of all manner of evidence that is left behind. This includes the destruction or obliteration of evidence by all manner of weather, as well as the effects of weather and climate on rates of body and biological transfer evidence decomposition.

Decomposition: Naturally occurring rates of decomposition, over time, can obscure, obliterate or mimic evidence of injury to a body. The clothing from a decomposed body will normally receive less attention for trace or transfer evidence.

Insect Activity: The actions of flies, ants, beetles, and other insects can obliterate the wounds on a body. They may also move, remove or destroy the transfer evidence.

Animal Predation: The feeding activities of all manner of indigenous wildlife from mice to coyotes and bears can relocate evidence, obliterate patterns, and further obscure, obliterate or mimic evidence of criminal injury to a body.

Fire: In cases were fire is involved, intentional or otherwise, the result can be the obscuring of all manner of physical evidence related to criminal activities, as well as its potential destruction. The evidence showing the actions of the offender regarding the primary offense are obscured if not eliminated by the subsequent arson. Evidence of the arson may remain.

Fire Suppression Efforts: In cases were fire is involved, there may be suppression efforts made. These efforts typically involve the use of high-pressure water, heavy hoses, perhaps chemicals, and firemen. Any of these, alone or in concert, can relocate the evidence, obliterate patterns, cause potentially misleading transfers, and/or add artifact-evidence, to the scene.

Police: The duty of the first officer on the scene is to protect life, not to preserve evidence. They must establish that the scene is secure from further attacks. Their actions may relocate evidence, obliterate patterns, cause transfers, and add artifact-evidence to the scene.

Emergency Medical Technicians: The actions of emergency medical personnel engaged in life saving activities in a crime may relocate evidence, obliterate patterns, cause transfers, and add artifacts mistaken as evidence. As well, they can add therapeutic injuries to the victim.

Scene Technicians: The actions of technicians working in the physical evidence recognition, preservation, documentation, and collection phases in a crime scene are expected to remove evidence without obliterating patterns, causing potentially misleading transfers, and adding artifact-evidence to the scene. The technicians must thoroughly document the scene prior to entering so the changes that occur are obvious.

Forensic Scientists: The actions of forensic scientists will also remove evidence, obliterate patterns, may cause potentially misleading transfers, and add artifact-evidence to the scene. This can occur by virtue of improper storage or destructive analytical techniques, or the addition of transfer and/or pattern evidence to a victim's body or clothing during transport and/or storage.

Coroners: The actions of the coroner in removing the body from the scene can move evidence, obliterate patterns, cause potentially misleading transfer, and add artifact-evidence to the scene. This includes the physical removal of the body from the location where it was discovered, the placement of the body into a "body bag," and the process of transporting the body from the scene. These actions will change pattern evidence on the clothing of the victim and may destroy potential valuable transfer evidence.

Case Examples

The following case examples have been taken from the authors' case files:

Example #1 - Fire and Suppression Efforts

A young female arrived at her older boyfriend's home, where he lived with his elderly mother and two teenage children. A confrontation ensued. The boyfriend and his mother, who were the only ones home at the time, were both killed, dying of exsanguination from multiple gunshot wounds.

The boyfriend's body was found outside of the residence with an associated blood trail. After the girlfriend removed some items of value she set both the house and the body of the boyfriend on fire.

Some of the actions and circumstances involved in the crime were evident, given the body outside of the home, associated transfer evidence, and blood patterns. However, a sequential reconstruction of the shots fired within the house, as well as the relative positions of the shooter and the victims, was significantly impaired. This was due to the movement and destruction of walls, furniture, flooring, household items, the body of the mother, and blood evidence in the scene. A crime analysis of the case reads in part:

...precise reconstruction efforts are hampered in this case due to the numerous destructive and evidence-altering variables that were imposed upon the scene in the interval after the deaths occurred and before it was safe for forensic efforts to take priority. These destructive and evidence-altering variables and elements, documented in part by a video made of this scene during and after suppression efforts were engaged, include, but are not limited to:

- the destructive nature of the fire itself, which involved both stories and many rooms in the house;
- the destructive nature of the suppression efforts, which involved water being pumped into the home at approximately 1000 gallons per minute, the destruction and movement of items in the home for both suppression and salvage purposes, as well as unintentional damage that may have been caused by heavy fire hoses in various locations within the home;
- the number of personnel venturing in and out of the home during and after suppression efforts, which some estimate may have been more that 50 individuals.

Example #2 - Decomposition & Insect Activity

An adolescent female was missing for approximately two weeks before investigators found her body. It was located in a slightly concealed area of foliage behind an unoccupied residence. Her deceased body had been placed inside of a piece of recently discarded carpeting, beneath a heavy metal water tank, and then covered by several more layers of older discarded carpeting.

According to the autopsy report, and visible in the autopsy photos, the victim's underwear was found in her mouth. The cause of death was determined to be "asphyxia by gagging" possibly in combination with a violent blow to the victim's jaw as evidenced by a fracture to the mandible.

The question arose as to whether there was evidence of manual or ligature strangulation. Due to the overall advanced state of decomposition, and the fact that maggots had consumed the soft tissue associated with the neck, a determination on this issue was not possible. In the absence of evidence to examine, one cannot make a legitimate determination as to whether or not manual or ligature strangulation occurred. This did not exclude the possibility that it may have occurred; merely that it could not be established and therefore should not be assumed for the purposes of analysis.

Example #3 - Secondary Transfer and Scene Technicians

The body of an adolescent female was found on a couch in her home where she lived with her mother and younger brother. She was wearing only a shirt and bra at the time of discovery. She was determined to have died of "asphyxia secondary to manual strangulation." She had a history of sexual abuse, suggested by the absence of her hymen and numerous anal scars, as well as a history of promiscuity. The DNA of one of her mother's lovers was found on her perineum, in the form of sperm.

Given the location and circumstances of the crime, the precise conditions of this exchange could not be reliably established. One possibility is that the suspect was engaged in some form of sexual activity with the victim, and that sperm transferred to her perineum as a result. However, the suspect and the victim's mother had sexual relations in the mother's bed, where the victim had been playing previously with her brother. There were also reports that the suspect and the victim's mother may have had sexual relations on the couch, were the victim would have been sitting. Additionally, a review of the crime scene video shows several evidence technicians moving evidence around on the couch and other locations, and then touching the victim's body in multiple locations, examining her body as it is being photographed, with and without gloves.

Given these circumstances, and the victim's history, the following are potential evidence transfer relationships in this case:

- From the suspect to the victim during a forced sexual assault;
- From the suspect to the victim during a consensual (but unlawful) sexual encounter;
- From the couch to the victim's perineum;
- From the mother's bed to the victim's perineum;
- From the scene technician's fingers to the victim's perineum

Example # 4 - Emergency Medical Technicians

A youth was stabbed several times by rival gang members. He ran for a home but collapsed in the walkway. A photo of the scene taken prior to the arrival of the EMT team shows a blood trail and that the victim was lying face down. Subsequent photos show the 5 EMTs working on the body on his back. He had been rolled over onto the blood pool. It became impossible for bloodstain pattern interpretation to be used to reconstruct the events leading to the death of the youth.

Example # 5 – Coroner Activities

Photos taken of the deceased showed isolated bloodstain patterns on the clothing of the victim of a rape homicide. She had been sexually assaulted and her throat was cut. The patterns on her panties appeared to be bloody transfers from a hand. The coroner refused to remove the clothing at the scene. When the panties were submitted to the laboratory they were soaked in the victim's blood from transporting her in the body bag. The patterns were destroyed as well as making it impossible to isolate the stains for identification purposes.

Example # 6 – Victim Activities

In this case the victim's actions prior to a crime caused "false evidence" to be present. A woman had sex with her boyfriend in his vehicle. He dropped her off at her apartment. As she enters her bedroom she surprises a burglar. A struggle ensued causing tears in her clothing before the burglar strangled her and fled. The boyfriend is suspected of the "rape/homicide." His DNA is found in her vagina. This would be considered proof of his guilt in many courts.

Fortunately, the boyfriend had an alibi; he was stopped for DUI a couple of blocks from the house. He was in police custody during the time the screams were heard by the neighbors.

Example # 7 – Family Activities

The body of an elderly man was found "in his bed." Upon examination, strangulation marks were found on his neck. These marks were consistent with a hanging. When questioned the family admitted that he had hanged himself. They didn't want the "shame on their family," so they had cut him down, changed his clothing and put him to bed. The evidence was destroyed for cultural reasons.

Conclusions

The failure to consider *Evidence Dynamics* as a part of any crime reconstruction process has the potential to provide for misinterpretations of physical evidence, and inaccurate or incomplete crime reconstructions. Any subsequent use of the reconstruction for investigations, trial or behavioral analysis would have a diminished foundation and relevance, compounding the harm in legal, investigative and academic venues. It is the responsibility of the forensic scientist to perform reconstructions of the circumstances and behaviors involved in a crimes with care, and to be aware of the possibility of *Evidence Dynamics*, in order that opinions regarding reconstruction of the crime reflect the most informed and accurate rendering of the evidence.

12

The Importance of Careful Interpretation of Shell Casing Ejection Patterns

Abstract: An experiment was conducted to gain information about shell casing ejection patterns. The research project showed that shell casing ejection patterns are dependent on a number of variables: type of firearm, stance, hand and weapon position (grip), and movement.

BACKGROUND

A review of the literature indicated some disparity in the opinions of crime scene investigators concerning the position of casings related to shooting incidents.

Ogle notes that the "location of fired cartridge cases may be valuable in a reconstruction attempt of the shooting incident. The location(s) of the shooter(s) may be determined by the analysis of the locations of the fired cases". Gardner writes that firearms examiners conduct, on occasion, ejection studies with the purpose of determining the distance and direction that a casing will eject when the weapon is held in any given orientation. He continues by noting that ejection studies have limited value, because casings will roll when they hit the ground or ricochet from walls or objects.

Garrison conducted a study on the position of casings dropped from a moving vehicle. He posited that some of the variables that can affect the final location of ejected casings are speed, road surfaces, vehicular traffic, crowds that might move the casings, and cartridge types. One of his observations was that, under similar circumstances, rimmed casings tend to travel less distance. Other research suggests that depending on many variables, extracted casings can end up virtually anywhere.

Case History

A patrol officer observed a black Cadillac with expired license plates driving on the city streets. The officer attempted to initiate a traffic stop. The vehicle f led, the officer began to pursue the vehicle and, within a few seconds, the suspect lost control of the Cadillac, which jumped a curb and came to rest in the yard of a residential neighborhood. The officer stopped behind the vehicle and exited his cruiser to make contact with the driver. The suspect exited his vehicle and fired two shots from a handgun. The officer took cover between the two vehicles and returned fire. (The officer later said that he thought he had fired his weapon four times.) The suspect then ran from the scene, entered a trailer park, turned, and fired three more shots in the direction of the officer. The officer radioed for assistance.

A second officer observed a person matching the suspect's physical description running through the trailer park. The second officer identified himself, ordered the suspect to stop, and gave foot chase. The suspect was subsequently taken into custody, and was later identified by the initial officer. Neither the suspect nor the officer was injured during the shooting. The suspect was intoxicated, had narcotics on his person, and had six live.357 caliber rounds in his pocket. During a search of the area, a.357 caliber Ruger 6-shot revolver was located on the ground between the initiating officer's cruiser and the location of arrest. One live round and five spent shell casings were located inside this handgun.

During the investigation of the crime scene, two bullet strikes were located on the police cruiser, one in the hood and one in the windshield. Two bullet holes were also located in the siding of a nearby trailer. The officer's weapon, a department-issued Smith & Wesson, model 5906, 9 mm semi-automatic pistol, with two additional magazines, was secured at the scene. Fully loaded, his weapon and magazines would contain forty-six rounds. Thirtynine rounds were recovered from the officer's weapon and magazines. Seven shell casings were located on the ground west of the suspect's vehicle. The shell casings were located between five feet and thirty feet from the suspect's driver's door, in grass and on an asphalt roadway (Figure 1).

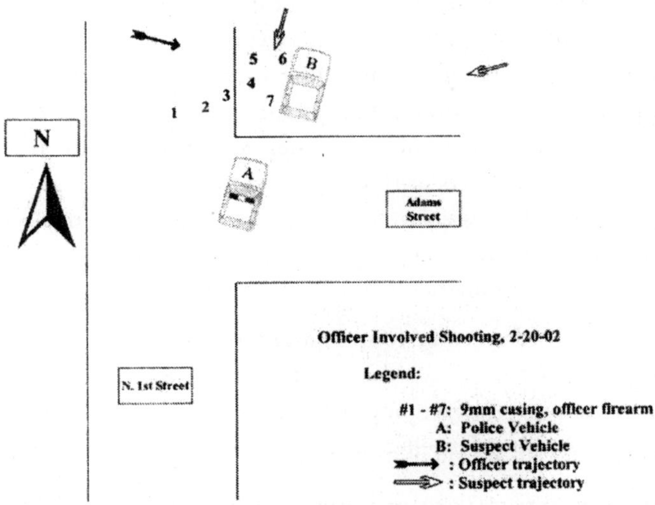

At trial, the defense argued that the officer was lying about the incident because he had stated that he had fired only four times. The defense theorized that because of the location of the shell casings near the suspect's car, the officer had fired the first shots and had done so as he contacted the driver. A defense witness with 25 years of police experience was asked whether he could determine the exact location of the parties at the time of the shooting, given the location from which the shell casings were recovered. The witness answered, "Yes, within a few feet of their location." He was also asked whether he knew the reason the numbers did not add up on the bullet count. To this he simply answered, "No." The defense attorney alluded to a "police cover-up" of the shooting events "because things just didn't add up".

In rebuttal, the supervising crime scene investigator (S.C.S.I.) took the stand and testified that the location of shell casings could give only a suggestion as to the general area of the shooter and that there are many variables that could account for the movement of the shell casings.

The S.C.S.I. listed variables such as surface type; weather conditions; pedestrian and vehicular traffic in the area, including the arrival of additional officers and medical personnel prior to securing the scene; the condition of the weapons; types of firearms ammunition; differences in shooting experience and training; the movement of the shooter at the time that the shots were fired; and other alterations (intentional or unintentional) concerning the crime scene. The S.C.S.I. also testified that, because of the high level of stress that the officer was most likely experiencing during this shooting confrontation, he may simply have not counted his shots correctly while trying to simultaneously take cover and return fire.

The defendant was found guilty on all charges. This trial experience gave the S.C.S.I. the idea for this research project, as well as an opportunity to give newer C.S.I.s some hands-on training in the interpretation of shell casing evidence at shooting scenes.

ANALYSIS OF BULLET WIPE PATTERNS ON CLOTH TARGETS

Abstract: This study was conducted to determine the reliability of bullet wipe patterns on cloth targets for use by the investigator in analyzing and reconstructing the events in a crime scene investigation. The study included variables such as ammunition, distance to target, and angle of impact.

The study examined the coloration and measurements of the bullet wipes and the effect of the variables tested. Although bullet wipe patterns can assist in reconstructing the events, the investigator should exercise caution when interpreting bullet wipe patterns.

Introduction

This study was conducted to evaluate the usefulness of bullet wipe patterns in investigations. Bullet wipe is a gray or black ring around the circumference of an entrance bullet hole. It consists of bullet lubricant, by-products of propellant, traces of metal from the bullet, and any residue in the barrel from previous use. Bullet wipe is present on lead and full metaljacketed bullets. Figure 1 illustrates bullet wipe around the margin of an entrance bullet hole. When a weapon is fired from a distance of greater than three feet, there usually will not be any visible gunshot residue on the target's surface. However, a dark ring around the hole is characteristic of a bullet entrance hole. Bullet lubricant and propellant by-products are wiped off around the margin of the hole as the bullet passes through the target.

Figure 1: Uniform bullet wipe around the margin of an entrance bullet hole. Shot was fired from 3.04 m (10 ft) at 90 degrees angle of incidence.

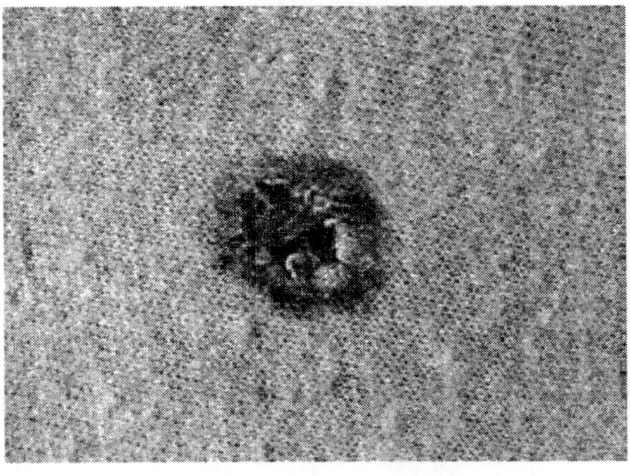

The sodium rhodizonate test can be used to test the dark gray ring around the hole's margin for the presence of lead. Even though bullet wipe may be left on materials such as doors, walls, and other solids that the bullet passes through, this study deals only with bullets passing through cloth targets. Bullet wipe patterns can be useful as investigative aids because investigators attempt to reconstruct the sequence of events at a crime scene to identify types of physical evidence that may be present. Also, physical evidence can be used to corroborate or expose deception in statements from suspects or witnesses.

Methods

Square cardboard targets approximately 12.38 cm by 12.38 cm (12 x 12 in.) in size and .64 cm (1/4 in.) thick were prepared and covered with 100% white cotton fabric. The fabric was wrapped around the cardboard target, stapled in place, but was not stretched.

A Smith & Wesson, model 686, revolver with a four-inch barrel was used to conduct the test. Because a clean weapon might yield inconsistent results for bullet wipe patterns for the first shots, ten shots were fired from the revolver before testing targets to maximize propellant by-products in the weapon's cylinder and barrel.

Figure 2: Light bullet wipe color at 9.14 m (30 ft) at 90 degrees.

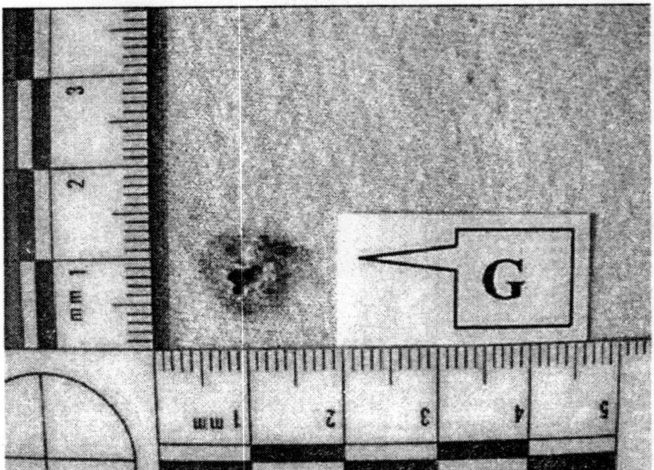

The first set of tests was conducted to determine whether bullet wipe coloration on the fabric varies with target distance. A single shot was fired at six distances to determine whether there were any observable differences in bullet wipe coloration. The ammunition used was Winchester .38 Special with a 150-grain lead round nose bullet (RNB). Six distances were tested at 90 degrees to target. They were 1.52 m (5 ft), 3.04 m (10 ft), 4.57 m (15 ft), 6.09 m (20 ft), 7.62 m (25 ft), and 9.14 m (30 ft). Two additional test shots were taken at 9.14 m (30 ft) to determine whether the bullet wipe coloration remained similar. An evaluation of the bullet wipe coloration indicated that the bullet wipe from shots fired from 1.52 m (5 ft) to 6.09 m (20 ft) is darker in color than the bullet wipe coloration from shots fired from farther distances. However, some of the shots that were repeated at 9.14 m (30 ft) did not consistently produce the same color bullet wipe on the cloth. See Table 1 for a summary of bullet color evaluation. See Figures 2 and 3 for examples of bullet wipe color at the same distance. The temperature of the barrel was not measured but there was a delay of several minutes between each test shot to observe and record the results.

Figure 3: Dark bullet wipe color at 9.14 m (30 ft) at 90 degrees.

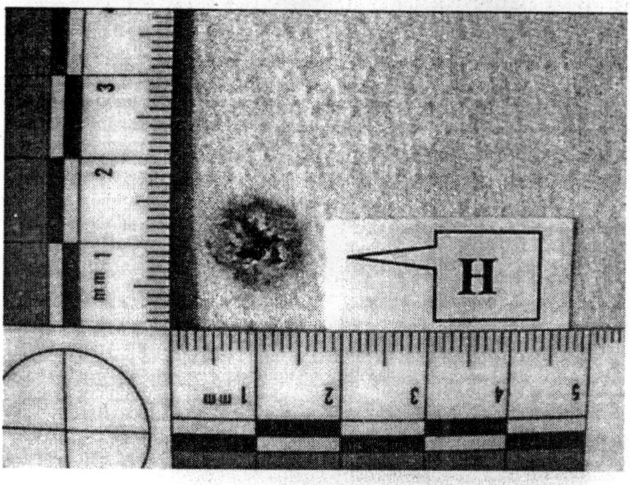

The second set of tests was conducted to determine whether bullet wipe measurements on the fabric varies at different distances to the target. The ammunition for this test was Winchester .38 Special with a 150-grain lead RNB. Six distances were tested at 90 degrees to target. They were 1.52 m (5 ft), 3.04 m (10 ft), 4.57 m

(15 ft), 6.09 m (20 ft), 7.62 m (25 ft), and 9.14 m (30 ft). A single shot was fired at each distance and two additional test shots were taken at 9.14 m (30 ft) to determine whether bullet wipe measurements remained consistent at this distance. The bullet wipe measurements ranged from 10 mm by 10 mm to 12 mm by 13 mm. See Table 2 for a summary of bullet wipe measurements.

Figure 4: Examples of bullet types and bullet wipe patterns. First cartridge in back row on left is the 3-D remanufactured .38 Special with 125-grain SWC. Second is the Winchester .38 Special with 158- grain LRN. Third is the PMC .357 Magnum with 158-grain JSP. In front is the Remington .38 Special with 125-grain SJHP.

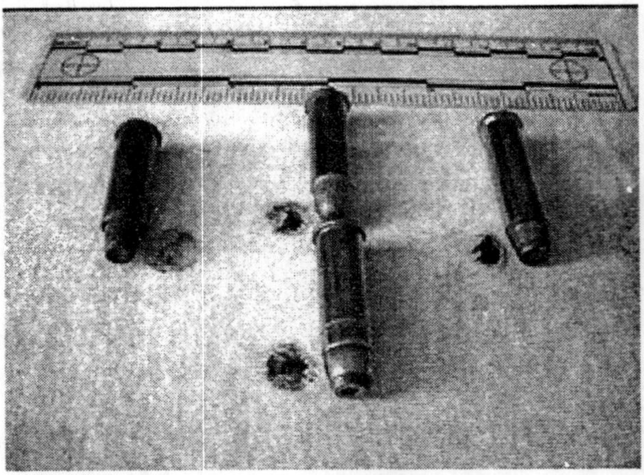

The third set of tests was conducted to determine whether bullet wipe measurements on the fabric varies with four types of ammunition at a specific distance. A distance of 3.04 m (10 ft) was used at 90 degrees to the target to test the ammunition. The ammunition tested included 3-D remanufactured .38 Special with 125-grain semi-wad cutter (SWC), Winchester .38 Special with 158-grain LRN, Precision Made Cartridges (PMC) .357 Magnum with 158-grain jacketed soft point (JSP), and Remington .38 Special with 125-grain semijacketed hollow point (SJHP). Figure 4 illustrates the bullet wipe impressions from four different bullet types. The 3-D remanufactured .38 Special with 125-grain SWC measured 12 mm x 12 mm. The Winchester .38 Special with 158-grain LRN measured 10 mm x 10 mm. The PMC .357 Magnum with 158-grain JSP measured 8 mm x 10 mm. The Remington .38 Special with 125-grain SJHP measured 10 mm x 11 mm.

The fourth set of tests was conducted to determine whether bullet wipe measurements on the fabric varies with different muzzle to target angles. The tests were conducted at a distance of 3.04 m (10 ft) using Winchester .38 Special ammunition with a 150-grain lead RNB. Five rounds were fired into cloth targets positioned at 90, 85, 80, 75, 70, 65, 60, 55, 50, 45, and 40 degrees to the bullets' paths. Tables 3 and 4 list the average measurements of the bullet wipe patterns. The width of the bullet wipe ranged from 7 mm to 11 mm and the length from 10 mm to 14 mm. Figure 5 illustrates elongated bullet wipe patterns at a 40 degree angle of incidence at 3.04 m (10 ft).

Figure 5: Bullet wipe patterns 40 degree angle of incidence at 3.04 m (10 ft).

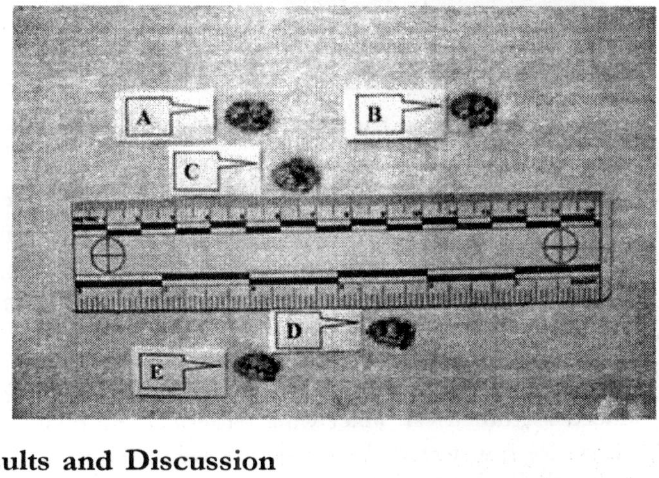

Results and Discussion

Bullet wipe does not always leave a uniform deposit around the margin of the entrance hole when fired at 90 degrees to the target. Figure 6 illustrates asymmetrical bullet wipe patterns fired at 90 degrees to the target. Therefore, investigators should not assume that the angle of the weapon to the target is greater than or less than 90 degrees based on symmetry. A possible cause for asymmetrical bullet wipe patterns on fabric for bullets fired at 90 degrees could be because the bullet exerted force on the fabric and the fabric gave way at the weakest fibers.

Figure 6: Asymmetrical bullet wipe pattern color shown in shots A, D, and E at 3.04 m (10 feet) at 90 degrees to the target.

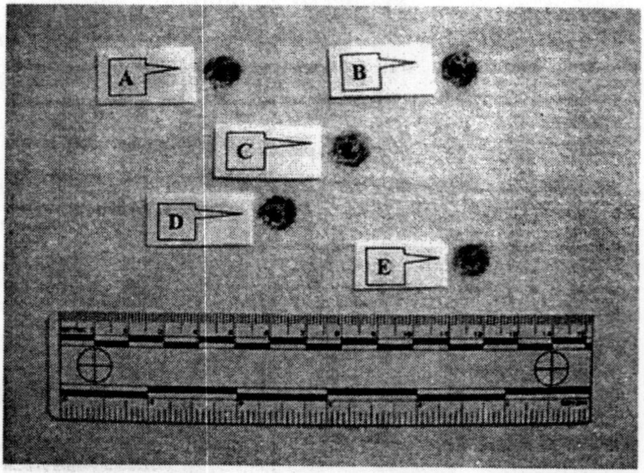

The color of bullet wipe for lead round nose bullets varied with each shot. A possible cause for variations in bullet wipe color could be because of different levels of oxidation on lead bullets or the friction between the fabric and surface of the bullet as it contacted and exited the fabric. Bullet wipe from jacketed bullets was lighter in color around the margin of the entrance hole compared to the color of bullet wipe from nonjacketed lead bullets.

The amount of tension for the fabric on the cardboard forms also produced asymmetrical bullet wipe patterns. The bullet wipe measurements for nonstretched cloth targets were 10 mm x 10 mm and, when stretched tightly over cardboard forms, they were 11 mm x 12 mm. Therefore, the investigator should consider whether the fabric was stretched tightly or loosely when examining a bullet wipe pattern. An asymmetrical pattern may indicate stretched fabric instead of an increased angle of muzzle to target.

Using lead round nose bullets at a distance of 3.04 m (10 ft) for 90, 85, 80, and 75 degrees, the bullet entrance hole averaged 11 mm x 11 mm. At 70, 65, and 60 degrees, the bullet entrance hole averaged 10 mm x 11 mm and was elongated by 1 mm. At 55 degrees, the bullet entrance hole averaged 9 mm x 16 mm and was elongated by 7 mm. At 50 degrees, the bullet entrance hole averaged 9 mm x 14 mm and was elongated by 5 mm. At 45 degrees, the bullet entrance hole averaged 7 mm x 13 mm and was elongated by 6 mm. At 40 degrees, the bullet entrance hole averaged 9 mm x 14 mm and was elongated by 5 mm. The findings indicate that there is a general tendency for the bullet wipe pattern to be elongated; however, specific bullet or target angles cannot be accurately determined on the basis of the elongation of the bullet wipe pattern. In the experiment, the first observable elongation in the bullet wipe pattern occurs at 70 degrees and is elongated by 2 mm. The elongated bullet wipe pattern is not directly proportional to the angle of incidence. As noted in Tables 3 and 4, some increased angles of incidence produce lesser degree of elongation.

Figure 7: Tapered end of bullet wipe pattern indicates angle of incidence.

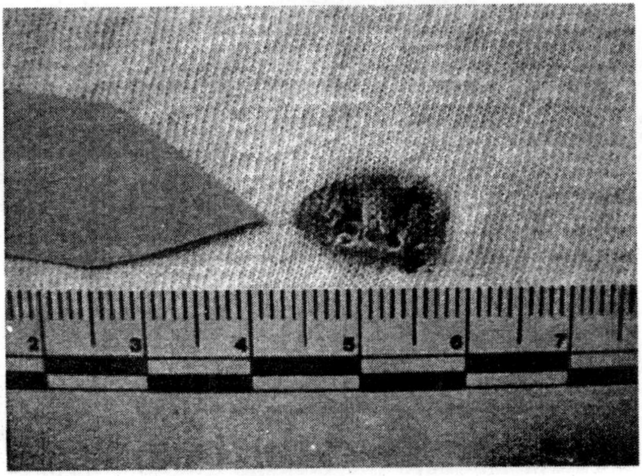

The tapered end of the elongated pattern indicates the angle of incidence of the weapon's muzzle to the target. (Figure 7 illustrates the tapered bullet wipe pattern.) This may be due to the bullet contacting the fabric at an angle and stretching it until the fibers give way. A darker colored bullet wipe was also observed on the opposite side of the angle of incidence at 60, 65, 50, 45, and 40 degrees. Figure 8 illustrates a darker colored bullet wipe pattern on the opposite side of the angle of incidence. This may result from the square area of the bullet's surface contacting the fabric. Another observation is that the fabric around the circumference of all the bullet holes was turned inward into the cardboard target. This feature is consistent with the direction of travel for the bullets.

Figure 8: Dark colored bullet wipe pattern on opposite side of angle of incidence.

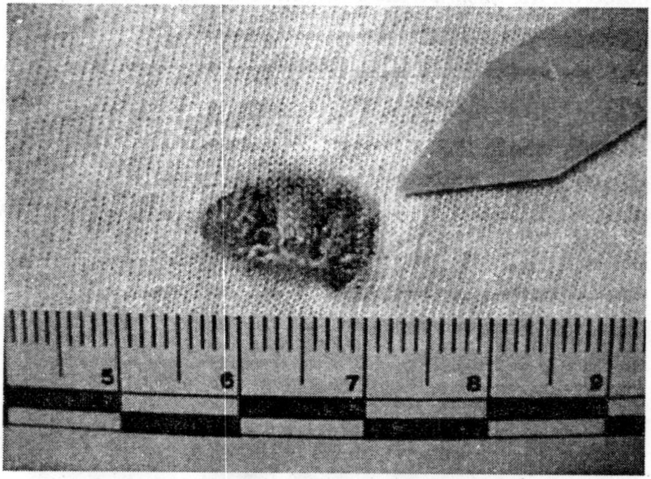

MULTIPLE EXPOSURE METHOD IN DIGITAL Photography of Fingerprints

Abstract: Forensic latent fingerprint photography, performed with evidence that has a substrate that is not uniform in terms of shape, color, and so forth, requires the use of various techniques. This report will introduce the multiple exposure method using digital photography and computerized image processing using layers methodology.

Background

Latent fingerprint (latent) photography normally requires the use of various lighting techniques to overcome the problems encountered with some surfaces upon which latents are discovered. Sometimes it is difficult (or impossible) to capture, in a single exposure, all of the detail using a single lighting technique. This problem is frequently encountered on curved surfaces because multiple light angles cannot provide the optimum simultaneous illumination to all portions of the print. Problems may also be encountered when multiple excitation wavelengths or different filters are needed to provide proper exposure for different areas in the same latent.

In conventional forensic photography, there are various solutions to the problems mentioned above. For example, when a light source does not cover the total area of the latent, the painting with light technique can be used. Another technique that is used in such cases is superimposition (i.e., double exposure of two images, one on top of the other, exposed on the same film frame). This technique is complex and is not frequently used in forensic photography. On the other hand, the digital multiple exposure technique is simple and productive because the merging of multiple images is more easily controlled in the computer. To the best of our knowledge, this digital method is a new application of an old technique and has not been previously reported.

Introduction of the Method

The main advantage of multiple images combined into one image is that this allows improved visualization of selected portions of a latent without affecting the rest of the image. The layers are similar to transparency pages that can be superimposed or placed one on top of the other. When there is an image on an upper layer, it is possible to see the lower layer through the use of a layer mask.

The multiple exposure technique is the superimposition of two or more separate photographs of the same latent, taken with a digital camera, while the physical position of the camera and the subject (the latent) are absolutely steady. Because several parameters may vary, the entire process must be fully documented. The parameters that may be changed between the different photographs include the light source angle, the light source, the wavelength of illumination, and the exposure. Ideal parameters vary according to the topography of the surface area, the nature of the surface, or the location of the latent within that area. Because the photographs are taken with a digital camera, it is very important to keep the file format (the RAW format should be used when available) and size constant. The reason for this is that a change in file size may prevent the precise alignment between the photographs when they are superimposed on separate layers. After the photographs are taken and a separate original file is retained for each photograph, a composite Photoshop Document (PSD) is created with the Adobe Photoshop software; this file format will allow a separate layer for each image. (Other image processing programs may have similar functions and capabilities.) When creating the composite file, it is important to understand that the alignment of the different layers is critical.

The next stage is to create masks for each layer. The masks for each layer can be created to either hide the selected area or to reveal only the selected area. The image areas can be selected with any of the conventional tools (e.g., the Marquee, Lasso, Magic Wand, or Paintbrush). On each layer, the layer must be masked to allow the latent area that was optimally captured in the image to be displayed, hiding the other areas that were captured but shown on different layers. In cases where the information in a certain area within two or more layers is complementary, there is an option to specify the top layer mask as a percentage (e.g., 50%), so the result will include as much information from each layer as possible. Often the final results can be improved by changing the order of the layers, thus creating an improved blending of the composite image. Other options allow for the merging of layers, the addition of adjustment layers, and the use of layer styles. The last phase of the process includes achieving uniformity in all of the layers by adjusting colors, brightness, and contrast; merging all the layers; and converting the final file to grayscale. The result is an image of the latent that is a computerized merge of the best portion of each image taken in order to display the maximum information available within the original latent fingerprint.

0-DIFFERENT EXPOSURES AND PHOTO SUPERIMPOSITION TECHNIQUE

This technique is recommended in cases where the object includes strong differences in the brightness levels of various areas within the latent, and the exposure differences are three aperture stops or more. Usually this phenomenon occurs when the latent appears partially upon a dark area and partially upon a light area. The quality of detail in the dark areas should be checked before using this technique.

Case Study

In this example, a latent print was developed on a beer can in a murder investigation, using basic yellow 40 (Figure 9). The latent fingerprint was located on top of the can, on a background that was part dark and part light, so the difference between the correct exposures was 3 to 4 aperture stops.

Figure 9: Beer can evidence.

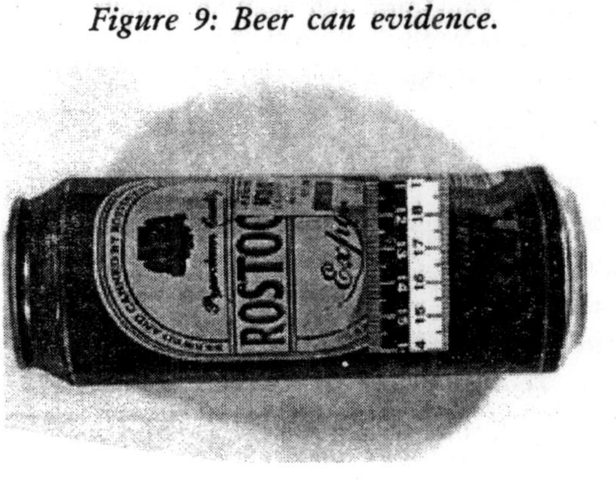

In the classic method, we used a conventional camera, centerweighed light meter, Plus-X 125 ASA black and white film, f/11-16 aperture using the shutter aperture priority, 450 nm wavelength Polilight illumination (which gives fluorescence), and an orange filter. The result was insufficient because of the difference in f luorescence that leads to the absence of information in the dark surface area (Figure 10).

Figure 10: Fingerprint luminescence at normal exposure.

To solve this problem, we took two photographs using a Fujifilm S1 digital camera and Micro-Nikkor AF lens. The two exposures were taken while the position of the camera and the position of the beer can were not changed. The first photograph was taken with the correct exposure (according to the fluorescence of the bright area of the can surface), and the second photograph was overexposed by 3 stops to record the detail in the dark area.

Using Photoshop, we opened a PSD file. The first photograph (normal exposure) was defined as the background layer and the second photograph, which recorded the detail in the dark area, was pasted on top of the background as a second layer. Working on the background layer, the letters on the beer can were selected using the Magic Wand tool. (The dark uniform coloration of the letters made them easy to select with this tool.) After a selected area is defined, the selection borders appear on any active and visible layer and can be used on the second layer. (As explained above, this layer contained the latent information on top of the dark letters because this photograph was overexposed). To get rid of the unusable information on the second layer, we used the Add Layer Mask and Reveal Selection commands and hid the overexposed portion of that image (the areas other than the selected letters). By using the Levels command, the two layers were brought to the same level of brightness and contrast. At this stage, the two layers were ready for merging into one layer, containing the full information of the latent fingerprint (Figure 11).

Figure 11: Composite of two different exposures.

Merging Photographs that were taken from Different Light Source Angles

This technique is recommended in cases where the latent fingerprint appears on top of objects that do not have a uniform surface topography (e.g., a convex or concave surface). If the surface is shiny, then the reflection problem can be corrected by controlling the angle of a single light. On this kind of surface, it is usually impossible to see the complete latent at the same time, and the light source must be adjusted in order to emphasize different areas of the print. Sometimes a different light source angle is not sufficient and different light sources must be used. The same technique procedures would apply.

Case Study

This example is from a terrorist attack investigation. Prior to fingerprint processing, a visible fingerprint was located on the aluminum clip on a cellular phone holster. Because the print was located inside the concave portion of the clip (Figure 12), it was impossible to see the whole of it from a single angle, and only parts of the information could be made visible by changing the angle of illumination.

Figure 12: Position of fingerprint on cellular phone holster.

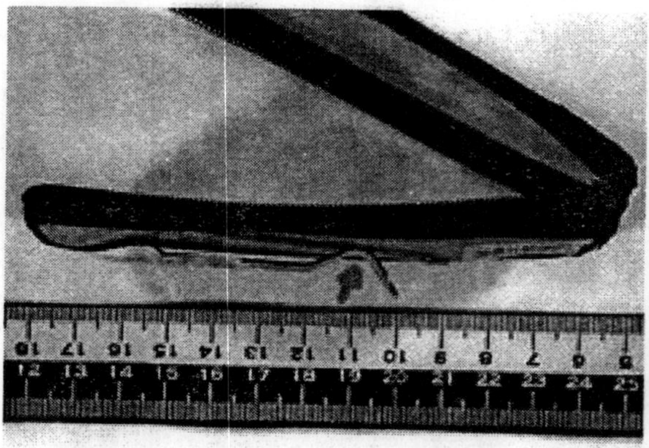

In addition to this difficulty, and to avoid any risk that the print could be damaged and lost during the chemical development process, it was photographed prior to any processing techniques. All photographs were taken while the location of the camera and the subject remained unchanged, and only the angle of the light source was adjusted. We used a Fujifilm S1 Pro, Micro Nikkor AF 60 mm lens (aperture f/16), and concentrated white light (using a Polilight device). The resulting photographs provided views of the two different parts of the latent fingerprint on the clip (Figures 13 and 14). The purpose of the computerized processing was to merge the two parts of the latent into one complete latent fingerprint with no distortions.

Figure 14 was selected as the background layer and Figure 5 as the top layer. A mask was created for the top layer using the commands Add Layer Mask and Hide All. After creating the hidden mask, we selected a brush with the needed characteristics of size and softness. It was necessary to choose white as the front color, in order to use the brush efficiently to "scratch" the opaque layer, which exposes the information from the hidden layer underneath. (By selecting the front color as black, the mask can be repainted to restore the masking effect.)

Figure 13: First part of fingerprint.

These steps require a lot of care; therefore, it is recommended to work with a small diameter brush. Because the two parts of the latent were overlapping (Figures 13 and 14), we achieved a smooth joining of the fingerprint ridges. The Levels command was used to reach the same levels of brightness and contrast in the two layers. The process was completed by merging the two layers and saving the final result as a flattened file (Figure 15).

Conclusion

Implementing the multiple exposure techniques in digital photography and using image processing, as described in this paper, provides a lot of opportunities to produce better photographs of latent fingerprints. We strongly recommend using this technique when taking photographs of latent fingerprints on ref lecting surfaces (e.g., metals or glass) or fluorescent surfaces, especially when the use of one light source or light source angle is not sufficient for obtaining all the details from the latent.

Figure 14: Position of fingerprint on cellular phone holster.

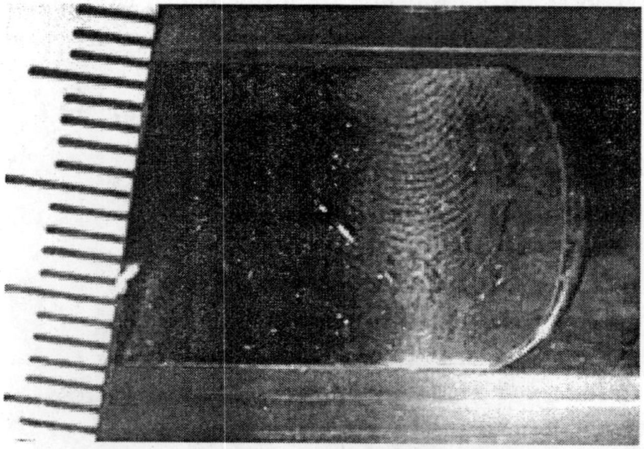

Figure 15: Composite of two light source angles.

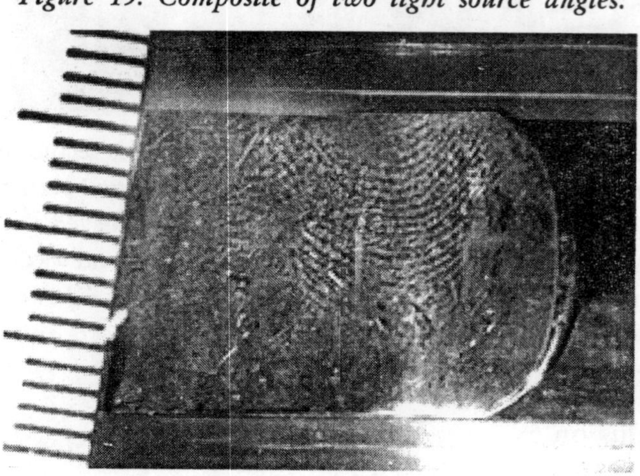

Great care should be observed in maintaining the chain of evidence. For every job, we recommend the use of a separate source folder that should contain the original untouched photographs. All digital photographs should be processed using copies of the original photographs, preferably in a separate folder named "image processing". The final processed image should be inspected and compared to the source images to ensure that no artifacts were introduced. The person doing the processing should be able to show in court the origin of every part of a composite image and explain the techniques involved.

REMAINS TO BE SEEN!

Abstract: Unidentified human remains present a multitude of difficulties to investigators. Positive identification is often chief among these. When law enforcement personnel and the Medical Examiner - Coroner have exhausted traditional means, such as fingerprints or dental comparisons, a forensic artist may be called upon to render a likeness from skeletal, badly decomposed, or disfigured remains. Usually, the forensic artist has not been to the scene or autopsy and must rely solely on photographs, physical evidence, and information provided by other personnel. Often, a significant amount of time elapses between the initial investigation and the decision to use a forensic artist. How successful the finished likeness is depends on the condition of the remains and the quality of physical evidence or photographs provided to the artist.

Introduction

In any death investigation, particularly homicide, the timely identification of the decedent is crucial to a successful conclusion of the case. In most instances, an identification is made through the conventional means of fingerprint, dental, or DNA comparisons. When an identification does not occur, a forensic artist may be called upon to produce a likeness that is suitable for a media release to the public. Any leads thus generated may then be compared to the deceased by using the conventional means.

A significant amount of time can elapse between when a body is discovered and when an artist is called in. How exact the likeness is can depend on the materials provided to the artist. Crime scene investigators should always remember that the deceased may not be readily identified and that the quality of the investigator's photographs and collected evidence will become very important. Particularly in cases of near or complete skeletonization, developing a mind-set to find evidence is crucial, and evidence that is found can be invaluable to a forensic artist. In cases where a body has been found after a lengthy period of time, hairs and clothing fibers of the decendant can often be found in birds' nests adjacent to the site. Even one hair can indicate the length and color. If the remains are scattered, an attempt should be made to find the "soak area" (i.e., where the body was initially located and the f luids from decomposition permeated the soil). Other areas to search for trace evidence would include windbreaks (i.e., areas where loose evidence may be blown by the wind, such as brush, vegetation, spider webs, or fence lines) and water breaks (i.e., areas where water tends to pool).

Some items can assist in determining the look and cultural lifestyle of the victim. Pieces of fabric and shiny objects, such as jewelry, buttons, or even eyeglasses, can be found in the middens of pack rats. Note: Care should be taken by anyone digging into a rodent area. Hantavirus, a potentially fatal disease, is spread through contact with rodent feces, urine, and saliva.

Methodology

Forensic facial images of deceased persons generally fall into two categories: postmortem renderings or full facial reconstructions. The deciding factor for which method the artist chooses to use is the amount of trauma or decomposition to the decedent's face. If the face is recognizable, but sufficient trauma or decomposition precludes posting the image to the public, a postmortem drawing or photographic enhancement can be used. If the remains are skeletal or badly decomposed, the preferred method is a full facial reconstruction upon the skull. In both postmortem and full reconstruction cases, specific photographs of the remaining eyes, nose, ears, facial or head hair, or anything unique about the decedent can be most valuable.

Of equal importance is the artist's close collaboration with the forensic anthropologist. In most cases, but particularly those involving bare skeletal remains, it falls to the expertise of the forensic anthropologist to be able to determine the race, sex, and age. In more subtle findings, such as the area of attachments to the bone, the experienced forensic anthropologist can offer insights into the victim's stature and, possibly, lifestyle. In cases of severe decomposition, it is necessary for the forensic anthropologist to clean the skull of all tissue prior to the reconstruction. If the artist has not been to the scene or has not seen the remains prior to the cleaning, it is important to consult with the forensic anthropologist to gather impressions, notes, photographs, and perhaps skull x-rays.

Postmortem Renderings

The artist completing a postmortem rendering has two options. One is a likeness completed in graphite or another art material of the artist's choosing. The second is an enhancement of the actual photograph, using a computer photo software program. In either case, the artist will be working directly from a photograph of the face; the better the photograph, the more likely the chance of a successful image. If possible, oblique lighting should be used to enhance the shadows of the facial features. Direct f lash will cause a washed-out effect. Because the artist will be working from a two-dimensional reference (the photograph), it is important that the photograph be taken without distortion. The lighting and lens angle should be similar to that used when one is photographing shoe or tire impressions (e.g., oblique lighting and perpendicular camera angles).

Figures 16 through 19 are simple line illustrations. All are drawings of the same face, but made from various angles. Figure 16 is drawn from the ideal angle. Taking photographs from odd angles, such as above or below the face, should be avoided (Figures 17 and 18). The best frame of reference to use is the Frankfurt horizontal plane (Figure 19) which is accomplished by imagining a horizontal line extending along a plane from the top of the exterior auditory meatus (i.e., bony ear opening) through the lower edge of the orbit of the eye. The camera lens should be perpendicular to the plane of that line. Ideally, there should be at least one quality frontal, lateral, and three-quarter shot of the face and head, enabling the forensic artist to choose the best photograph to use.

Figure 16: Photograph of the face taken from an ideal angle without distortion.

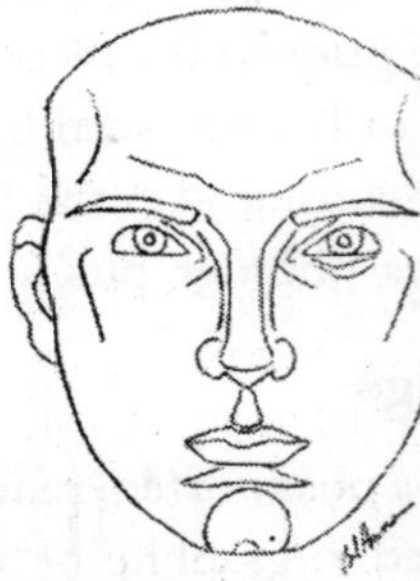

Figure 17: Photograph taken at an odd angle from above shows distortion to upper face.

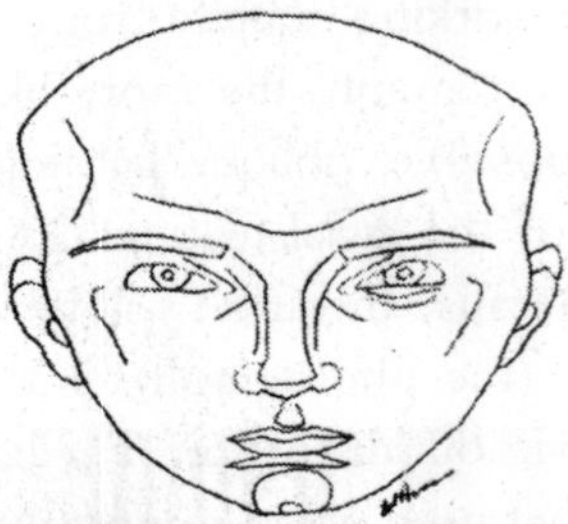

Figure 18: Photograph taken at an odd angle from below shows distortion to lower face.

Figure 19: Illustration of the Frankfort horizontal plane.

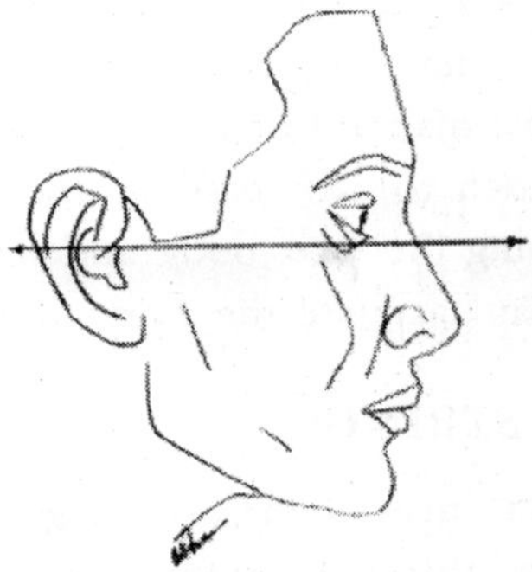

The "slack jaw" effect should be avoided. When the deceased is in a supine position, the mandible will often recline from its natural position, causing the false impression of a severe overbite. This can be avoid by having a medical examiner or assistant hold the jaw in its natural position prior to taking the photographs.

Full Facial Reconstruction

A full facial reconstruction is completed using the skull for reference.

The two-dimensional technique incorporates drawings done over life-size frontal and lateral photographs of the skull. In the three-dimensional technique, clay is applied directly on a cast of the skull or on the skull itself. In both techniques, although the skull is the basic reference, good photography and evidence collection at the scene and autopsy are important.

In cases with partial or extreme decomposition, photographs should be taken of the decedent's head and face as well as the area immediately surrounding the body prior to any movement of the body. Even in cases of extreme decomposition, facial proportions and details of unique features can often be seen by a practiced eye. Several photos taken with a scale of the areas of the face give a feeling of actual size. Specific photographs of any remaining features or anything unique should be taken.

Conclusion

In any death investigation, investigators, keeping in mind the fact that the individual may not be easily identified, should apply a commonsense approach to each case. A few extra minutes spent properly photographing the face, body, and scene and looking for any trace evidence can facilitate the work of the forensic artist.

COMPUTERS VS STRINGS

Case #1: A white male with a single gunshot wound to the head, back to front and through and through. Forward bloodspatter in the immediate area of the shooting with transfer and projected available in the area where the body was found. Manually stringing bloodstains within the pattern area was used in the courtroom to display the point of origin.

Case #2: A white female with a single gunshot wound in the mouth; front to back and through and through. This is an outdoor scene with multiple bloodstain patterns and multiple directions of impact spatter. The computer gave a more applicable view of multiple directions/multiple points of origin, within a small area where stringing the stains would have been difficult at best.

Introduction

In case number one, a white male was found shot in the back of the head, lower center area, with a .45 bullet exiting the top front center area of the forehead. The scene was in the bedroom of a residence with 90° bloodspatter being located on the bedroom dresser and items found on the dresser. The left second drawer of the dresser was partially pulled open with measurable bloodspatter located on a white cardboard photo frame.

After manually stringing the bloodstains on the cardboard photo frame, the point of origin (the head of the deceased) was found in such a position that the body was bent forward at the waist consistent with retrieving an item from the partially open drawer. The girlfriend of the complainant (deceased) stated that the complainant committed suicide inside the bedroom with the door closed. Positioning the complainant became a pivotal point in the case investigation displaying a position inconsistent with suicide.

On top of the dresser on the left side, directly above the partially open drawer, was a white shoe box and a multi colored popcorn box. The front facings of these boxes contained bloodspatter consistent with forward spatter in and near 90°. The white cardboard photo frame was the top layer of items within the drawer with measurable stains and with bloodspatter consistent with forward spatter. After removing the white cardboard photo frame from the drawer, a void line was present allowing the item to be place back in the drawer for reconstruction purposes.

The outside of the bedroom door, the side facing the hallway, contained projected bloodstain patterns, transfer bloodstains and these both showed movement left to right and downward (the door open and movement from the bedroom toward the hall) where the body was found in the hallway.

The limited amount of measurable stains on the white cardboard photo frame, made the use of the computer limited in program ability, therefore, stinging was the method to give a visual display for the point of origin.

During the trial, the bedroom furniture was brought into the courtroom where a recreation of the stringing was done in front of the jury. After positioning the complainant, the Medical Examiner and the Firearms Examiner reinforced the bloodstain pattern testimony that I had already given.

The jury found the defendant guilty of murder with a sentence of ten years in the Texas Penitentiary.

In case number two, the crime scene is located at an apartment complex with the scene located outside next to one of the apartment buildings. The complainant (deceased) was found on the ground with a single gunshot wound into the mouth and exiting the top rear area of the head. Located against the wall/doors next to the complainant were multiple bloodstains patterns, multiple directions/ multiple points of origin and multiple bloody types.

After evaluating the crime scene, an attempt to string the bloodstains was made. This immediately became difficult and was obvious too many directions and locations within a small area would make the visualization confusing.

The computer displayed several different points of origin, all within a relatively small area, where the strings appeared to be disorganized. Viewing the computer displays, bloodstains with the same points of origin were visible and easy to view.

The case was ultimately ruled a suicide by the Medical Examiner's Office, yet a serious event occurred at or near the time of the suicide.

Discussion

The crime scene investigator needs to keep his options open and be aware of the tools available. These two cases are examples where the availability of technology and the manual use of stringing was utilized and the right tool was used for the right circumstance.

13

Sex and Crime in the Media

Settle up and lean out. Make down your mind and peace in. C'mon baby, lay forward a bit and massage your inner thighs. Tell your conscience I said, "Don't worry. Everything is silky smooth like butter." Don't bother getting dressed; just sit over there, by the window, and bask in whispered desires. Forget everything and remember this little something: *sex sells*. And *sex* is everywhere—on advertising billboards at every stoplight, in magazines devoted to every perversion, throughout films targeting every demographic from infancy to adulthood.

As with any other external stimuli, it may be reasoned that overtly sexualized mass media is having some effect on American culture and society. But just what exactly might that effect be, and is it positive or negative? Unfortunate as it may be, research shows that people's preconceived notions of self-image and conduct are being grossly distorted by unrealistic sexual imagery and suggestion in mass media. Likewise, there is an overwhelming amount of evidence to argue that the majority of overtly sexualized imagery used in mass media is unethical, particularly with reference to its use in targeting our nation's most impressionable market: the adolescent to young adult demographic.

With merely the tiniest of public outcries, sexuality in advertising and the media has become a centerpiece of American culture and for good reason. Selling everything from brand-name clothing to bars of soap to vacuum cleaners to activism against animal cruelty, human sexuality may be likened to the Holy Grail in peaking consumer interests. Those who might associate sex with the color red, commonly associated with love, are dead wrong—sex is greener than any pasture, lining the pockets of business executives like black coal compressed into a diamond. Continuing along this line of reasoning, it almost seems ideal that most sexuality used in mass media should be targeted at our nation's youth; they are just beginning to discover their bodies and sexuality while simultaneously riding an emotional rollercoaster caused by pubescent hormonal chaos. However, this latter notion is exactly what makes them so susceptible to mass media depictions of gender roles, sexuality, and appearance.

Additionally, data collected in 1999 show that young people spend on average of 6-7 hours a day with varying forms of mass media (Brown, Mass Media Influences on Sexuality pp. 42). During this stage, the most prevalent concern of adolescent youths is one of self-definition and role experimentation, which often results in the emulation of desirable external depictions of happy, intelligent, and successful young adults who, of course, are sexually mature and satisfied (Steele, Teenage Sexuality and Media Practice pp. 335). But as sexuality becomes an increasingly dominant influence on the psyche of a developing youth culture, it is of the utmost importance that we step back and take an objective look at sex in the media and the dire consequences it may pose to the future of our American society and culture.

In order to best understand contemporary fascinations with sex in the media, we must first identify its origins. In 1924 the American Association of Advertising Agencies established a code of ethics, which outlined the standards that were necessary to uphold in advertising media. This included code maintaining comparative truth in product expectations and admonishing the use of statements, suggestions, or imagery offensive to public decency (AAAA.org). Nevertheless, the vaguely defined standards of the AAAA code and ambiguous circumstances surrounding its conception provided advertisers with just the right amount of leniency to all but disregard its existence (Rodman, Making Sense of Media pp. 309). After all, very rarely does ethical conduct positively correlate with increased revenue. Predominant gender roles extending to farther back than the study of communication itself provided the foundations necessary to create a cookie-cutter recipe for the appearance of models that would be used by advertisers: woman were cast as ladylike submissives, clean, beautiful, and inviting and men were cast as authoritative smooth-talkers, intelligent, independent, and cool (Media Awareness Network).

Up until the 1940's, these gender roles that were imposed upon American society by advertisers remained relatively static with only slight variations due to coordinating media influences on trends in style and fashion. Then, following WWII and the subsequent return of American troops to their wives, the Baby Boomer generation was born. Middle-class families took up residence in an emerging suburban environment at the outskirts of major cities, where they could provide their children with a safe, relaxing atmosphere away from the hardships they endured growing up in the city, many as struggling immigrants, during the early 1900's.

The Baby Boomer generation would be the first to experience a new ideological reiteration of the American dream that developed with a heightened emphasis on leisurely activity, social networking, and public education. The *teenage years* became a critical stage of childhood development just around the same time as the 1954 Brown v. Board of Education U.S. Supreme Court ruling desegregated public schools, which inevitably would be a critical stimulus for changing American cultural notions of diversity and self-identity within the already confusing stages of adolescence (Advertising Age, *The Advertising Century Report*).

In the case of the Baby Boomers, these first-generation teenagers were experiencing an American culture unlike any other previous generation. The 50's gave way to perhaps the most pivotal year of the 20th century, 1968, during which time preconceived notions of human sexuality and its societal acceptance became popularized by a youth culture fueled by sex, drugs, and rock and roll. Unfazed by the aggressive rebelliousness of this emerging demographic, the advertising industry acclimated and indeed took advantage of their internal desires. Using techniques far inferior to those used today, advertisers began to manipulate and "enhance" the appearance of models to make noticeable changes in their natural body structures that emphasized perfection over attractiveness—beings that are more human than human (Shenk, *Every Picture Can Tell a Lie*).

This radical shift in sexual imagery and suggestion reciprocated the disturbance caused by such a drastic cultural shift occurring as many young adult Baby Boomers started attending large public universities such as U.C. Berkley, where an increasingly sexually charged atmosphere inspired student activism and experimentation in the early 70's (Brokaw, *Boom!*). Soon enough, the strategy of exploiting sex in advertising was spreading to other forms of mass media, including modern technologies that were just beginning their infancy, such as the Internet and cable television. And so was birthed modernly dominance of sex in the media.

Still the question remains of how American youth culture has been affected by this contemporary environment supersaturated by sexuality—in which the primary interests of an entire generation have been monopolized by a mass media peddling tabloid journalism focused solely on promiscuous celebrity role models, pornographically inspired popular music, television dramas, and movies driven by sexual desire, countless *teenage* magazines saturated with sexual improvement tips and beautification, and online social networking websites that seemingly approve of pre-teen casual sex and dating. Sometimes it takes a quiet moment of self-reflection in order to rationally fathom the implications of entire decades o individuals, nursed from infancy by false impressions of human sexuality, who must someday take ownership of and be responsible for the future of our country, never mind entire world civilizations harrowed by one endemic after another, never mind the continued survival and inevitable expansion of the human species in forthcoming millennia. Juxtaposing these issues within the context of objectivity, with nothing but the highest respect for the philosophical prowess of Ayn Rand, sex simply seems so selfish, so secondary, so silver-spoon. And yet it is because of the convergence of these circumstances and the media's virulent use of sexploitation that it is critically necessary to identify the present-day sociology of its causes and effects.

Robin Gerber, multiple author, motivational speaker, and advocate of the Elephant Man Foundation's Inner Beauty Campaign famously remarked during one of her workshops, "We don't need Afghan-style burquas to disappear as women. We disappear in reverse-by revamping and revealing our bodies to meet externally imposed visions of female beauty." While Gerber's maturity and intelligence allow her to insightfully reflect upon the concept of beauty, many female adolescents continually bombarded by unrealistic media depictions of appearance are left without such perspective, considerably more so if they live in impoverished or abusive family environments (Steele, pp. 339). Using a rigorous method for analyzing the media's effect on self-image, The Adolescents' Media Practice Model, a psychological profile can be attained from normative interaction with everyday media imagery. The data received from testing a representative sample of black females between the ages of 13-16 living in an inner city, high-crime neighborhood provides a significant positive correlation between increased media exposure, decreased sense of beauty, and increased sexual promiscuity starting at an early age (Steele, pp. 340).

But it is not only those adolescents living in harsh environments who are affected by sexually explicit imagery in the media. One such study published in the Journal of Advertising asked the question of how popular magazines might affect the perceptions of teenage girls living in middle to upper income households. Utilizing Chi-Square analysis to interpret the frequency of appearance between various types of beauty represented by models in sexually oriented magazines such as Cosmo, Glamour, Seventeen, and Vogue, all of which are well-known by industry professionals for their use digitally manipulated images of models (Schewe, *Digital Ethics*). Those types of beauty defined by the researchers were divided into six categories: exotic, cute, girl-next-door, trendy, sex kitten, and classic, of which the most frequently depicted were exotic, trendy, and classic. After contacting monthly teenage subscribers who confirmed their consistent readership, it was not surprising that most of those interviewed also displayed the same preference for these styles of appearance, clothing, and accessories. Furthermore, an overwhelming majority admitted to having previously battled eating disorders, addiction to weight loss supplements, having a below average self-esteem, and asking their parents for plastic surgery in order to attain such standards of beauty (Englis, Solomon, and Ashmore, *Beauty Before the Eyes of the Beholder*).

Another study confirming the adverse effects of unrealistic appearances imposed by beauty magazines was accidentally performed by Vogue itself. In an attempt to identify the average demographic of its readers, editors were astonished to discover the results its survey, which found that 20 percent of Vogue readers wore a size 16 or larger and 49 percent wore at least a size 12 (Barthel, *Putting on Appearances* pp. 232). These results outline the disparity between media images and the average adolescent who is subjected to the implicit message that *this* is ideal beauty. Similarly, a social dichotomy is created between those who are naturally born with these body proportions and those who are not.

Perceptions of self-image that are attained from mass media imagery essentially falsifies the notion of an average appearance that is not average and an above average appearance that can only be achieved through the use of concealment products marketed by advertisers in these magazines—clothes, make up, skin treatments, dieting supplements, and cosmetic surgery. Sadly, these magazines and their editors seem to promote a lifetime of shame, self-consciousness, and embarrassment amongst those adolescents born with any sort of alternate proportions that may differ from their hegemony on appearances.

If the majority of female adolescents are so adversely affected by the media's imposed standards of beauty, it would be logical that adolescent males would experience many similar pressures, albeit with less potency due to less time spent interacting with media and more time spent engaging in the external world. However, extensive research concludes that not only do the majority of males have identical concerns to that of females regarding their appearance, but there is a increasingly heightened sense of stress from mass media emphasis of masculine gender roles. In one study, a representative sample of adolescent males in various age groups ranging from 6-19 years old were surveyed regarding media preferences and idealistic male role models. The majority of males showed a significantly greater viewer favorability of athletic sporting events as well as the images of contemporary, muscularly built role models such as Arnold Schwarzenegger, who was chosen as a more motivational role model than great historical icons such as Abraham Lincoln, Alfred Einstein, William Shakespeare, and Bill Gates (Hirsch and Thompson, *Why Media Matter* pp. 48).

In such a case where adolescent males are being convinced that a trained, muscular build is more desirable than being gifted with a genius intellect or extraordinary artistic ability, researchers believe that there is a very pertinent suspension of disbelief at work. Similar to unrealistic depictions of womanly beauty, media imagery of men with superior physiques provide an example for which they rationalize as ideal if they are to be sexually appealing to the opposite gender. This environment is particularly dangerous to the male psyche, as the desirability of visible strength implicitly promotes the use of that strength, such that oftentimes it may result in the acceptance of violent behavior as an essential aspect of masculine gender roles.

David Winter, esteemed political psychologist, examines the military as a predominantly youthful masculine environment fueled by overtly murderous tendencies due to sexual frustration, quoting several military soldiers as commenting, "[Killing is] like getting screwed for the first time," "...it's like the best dope you ever had, the best sex you've ever had," "Weeks of bottled-up tensions...released in a few minutes of orgiastic violence;...an ache as profound as the ache of orgasm," "The highest status was given to "double veterans" (rape followed by murder)." (Winter, *Power, Sex, and Violence* pp. 392)

Such an environment of increasingly disappearing morality and inhibitions might also be contributed to mainstream journalistic media coverage of sexually related misconduct. Shocking as it may be, sex scandals involving sexual deviance amongst religious ascetics, celebrities, politicians—all the way up to Presidents of the United States—and other public figureheads have become even less of a shock due to the frequency of journalism coverage over the past few decades. Similarly, coverage of sexual harassment in the workplace has been a topic of newsworthy discussion ever since provisions of workforce equality were set forth by the Civil Rights Act of 1964.

The subsequent stigmatization of sexuality that results from predominant coverage of sexual deviance instead of sexuality as an aspect of human activity sends mixed messages about the morality of sex to a confused youth culture. Separate from journalistic stigmatization of sex is the American societal stigmatization of pornographic media, which is quite readily available to internet-savvy adolescents—for example, the word *sex* has been the most popular search query on the internet for the past decade (Brown, Mass Media Influences on Sexuality pp. 42). Coinciding with these messages of sexual lewdness are the advertising and film media in which the subtext teaches sex as a desirable activity. For the developing psyche of the adolescent mind, an overwhelming sense of cognitively dissonant messages creates a social ambiguity surrounding the overall morality of sex (Gamson, Sex Scandal Narratives as Institutional Morality Tales pp. 185-205).

Indeed, while it might be somewhat melodramatic to visualize only the gravest of consequences the amount of sexual imagery in mass media may have for the future of our nation's youth and future generations of youth culture, it is difficult to ignore the continuing trend of ever more risqué material being introduced without an overall sense of public dissent. But it is just as difficult not to put hindsight to good use and purvey the effects sexualized mass media has had during the 20th century. We can justify our fears as negligible in response to the powerful societal breakthroughs that overshadow such trivialities as a change in media imagery. Marvelous achievements in science, medicine, and technology have provided us with a quality of life unparalleled to any period in history. Likewise, the racial and gender equality movements have never seen a more prodigious presidential election than in 2008, and American democracy has never proven more adept at proving that we can endure tragedy and hope for a brighter tomorrow.

Nevertheless, discussing the implications of the ever-changing sexual atmosphere imposed by mass media is most important to the subjunctive understanding of whether or not we must take up an opposition against its habitual presentation of unrealistic appearances, sexual suggestion, and pre-conceived notions of gender conduct. Likewise, it must be duly noted without mention of slippery slope that public acceptance of sexual imagery is a barrier that over the course of the last century has constantly expanded in favor of American mass media usage. And it is most important that this issue be particularly emphasized within the context of *American* culture, as cultural attitudes in American are what set our media consumption apart from any other.

In many overseas nations, cultural perceptions of sexuality and individual self-image are an altogether different terrain, such that in Saudi Arabia a woman must have her entire face and body hidden from public view whereas Italy is known for having the largest population of habitual nudists and very few laws against public indecency (Nagel, *Ethnicity and Sexuality*). Therefore, it comes as no surprise that Italian advertisements can display bare-chested models to sell products that have little relevance to a woman's breasts, such as in an ad campaign for yogurt by Danone Activia (Martin, *Janet Jackson's Right Breast and European Sexual Attitudes*). On the other end of the spectrum, Saudi Arabia has within the past decade seen the allowance of women to be both the target of and depicted in public advertisements, albeit nothing more revealing than their faces (Pfanner, *Ads for Saudi Bank Focus on Women*).

As other cultures of the world undergo radical change in their attitudes toward sexuality, we must wonder whether our own continued liberalism regarding sex in the media can have a positive outcome on the future of our society. Can there be designated line, which once crossed, would send American culture spiraling down some degenerative path of debauchery and sexual apathy? Young people's willing acceptance of mass media ideology certainly raises concerns of a future in which casual sex between people could become as innocent as a first kiss or holding hands.

Furthermore, as young girls continue to push the boundaries of acceptable amounts of clothing, who knows when belly shirts might be considered conservative? And can we truly say that mass media inspires the standards of beauty it promotes, or perhaps these are mere reflections of our innate biology. Do I prefer blondes over brunettes because of the frequency in which they appear in the mass media I consume, or instead because of some subconscious primal caveman urging, "yellow, pretty". Such a digression along the so heavily trodden, enigmatic path that is the debate of nature vs. nurture will not help us reach a conclusion. Once again, the question begs repeating, is sexuality in mass media bad for society?

While it may be reasonable to decide that if any evidential harm is being done to our children, explicit sexuality in the mass media warrants an immediate reiteration of standards and limitations. However, while it can be proven that sexual imagery does have a significant effect on adolescents and youth culture, it would be hastily generalized to reach the conclusion that these effects could be inherently harmful. Yes, there is the fear that perhaps the repercussions of even spending time to debate this issue will not affect our children, or even our children's children, but one day the descendents of present-day society may look back at their ancestors and curse our inaction. And this would indeed be the saddest of days on which mankind should face the consequences of his incompetence.

Yet there is this glimmering sense of assurance that regardless of how culture may deviate away from ethical decency, our uniquely human sense of morality will always remain intact. Mass media itself cannot be held accountable for capitalizing upon adolescent sexual insecurities. Instead, these inadequacies seem more so to be rendered by the innately human psychological need to be an accepted member of a group. If this is the case, then the false images imposed by mass media are not only beneficial to individual self-discovery, but create an environment in which such an individual can identify with a society that sees beyond the glamour; for those who can never see further, they will never know of real beauty.

AS A MAN THINKETH: EFFECTS OF THE MEDIA

The world is awash in visual and auditory stimuli: television, films, radio, books, newspapers, magazines, and advertisements clamor for attention, and we give them a great deal of our time. Generally we believe that what we see and hear, particularly for entertainment, has no actual effect on us; that whatever goes on in our minds and emotions is a private experience which does not impinge upon others. Counselors commonly recommend using fantasies as a harmless means of fulfilling desires which should not or may not be acted out. Here thoughts and feelings are considered abstractions with no objective reality or consequences in themselves. Only what we do and say, what can be perceived through the physical senses, is considered real.

Mankind, however, exists primarily in a psychological, not a physical, world. The physical world exists undeniably, but we know it only through our mental interpretations of sense impressions. While we exist in several spheres — physical, psychic, psychological, and spiritual — our main sphere of activity is our feelings, thoughts, desires: the psychological universe which we experience directly. From the theosophical point of view, the building blocks or "atoms" of the psychological world are thoughts and feelings, which are not abstractions but elemental living beings with their own rudimentary consciousness. Physically imperceptible, these relatively unevolved entities or energies are just as real and influential as electricity, light, or magnetism but directly affect us psychologically rather than physically. In the course of our life, we are each aware of continually drawing on and adding to our individual consciousness. But humanity as a whole also exists in a global field of consciousness, each person drawing on and contributing to this great sea of human thought as well as to the vortices and currents within it formed by the psychological effluence of particular cities, nations, and other groupings of people.

The films and television we watch, what we read and hear, involve thoughts and feelings which are drawn from the psychological atmosphere of the earth and which return to it stamped with the results of their stay with us. When a particular thought or feeling occupies our attention, we either strengthen it so it is easier for others to pick up in its circulation through the thought-atmosphere, or weaken it so it is not so energetic and easily available. We color it by our positive, negative, or neutral use of it, and so bear a responsibility both to the entity that is manifesting as that thought and to the rest of humanity to whom we automatically make it available in that form. We have, of course, a responsibility to ourselves as well. Our future self is the direct result of our psycho-spiritual life, which directs the growth of our character.

We constantly impress our being with what we allow our consciousness to focus on. Thought and imagination are powerful tools in human evolution. We have not yet begun to understand the profound effect that our imagination has on our spiritual development, for as Katherine Tingley remarks: I hold that the imagination has a wonderful and creative power. I hold that if we let it soar in the world of spiritual and creative thought ... it can create what truly seem to be miraculous things.... Visualize! Visualize! You touch a mystic law when you create in imagination the picture of mighty things, for you open a door to new powers within yourself. Something in the way of potent energies is awakened and called into life and strength both without you and within.

If you aspire, visualize your aspirations. Make a mind-picture of your spiritual ideals, a picture of the spiritual life as you know it to be, and carry that picture with you day by day. Cherish it as a companion. Carry it with you for breakfast, dinner and supper, and before you know it a new life has been born. Before you know it the ideal has become the real and you have taken your place as a creator, truly, in the great, divine scheme of life.

The transforming power of imagination when serving either our spiritual impulses or our lower aspirations and desires may not be widely accepted, though the effects of deliberate visualization and imaging are being recognized. Intense focusing of consciousness and the mental picturing of certain results are beginning to be used in many situations, from healing to seeking particular opportunities or circumstances in life. All our thoughts and feelings also have effects, though not as dramatic as when we put our conscious will strongly behind them. Once we acknowledge the power of thought to influence directly even the physical world, it is obvious that it is not enough for a person to be responsible outwardly while behaving irresponsibly in his thoughts. "As he thinketh in his heart," says the Proverb, "so is he."

The Hebrew word translated as heart is nephesh, meaning our lower, animal nature, so that the phrase actually means, As a person thinks in his lower nature, that he is or becomes (cf G. de Purucker, Fundamentals of the Esoteric Philosophy, p. 200). While we may feel we are indulging in harmless escape or fantasy, we are actually dealing in causal realms. We will feel the effects in our being by the kind of person we cause ourself to become, and eventually will also receive back from the environment the consequences of all our psychological output, not just that from our "serious" moments. Because the media affect directly the content and tone of our consciousness, they exert a powerful influence on individuals and society. Our auric atmosphere and the psychological atmosphere of the earth are filled with the thoughts, images, and impulses we allow into our psyches.

The various mass media induce psychological energies and impulses which are magnified and reinforced by the hundreds, or even millions, of people who share them. If the content of the media was mainly positive and uplifting, this might be a distinct benefit, but the largest segment of the market goes toward satisfying the demand of the lower human appetites, as a peek at the local video store, supermarket book and magazine racks, or the evening's television amply attest.

Advertising, too, so ubiquitous as to be scarcely noticed, usually plays on the lowest common denominator of its audience. We are accustomed to being manipulated, to being bombarded with appeals to our selfishness and insecurities, and to having our appetites stimulated to want ever more and more. Impersonal, institutionalized flattery, unrealistic claims, illusions of violence and sensuality, and glorified selfishness have become so commonplace that they do not shock or disturb many of us.

When we experience violence and immorality through film or print, we excuse it as harmless because it is only a portrayal. But, as Jesus said, to not commit adultery is insufficient; we must reject it in our minds and hearts for "whosoever looketh on a woman to lust after her hath committed adultery with her already in his heart" (Matthew 5:28). By our indulgence in such spectacles vicariously through technological illusions, we participate in that psychological reality as if we were witnessing those events in person.

And moving from illusion to reality becomes increasingly easy with familiarity, especially when traditional moral standards have little hold on society. Certainly our consciousness has been coarsened by the onslaught of the petty and degrading to which we subject it. By their content the various media contribute significantly to the psychological smog that hangs over our civilization, polluting our thought-atmosphere and eating away at our collective inner health and well-being.

This atmosphere creates and reinforces further demand, which will never be satisfied since it is based in human appetites. The Roman circuses, for example, began as innocent entertainment, only to degenerate over time into terrible excesses of brutality, torture, killings, and sex acts as it pandered to jaded viewers. Such events are commonplace now in popular fiction and film.

Can we long maintain our ethical sensitivities when we surround ourselves with such material? What can we do if we do not like the current trends? Censorship by some authority is not the answer; rather, we need to cultivate a more realistic perception of what is healthy and what is damaging to ourselves and others.

Such shifts of popular viewpoint have had an effect with physical problems: the connection of heart disease with diet, for example, has altered the eating patterns of many people and the proliferation of AIDS is changing popular attitudes toward casual sex. Again, the obvious results of pollution and unwise industrial activity are beginning to affect people's opinions and way of life. These, however, are diseases of our physical body and environment, and changes have come only after irrefutable evidence of deadly consequences.

Will we recognize the psychological malaise that infects our society and trace its causes to the actions of human consciousness? Or will we continue to believe that only that which is perceived by our physical senses is real? Negativity feeds on itself; we must be willing at some point to discipline our own consciousness as a contribution to our health and that of humanity.

The cesspool of mankind's consciousness can be purified — but not by adding ever more destructive material or by rationalizing material that panders to the lowest in us as harmless entertainment which has no objective consequences. The media, neutral in themselves, become constructive or destructive by our use of them. Our own reactions to the various media show the tremendous power of their products to elicit either nobility or meanness. While it is easy to indulge our negative aspects, which can be so powerful, we owe it to ourselves and to our fellowmen to minimize the hold of the lesser self over our consciousness and to nurture the wonderful, worthy aspects of ourselves by thinking toward the greatness in every human being. For the quality and content of our individual consciousness is our most important contribution to human and planetary evolution.

Bibliography

Alan, B.: *Management of Electronic Media*, Belmont, Wadsworth/ Thompson Learning, 2002.

Arant, David: *Perspectives: Ethics, Issues and Controversies in Mass Media*, St. Paul, Coursewise Publishing, 1999.

Bagdikian, Ben: *The Media Monopoly,* Boston, Beacon Press, 1997.

Berry, David: *Ethics and Media Culture*, Woburn, Focal Press, 2000.

Berry, David: *Ethics and Media Culture*, Woburn, Focal Press, 2000.

Cannadine, David: *History and the Media*, New York, Palgrave Macmillian, 2004.

Chermak, M.: *Victims in the News: Crime and the Indian News Media,* Boulder, Westview Press, 1995.

Christians, Clifford G.: *Media Ethics: Cases and Moral Reasoning,* Boston, Allyn & Bacon, 2004.

Daniel, Webster: *The Media in America,* Santa Barbara, ABC-CLIO, 1995.

Darrell, M.: *The Rise and Fall of the Media Establishment,* Boston MA: Bedford/St. Martin's, 2001.

Day, A: *Ethics in Media Communications*, Belmont, Wadsworth, 2003.

Dizard, Jr. Wilson: *Old Media/New Media: Mass Communi-cation in the Information Age,* New York, Longman, 2000.

Ericson, Richard: *Crime and the Media,* Brookfield, Dartmouth Publishing, 1995.

Fallows, James: *Breaking the News: How the Media Undermine American Democracy,* New York, Pantheon, 1996.

Fiske, John: *Media Matters: Everyday Culture and Political Change*, Minneapolis MN: U. Minnesota Pr., 1996.

Freedman, Warren: *Press and Media Access to the Criminal Courtroom*, New York, Quorum Books, 1988.

Gordon, A. David: *Controversies in Media Ethics*, White Plains, Longman Publishers, 1999.

Jewkes, Yvonne: *Media and Crime*, Thousand Oaks, Sage, 2004.

Land, Mitchell : *Contemporary Media Ethics*, Spokand, Marquette Books, 2006.

Langman, Larry: *The Media in the Movies*, Jefferson, NC: McFarland & Company, 1997.

Limburg, Val E.: *Electronic Media Ethics*, Boston, Focal Press, 1994.

Louis, A: *Ethics in Media Communications*, Belmont, Wadsworth, 2003.

Mouritsen, H.: *Case Studies in Media Management*, Boston, McGraw-Hill, 2001.

Nacos, Brigitte L.: *Terrorism & the Media*, NY, Columbia University Press, 1994.

Norris, Pippa: *Women, Media and Politics*, Oxford, Oxford University Press, 1997.

Patricia, A.: *Police and the Media*, Springfield, Thomas Books, 1987.

Patterson, Philip : *Media Ethics: Issues and Cases*, Boston, McGraw Hill, 2002.

Peter, Burke: *A Social History of the Media from Gutenberg to the Internet*, Malden, Blackwell, 2001.

Ripley, Jr. Casey: *The Media and the Public*, New York, H.W. Wilson, 1994.

Seiter, Ellen: *Gender, Race and Class in Media*, Thousand Oaks, CA: Sage, 1995.

Sohn, Ardyth: *Media Management: A Casebook Approach*, Mahwah, Lawrence Erlbaum Associates, 2003.

Surette, Ray: *Justice and the Media*, Springfield, Thomas Books, 1984.

Ward, Hiley H.: *Mainsteams of American Media History*, Needham Heights, MA: Allyn & Bacon, 1997.

Warner, Charles: *Media Management Review*, Mahwah, Lawrence Erlbaum Associates, 1997.

Index

A

Accident, 162, 165, 169, 170, 171, 184, 186.
Administration, 9, 86.
Advocacy, 21, 38, 39.
Applications, 116, 145.
Approach, 23, 84, 85, 126, 128, 137, 140, 149, 150, 234.

C

Cold War, 93.
Communicable Diseases, 130.
Communication, 14, 58, 103, 143, 149, 239.
Communications, 21, 23, 24, 108.
Community, 9, 15, 22, 36, 38, 39, 52, 53, 55, 91, 92, 99, 103, 110, 114, 186.
Consumer, 47, 82, 238.
Crime Profiling, 113, 114.
Crime Scene Reconstruction, 187, 188, 190.
Culture, 21, 86, 90, 92, 237, 238, 239, 240, 244, 245, 246, 247.

D

Development, 15, 19, 21, 43, 45, 50, 88, 191, 193, 194, 226, 239, 248.

E

Enforcement, 3, 21, 24, 80, 116, 120, 122, 139, 194, 229.
Environment, 3, 9, 22, 78, 92, 110, 112, 142, 165, 239, 240, 243, 244, 247, 249, 251.
Evaluation, 166, 215.

G

Governance, 98.
Guidelines, 111, 120, 156.

I

Improvement, 240.
Indian Elections, 97.
Information, 4, 7, 8, 21, 23, 31, 35, 36, 37, 39, 40, 58, 59, 61, 63, 65, 66, 69, 70, 72, 79, 80, 81, 82, 84, 90, 91, 114, 115, 117, 119, 121, 124, 128, 129, 131, 133, 134, 136, 137, 138, 139, 140, 142, 143, 145, 146, 149, 150, 154, 156, 161, 162, 165, 166, 167, 169, 171, 173, 184, 193, 198, 199, 209, 222, 223, 224, 225, 226, 227, 229.

Institutions, 4, 9, 58, 86, 90, 93.
Insurance, 171.
Investigation, 1, 113, 114, 115, 121, 126, 128, 130, 131, 132, 133, 135, 137, 138, 140, 150, 151, 166, 170, 171, 172, 174, 175, 176, 177, 178, 183, 193, 195, 196, 210, 212, 223, 226, 229, 234, 235.
Investments, 52.

J

Journalism, 2, 3, 4, 35, 36, 92, 100, 102, 103, 242, 246.

L

Leaders, 9, 11, 12, 55, 98.

M

Management, 53.
Mass Media, 4, 9, 15, 17, 57, 102, 103, 105, 110, 237, 238, 240, 242, 243, 246, 247, 248, 251.

N

Networks, 96, 106.
News, 1, 3, 7, 16, 20, 22, 23, 24, 25, 26, 27, 28, 29, 30, 31, 32, 33, 34, 35, 36, 37, 38, 39, 56, 57, 58, 59, 60, 61, 62, 63, 64, 65, 66, 67, 68, 69, 70, 71, 72, 73, 74, 75, 76, 77, 78, 79, 80, 81, 82, 83, 84, 85, 88, 90, 91, 92, 94, 95, 96, 97, 103, 138.

O

Organizations, 3, 21, 36, 60, 88.

P

Policy, 8, 12, 23, 30, 39, 50, 52, 94, 96, 174.
Production, 41, 42, 43, 44, 45, 46, 49, 64, 65.

S

Security, 13, 74, 78, 79, 80, 84, 110, 125, 154.
Society, 1, 2, 7, 9, 10, 11, 14, 19, 21, 22, 40, 41, 42, 43, 44, 45, 47, 49, 57, 58, 69, 86, 87, 88, 89, 90, 92, 100, 102, 103, 105, 107, 109, 110, 111, 114, 123, 124, 125, 237, 238, 239, 246, 247, 250, 251.

T

Tourism, 51, 54.
Treatment, 29, 177, 187.

V

Violence, 4, 5, 7, 8, 21, 22, 23, 25, 26, 27, 29, 30, 31, 32, 33, 35, 36, 37, 39, 40, 59, 61, 62, 74, 76, 102, 103, 104, 105, 106, 107, 108, 109, 110, 111, 112, 120, 124, 169, 244, 250.

□□□